Sbae

D0992218

JAN — — 2019

Almost a Murder

Jody Seay

Jim Lloyd

Koho Pono, LLC

ALMOST A MURDER

Published by Koho Pono, LLC
Clackamas, Oregon USA
http://KohoPono.com

Koho Pono is committed to publishing works of quality and integrity. In that spirit, we are proud to offer this book to our readers because the authors strove to present the events as truthfully as possible, as it was experienced. Trial transcripts and evidence photos back up memories; however, it's almost impossible to recall a conversation word-for-word and the authors have compressed some conversations and rearranged some time sequences for readability (flashbacks, etc.), but did not alter the meaning of events. As in life, the actions and motivations of others can only be guessed, so the reactions and motivations detailed in the book are based on the author's perceptions and may not be precise or factual, but they do contain the truth as the author experienced it. Some of the names have been changed, however, this case is an extensively studied in law schools around the country and was extensively covered in the press; thus the characters are already exposed to public scrutiny and commentary.

Hardcover Edition 22June2018

ISBN: 978-1-938282-21-8
LCCN: 2014022590

Koho
Pono

"There are writers and there are WRITERS; but every now and then a monster writing talent rockets into the literary world from seemingly out of nowhere. Such a writer is Jody Seay. I have known Jody for years, and have never ceased to be simply amazed by every piece of work that flows from this woman's pen... There is a depth to her work that simply defies description. Jody's stories are to be tasted, then munched, then gobbled up whole and juicy like warm pie. Writing just doesn't get any better than this. Sit down with her book, and get ready for a feast... This woman's work is marvelous. There is something about the way she magically strings words together that makes you just proud to be a member of the human race. Let's hope we all hear much, much more from this wonderfully gifted writer."

> *- Susan Chernak McElroy, New York Times best-selling author of "Animals as Teachers & Healers", "Animals as Guides for the Soul"*

"Jim Lloyd makes you believe you are sitting across the table from him while he passionately sets forth the emotions, motivation and legal reasoning which brings a jury to conclude there is reasonable doubt that his client had committed murder. Result: Innocent. His enthusiasm and confidence will challenge the reader to invest themselves absolutely in their convictions. Who wouldn't want a 'Jim Lloyd' to defend them when it really matters?"

> *- Mark Lindberg, Attorney & Business Law Professor at Oral Roberts University Tulsa, Oklahoma*

"Jody Seay is a story-teller extraordinaire. Her wonderfully funny and insightful work has universal appeal. With her page-turning writing, she has that rare gift of being able to touch the hearts and minds of a broad and varied audience."

> *- Nina McIntosh, MSW, author of "The Educated Heart: Professional Guidelines for Massage Therapists, Body-workers And Movement Teachers"*

"Forty years ago the law profession was much different; many of us gave lip-service to real 'justice for all'. However, you, Jim, at the risks of your reputation and financial disaster made it real – not always pretty – but real. And now, in this book, you capture for us the behavior of the characters involved and you shine a light that glimpses their soul... their very being. This makes it all the more overpowering."

- John W. Klenda, Lawyer

"[Jody Seay's] remarkably confident debut novel of heartache and redemption... Written with a firm command of vernacular speech and down-home metaphors, the narrative holds attention with charmingly quirky characters and a good sense of place."

- Publisher's Weekly review of "The Second Coming of Curly Red", October 1999

"Jim's unique understanding of the law brings this story of a young Thai woman who killed her husband to life. His struggle to balance the legal profession with his personal life in order to save his client makes this book a real page-turner."

- Ed Lutz, Attorney

"... a candid, compelling, compassionate and illuminating [book]. Highly recommended."

- Wisconsin Bookwatch review of "The Second Coming of Curly Red", February 2000

"Seay's characters are originals and well-developed. She has a good ear for how people talk and a gift for layering emotional impact into her chapters with a powerful yet light touch..."

- Oriana Green, Just Out, January 2000

"Jody Seay handed me her book [*Dead in a Ditch*] and said, 'I hope you laugh so hard you bust your spleen.' I'm happy to say that my spleen survived intact – but my pancreas is still in a splint. Jody Seay is ONE FUNNY WRITER."

- Jerry Juhl, three-time Emmy Award winner, former head writer for The Muppets Show and Jim Henson Productions

Dedication

This book is dedicated to those who never give up, and to the attorneys in my life I know, love and admire who do good things for the right reasons. (Here's a very special SHOUT-OUT to all the attorneys who worked, pro bono, sitting on floors in airports around the nation just a few months ago to help immigrants trying to get back to their families.)

Overall, I think lawyers get a bad rap and that breaks my heart, because that has not been my experience – at all – of most attorneys. I am lucky to know the ones I'd want on my side if I ever got in a jam. And so, to those good and brilliant people, I offer my sincere thanks for all that you take care of – in so many ways – and I offer my deepest bow.

Also this book is dedicated in loving memory of Georgia N. Ramay, (1934 - 2016) my 8th grade English teacher, who read to us on Friday afternoons and made words catch fire in my heart. Mrs. Ramay, thanks for being such a fabulous teacher. Clearly, this is all your fault.

AND THIS BOOK IS FOR STEF, AS IS EVERYTHING I DO.

- JS, 2017

I dedicate this book to my second grade teacher, Mrs. Helen Austin, who followed my career and told me over and over again that she was still proud of me. I hope she knew how much it meant to me to get those precious phone calls.

I acknowledge my friend, Rafe Foreman, who read the original rough draft of "The Old Tired Silk Tie", which was just a few paragraphs. Those few paragraphs became Chapter 11 (*A Special Souvenir: Almost Lost*) because Rafe kept asking me questions, which, in the end, helped me discover what made me tick, how I had changed, and how my experiences changed my life. His sheer persistence in questioning me made the story come alive in its present form and I am grateful to him for taking such an interest.

I wish to thank Gerry Spence for his amazing mentorship and, in particular, for his concept of "The Inquisitor of the Self". In Gerry's book, *"Seven Simple Steps to Personal Freedom: An Owner's Manual for Life"* he says, "Skepticism is the father of freedom… Question every truth, for what is true for the master is rarely true for the slave…" I named my childhood dragon, Quizzer (Quiz, for short), because he always gave me pop quizzes, but now that I am no longer a child, I like to think that my ideas about Quiz have matured to become more like Gerry's Inquisitor of the Self. Also this book is dedicated to all the lawyers who value a "good fight" over "the easy path", especially Melvin Belli, who sacrificed to keep our justice system fair - and the folks at the Innocence Project who reveal Exculpatory Evidence and work with new technologies to ensure that innocent people are not prosecuted and convicted.

And to my brother, Rex, my right arm, my friend: even though you got lost half the time, I'll be forever grateful that you were there when I couldn't be, taking the kids to soccer games and so much more. You were there for me even when it wasn't easy or convenient. I'll never forget. And for helping me lug those 98 trial exhibits up seemingly endless flights of stairs (5 stories). Why didn't we ever take the elevator? And for being my eyes; I'm so grateful that you can see into people and can always tell me what is going on.

And finally, I dedicate this book to Nancy. You are the secret to my success – you are my secret sauce – you are the sugar to my flour as we make our life together. Every time, Nancy, when you give me that look, I find it powerfully motivating. You have always kept everything together for us. I thank you for it all.

- JL, 2017

Acknowledgements

ALMOST A MURDER is a true story by Jody Seay, as told to her by Oklahoma attorney, Jim Lloyd; the gripping saga of one young lawyer who risked it all to fight for justice.

Without my friend, Jim Lloyd, this book would not be in your hands now. He lived this story, as unbelievable as the story itself sounds. I have had a staggeringly vivid imagination all my life. Creating stories is something I have done since I was a tiny child, and, I have been an award-winning author for many years. Still, even with those two distinct advantages, I don't believe I could ever have thought this story up. To bring this tale to life, Jim gathered the facts, clipped newspaper articles, ordered transcripts, dug through dusty, sweltering, cobweb-caked warehouses in search of long-lost evidence, and dragged me all over Tulsa and Creek Counties in Oklahoma so I could get a "feel" for the places most important to the proper writing of this story. Most crucial of all, he preserved an old, tattered, yellowed manuscript of dialogue and storyline from which this book emerged.

As a writer, my job was to make it flow – and I have. It is not like any book I have ever written. It has been easier, in some ways, because I didn't have to make the story up in my head – not that I would ever have thought this one up in a million years. That's also what made the writing of this book harder, because I needed to stay true to the story and to what happened – and I have.

Jim Lloyd, the Tulsa attorney who lived this story, and who took this first degree murder case to trial three times, is one of the most enthusiastic and optimistic people I have ever met. His unbreakable spirit compels him to be no less than that. So, for these reasons and other equally just reasons, it is right, fair and proper that he should be fully credited as co-author of this book. After all, he carried the weight for the vulnerable and tempest-tossed for so long.

Jody Seay – Roseburg, Oregon – 2017

TABLE OF CONTENTS

"Courage can come out from its hiding place when least expected, when it is needed most."

— Jody Seay

CHAPTER 1 – THE NIGHT I *ALMOST* KILLED MY SON

Fear is a weird dude, a sneaky bastard, like the guest who never leaves and, yet, the very same one who goes through my dresser drawers and cabinets when I'm not home, finding clues and mementos of my life, always looking for the soft underbelly of who I am. Fear is relentless. With this information, he can grab my heart from behind and squeeze so hard the hair stands up on the back of my neck. Fear, that sneaky bastard interloper, squeezes and squeezes until I almost pass out.

And, my neck! Oh, Jesus-God, I rotate it around so much these days trying to spot whomever is about to nail me that my head feels like it's on a swivel. I know it would be loose and bobbly if the tension in my shoulders – hard now as cinder blocks – wasn't keeping it in check.

On this night, this stormy, frightening Oklahoma night, it is very late. Dark greenish-gray clouds rolled in over Tulsa earlier in the afternoon and now the storm has unleashed itself over the city – right over my house, it sounds like – pelting every neighborhood with a deluge of thunder and lightning. There are raindrops the size of ripe figs slapping, pounding, exploding against the roof and windows. I noted on the ten o'clock news that there is flooding in Broken Arrow and Sand Springs, both suburbs of Tulsa, but no tornados – thank God! – just the lashing and unrelenting rain and high winds of this thunderstorm. I can hear the patio furniture getting whammed outside, grinding across the concrete with the wind. If someone comes to kill me tonight, I'm pretty sure I'd never even hear them break the front door down over the terrifying racket of this storm.

It is easier to get to sleep - I know from experience - when there's not a storm raging outside, one such as this, the type that bends the trees and makes limbs scratch across the screens. In the fall or winter, when it's cool, I like to crack the window open just a bit for some fresh air. In the summer, the hum of the central air conditioning feels almost soothing, restful.

I glance over at my wife, Nancy. She sighs every so often, a velvety sound from the back of her throat, like someone in a deep slumber. Nancy looks after our young boy and a new baby in addition to her work as a CPA, and she's just begun law school. She is *beyond* exhausted; she needs her sleep. If she could just quit worrying over every cent I have spent on this case it would be better.

The storm slams our window and I jump and glance at it. Then I go right back to my thoughts like a cart in a rut.

If Nancy could just quit worrying over every cent I spent on this case, I know we would all be better off. However, knowing Nancy, that wish seems impossible. She frets, and I know I have given her plenty to fret about. The trial, this whole thirteen month-long ordeal I have put her through, has taken a bigger toll on her than I would have ever expected. She murmurs again and my thoughts soften as I glance back at her. I am grateful my wife can sleep as deeply as she does right now.

When we sleep, our cells replicate and our body does its repair work. This is something I learned in high school biology class. It is different than rest. Rest is rest; sleep is repair. Knowing this, it feels good to me to see that my wife can slip into the deep sleep she needs to nourish her body. Sleep has never been easy for Nancy, so I know how exhausted she must be. I yearn for the same sleep experience, but it is not to be, not now, maybe not ever again.

Fear sneaks up again and grabs my heart with cold claws, pricking my skin ever-so-slightly, reminding me that, because of the choices I have made, my life may never again be truly my own, and, indeed, it may end the moment I let down my guard. I can't let that happen. I'm pretty sure I haven't taken a deep breath in over a month, not since I heard there was a contract out on my life with the Kansas City mafia, not since that Deputy Sheriff said, "Always carry a gun, young man, and don't go to work the same way each day. We intercepted a call made from the courthouse to Kansas City. You've got a contract out on you. Better get a remote starter for your car. Remember Judge Nelson? He got blown up. He didn't have a remote starter."

Nancy murmurs and I look back at her. She doesn't share my fears because I haven't completely shared with her. She just wants her family safe and I have assured her that it is. Just to be certain, though, I have stashed guns around the house in various places, places I could get at easily if the need arises, but not so accessible that a young boy could find them.

My gun collection is extensive, most of them passed down from my father and grandfather, but some newer and more powerful ones are recent purchases I made. Nancy doesn't believe in having guns in the home, nor did her parents. It's just one of the many differences between our two families of origin, but then, she didn't hear what I heard and wasn't privy to information I now have about the threats on my life. Nancy tends to think I'm a bit paranoid, and she's probably right, but there's an old saying in Oklahoma: TRUST IN GOD, BUT TIE UP YOUR HORSE. If I am erring, it's on the side of caution. It *has* to be in this case because I am determined to keep my family protected.

With the exception of those guns I've stashed in special hiding places around the house, all of the others stay locked up; only I know where the key is. The .22 pistol I slide under pillow each night goes back up into a lock-box on the top shelf in the closet behind a rolled-up Army blanket each morning as soon as my feet hit the floor. This is my new routine, as ubiquitous to my life as punching the button on the coffee maker, tying my shoes, or picking up my briefcase. I hate it, but it's there. The fear never leaves. The smell of gun oil stays in my nose like chlorine; no matter how fiercely I blow my nose, it stays. And, it has changed me, this fear. At first, in ways so subtle I hardly noticed, but then, suddenly, I realize I've acquired a startle response I didn't have before. This sneaky bastard, Fear, has changed my brain, I know it. Even my dogs have begun to mirror my jumpiness. Now, they have started peeing on the carpet whenever they get startled, something they never did before this case.

I never really saw myself as a fearful man but, of course, no officer of the law had ever taken me aside and said, "You'd better be watching your back. There are people who are going to be gunning for you from now on." Everything changed in that moment. *Everything.*

Bam, the wind slams into the window. Oklahoma thunderstorms are a thing of both beauty and terror. High up in the stratosphere, clouds slam and grind together. Lightning flashes and slashes across the sky from the friction of that collision. Seconds later, thunder smashes my ear drums, making me jump like a coyote instinctively hopping into the air at the crack of a rifle. I pull my head down to duck from what I'm pretty certain is a tree trunk coming through the window. It is exhausting, this terror, this waiting. I now live in the world of *might.* This awful thing *might* happen; that awful thing *might* happen. I have to be prepared to fight or to run at any moment. I'm sure my adrenal glands are going to shut down on me at any second from overwork.

I am staring at the window when I hear our bedroom door barely begin to creak open, just the faintest, horror movie kind of creaky sound, then it continues to creak open a half inch at a time. In the darkness, but illuminated by the lightning still flashing outside, I can see a head coming toward us. Instinctively, I move my right hand under the covers and slowly rest it on my sleeping wife's leg to protect her. She doesn't move, even at my touch, despite the feel of my clammy hand on her leg, even as blasts of thunder and the sound of rain lashes against the windows. I know, however, that Nancy has been so exhausted in the past several months that there's very little, beyond the cry of a child in the night, that could jolt her awake. At this moment, I feel myself being only slightly relieved about that.

My left hand I slide under the pillow and grip the .22 pistol, a relatively small gun, but one that could still pack a terrible wallop and fits easily in my hand. This gun is loaded with hollow-point bullets, which are designed to kill. The entrance wound is a small one, but the exit wound is massive from this type of ammunition, and the results are deadly. The cold, gun metal feel under my pillow still surprises me, almost startles me, even though I am the one who put it there, the one who keeps it there. This gun, the one I have decided to keep right below my head each night, is a dual-action revolver, so there is no safety device on it. The only two ways it can fire is either by pulling the trigger with enough pressure or by cocking the hammer back and then pulling the trigger. This, I'm fairly certain, is the safest of the bad choices I now have to make. I'd really rather not run the risks of shooting myself or my wife to death each night. I slip the gun out slowly and point it at the head, which is now even bigger, closer as I see it creeping across the bedroom, coming straight at us.

The killer had dropped to his knees before entering the room and is now slowly heading right toward our bed. My heart is beating so loudly, whamming against my chest wall like someone kicking a cardboard box. I'm surprised Nancy hasn't awakened from the sound of it. The whamming is relentless and thunderous; it sounds like someone banging a hammer on a trash can lid.

The vague, shadowy head is inching toward us, closer… and closer. My mouth has gone completely dry, tasting only of ashes and gun oil. I aim the pistol straight at the silhouette of the head I see coming at us in the darkness. My mind is screaming *"Kill the mother before he kills us!"* My hand is sweating, shaking, vibrating with terror, but I know if I cock the hammer back on this gun, he will surely hear it and start blasting away at both of us. I decide to keep pulling slowly on the dual-action trigger; just a few more ounces of pressure and I'll blow his brains all over the place. *God, what a mess that's going to make*, I think, but I know I won't give him much of a chance to do what he's been hired to do. *I will kill this sonofabitch, by God, before he hurts anyone in my family*; that is, of course, if my chest doesn't explode from my pounding heart. Lightning flashes again outside, slashing the night with just a tease of light, followed closely by a rumble of thunder. And, that's when I hear it – his voice, over the roar of the storm and the thundering of my pounding heartbeat – just barely above a whisper in the darkness. All he says is, "Daddy, I'm scared."

Fear almost took another life tonight. No, almost took two.

CHAPTER 2 – HOW I *ALMOST* LOST IT ALL

My name is Jim Lloyd. In 1982, I was an inexperienced young attorney in Tulsa, Oklahoma. At that point, I'd only tried one jury case and I lost.

My wife, Nancy, and I were the parents of our five-year old son, James R. Lloyd II, whom we called Buddy, and a newborn baby girl named Jamie. I was 32 years old; Nancy was 31. The previous year, 1981, we had lost our baby son, Brandon, who only lived for twelve hours after he was born, dying from a staph infection he picked up in the hospital.

"We're sorry Mr. Lloyd," the nurse whispered as she handed me my dead newborn son. My knees buckled as I struggled to sit in the neo-natal unit's wooden rocking chair.

I rocked my dead baby even though he couldn't feel it. Between cries of anguish and hysterical sobs, I tried to catch my breath, gasping for air like a carp on a river bank. *"Oh my God, why Lord, why?"* I screamed out toward the heavens, knowing, even then, that such beseeching was futile. Words can't describe my aching, heart-broken, crushed spirit and depths of despair. I might have been in shock. It took me a long time to come to grips with such a loss.

Sometimes, I think I never really did. All I learned to do was go on putting one foot in front of the other until the pain eased up enough and I could smile again.

It was a hard time for Nancy and for me. As I look at the successful lives of my children now, and as much as Nancy and I are both thrilled to be grandparents to five adorable little children, still, sometimes when I run my hand over a baby blanket, I can feel my tiny boy's back under my fingertips. I can remember whispering to him, "Brandon, your Mommy and Daddy love you very much. Hang on, son. Never give up – you're a Lloyd! We don't quit, and we don't back down from a fight. Come on, little guy."

For anyone who has ever lost a child, I'm sure you can relate to the pain, sadness, rage, and feelings of impotence in not being able to save your own baby.

We were desperate, Nancy and I, to ease the pain of loss. We thought by creating another life, another little baby for our family, it would help. And we were thrilled when we found out Nancy was pregnant again. However, the pregnancy was a roller coaster ride. It was tenuous and peppered with complications – it was still difficult to breathe. So, as much as Nancy and I were overjoyed a year later at the arrival of our beautiful baby daughter, Jamie, in truth, we were both still feeling raw and wounded when this case dropped into my lap in 1982.

Maybe how I moved through this case was a reaction to not being able to save my son. I don't know. I just knew I would not quit on it. This case would use up every resource my family had, take up all the time I could scrape together and squeeze out of each day. It took all of the energy and physical reserve I could muster. It would almost wreck my marriage. And it almost forced us into bankruptcy.

However, even though I couldn't see it at the time, it was my call to action, the beginning of my own journey toward becoming the man I hoped I would be but, secretly, was terrified that I never would become. It would wind up being a case that would change my life in unimaginable ways and is one which is taught – still, to this day – in law schools all over this country. Stranger still, of the six related cases of this particular client I represented, the one that I *lost* is the one which is most remembered, or, at least, most frequently cited in courts of law, and is the one taught in law schools throughout America. It is State Mutual Life Assurance Co. of America, v. Mitchell, 1985 OK 19, 696 P.2d 1027, Decided 03/06/1985, Modified 03/12/1985, Supreme Court of Oklahoma.

This murder case was full of almosts: I *almost* didn't take it. Once I took it, I *almost* couldn't get away from it. It *almost* ruined my marriage, *almost* cost me my law practice, and *almost* lost me my family. My client was *almost* guilty of murder, and she was *almost* convicted of that crime. I was *almost* sure she was innocent, and I was *almost* sure I could prove it in court.

Like being caught in a vortex, the trying of this case swirled me 'round and 'round through the course of three separate murder trials over thirteen months, *almost* pulling me completely under before I could break free from it and swim upward, toward The Light.

CHAPTER 3 – HOW SHE *ALMOST* GOT AWAY WITH IT

"Don't come in, Nancy," I said to my wife, "there's blood everywhere." With that, I left Nancy and our baby daughter, Jamie, in our 1978 Olds parked in the driveway.

Earlier this evening, Nancy had complained to me, "I never see you anymore. We never spend any time together."

"That's true," I agreed. I was spending more and more of what had been my "free time" digging around through evidence and rooting through files pertaining to this case. *I'm sure Nancy is feeling ignored*, I thought. So I suggested, "Let's leave Buddy with the babysitter and bring Jamie along with us to Noi's house." It was one of the first of many mistakes I would make in regards to our marriage before this case was through.

Once we pulled up in front of the house with its eerie look and violent history, I realized I didn't want my wife or baby daughter in there smelling that miasma of decaying blood and leftover food and trash. Besides, I felt I could just get a lot more done if I wasn't worrying about anybody else in that moment.

Just then Jamie awoke and began her cranky, fussy, baby-goat-sound – the sound of a hungry newborn.

"Why don't you stay in the car and feed the baby?" I said to Nancy. "I won't be too long."

"But, then, why did you even suggest I come along?" Nancy was starting to get mad; I could hear it in her voice. "I thought the whole point was to spend some time together."

Once again, I had let her down. I cut off her complaint. "I'll be right back," I said, forcing a smile at her as I closed the car door.

Just getting access to this house where Noi and Bobby Mitchell had lived was a triumph for me. It was Oct. 29, 1982, the first time I'd been able to enter the crime scene without the Broken Arrow Police, the District Attorney or the attorneys of the victim's father supervising my every move.

Without really wanting to and, certainly, without having tried to do so, I had become the attorney for Noi Kanchana Mitchell, a young woman from Thailand who was accused of murdering her husband, Bobby Mack Mitchell III in this home: of shooting him with a gun, whamming him in the head a number of times with a baseball bat, strangling him, dumping his body in another county with some help from a friend, and finally, throwing the gun into a lake. And *the police said she had confessed – they had it on tape.* By any stretch of logic, this young woman looked guilty as charged.

But, was she, really? After all, did she really understand what she was doing by confessing? And, what if there was even more evidence that had not been found? What if there was more to it all than just what we were hearing from the police and reading in the newspapers? Noi had told me it was an accident, so I'd hired a Private Investigator to help me find out if that was true.

Bright, moonlit nights in Oklahoma are hard to hide from. Everything looks illuminated as if by neon. On this night, standing in the foyer of Noi and Bobby's home, I waited for my Private Investigator, Tom Cook, to arrive. I could see what appeared to be a large patch of dried blood on the front porch.

Tom Cook was the best Private Investigator in Oklahoma. What made him that, in my eyes, was that he paid for our lunch when we first met, then he agreed to do all the work and to bill me only when I got paid, or, when I could afford to pay him. I knew he wouldn't do this for just anyone. Nice guy. I didn't have much money and I guess he could tell.

When Tom arrived, I felt braver. Something settled in my heart as we went into the house together. There was an aura of death in the place, more than just a stuffy smell. It was a sickening stench – sweet, like liver or old fruit left rotting in the sun. There was also a feeling of emptiness. Cobwebs were hanging in every corner and from the light fixtures. It was hard to believe that there had been a family living here at one time. The place felt haunted, spooky, *almost perfect for Halloween, which was coming up in a couple of days,* I remember thinking, then felt ashamed that the thought had even entered my mind.

There is an energy about homes when happiness lives there. The yard stays mowed, flowers grow in gardens or pots by the porch; there is an uplifted feeling of everything being in place and cared for, like the family members themselves.

Likewise, a home which absorbs the bad vibes of discord, drama and dispute between family members seems to almost sag under the burden of all that upset. Before you know it, roof shingles fly off in the wind; flashing comes loose and peels away; paint blisters and pops off in the heat of the sun; shutters begin to sag and come unhinged, then fall off into the yard. It's as if the house knows when the happiness leaves – that same happiness that was the cohesion, the glue, that's kept everything together. Now, without that glue, parts of the house have decided suicide is their only option and begin, bit by bit, jumping to their deaths. Weeds sprout up along and within the walkway; indeed, the walkway itself begins to crumble or buckle, reminding everybody just how much everything was already falling apart and turning to dust, right before their eyes, even if they couldn't see it themselves.

Noi and Bobby's home in Broken Arrow, Oklahoma, a Tulsa suburb, was such a place, just under five miles from where Nancy and I lived with our children. A wooden home of modern design, it had angles and rooms jutting out all over the place. Nothing about the house seemed to match, just as the design of the house itself didn't match any of the other homes in the otherwise conventional suburban neighborhood, like it had been flung with great force onto the lot by some dark entity anxious to get rid of it.

Once, not all that long ago, there had been two small girls living here with their Thai mother, Noi Kanchana Mitchell, and their American father, Bobby Mitchell III. Now, it was standing empty, as vacant and whistled-through as a con man's heart.

The electric company had cut off the electricity for non-payment. So Tom and I used the light from our flashlights and the glow of the moon to follow what remained of a bloody trail Bobby had made on Oct. 5, 1982. Most of the bigger blood spots had already been washed clean, causing us to stoop and scan as we made our way through this scene of death and mayhem.

Had this house taken on the personalities of its occupants? It had been the scene of deception, jealousy, resentment, revenge, coercion, rage, domestic violence and, finally, death. Even without the blood and the garbage left behind, I surmised, it would have smelled bad. As it was, there were dirty dishes, sacks of trash sitting in the middle of the kitchen floor, and partially-folded laundry lying on the sofa. A newspaper dated Oct. 6, 1982, was still in its plastic wrapper. It was clear that something drastic and unexpected had interrupted the normal routines of this family.

Tom and I spotted blood on the dark brown shag carpet and on the wall in the hallway. Following the droplets of blood to the linoleum floor in the hall bathroom, we then realized that the trail continued on into the master bedroom. There were dark spots on the dusty mirror – COULD BE BLOOD – and there was even more blood on the skirt of a green chair in the bedroom. Apparently, the chair had soaked up blood from the carpet. It shocked me to realize that the blood still felt damp and fresh almost a month after Bobby's death, so much so that it made the hair on the back of my neck stand up and bristle. Our shadows looked frightening as Tom paced off the scene while moving his flashlight from side to side.

There were dried towels in the dryer. Noi had used those towels to mop up the blood and gallons of water she had poured onto the carpeting. Now, the hall closet was empty where the towels had once been.

Then, I noticed it. I was drawn like a magnet to a hole in the east wall of the bedroom. My Cherokee blood stirred deep within me and I felt this was important. In fact, it turned out to be the most important evidence in the entire case and I walked right to it! In the world of Spirit, there are no accidents. This hole was my first *"Godplop!"* for this case, and, there would be more before all was said and done.

The wall had blood spatters beginning about five feet from the floor and continuing on up to about nine feet high. According to Tom's measuring tape, at precisely seven feet five and a half inches from the floor there was a hole in the wall. It appeared that a bullet had entered the wall sideways.

In the bumpy terrain that is the law – in particular, in criminal law – this was precisely what we had been looking for: something concrete, some physical evidence to prove that the gun had fired accidentally. My hope was that ballistics tests would prove that this could only have been an accident and, thus, verify Noi's story.

Wondering if the bullet was still embedded in the wall, Tom stood on a chair and peeked into the hole with a flashlight. He said he couldn't see anything, but that the bullet might be behind the insulation. Magnets do not attract lead or copper-jacketed slugs, so a magnet wouldn't work. While a metal detector would pick those up, so would it also pick up every nail within several feet. When we checked outside, we determined that the bullet had not penetrated the east wall; it had just penetrated the sheetrock inside. If we were to cut the wall out and remove the bullet, we could then have our experts verify that it was, indeed, fired from Bobby Mitchell's own gun and maybe give us the trajectory of the bullet that killed him, judging from the angle and height of the bullet hole.

Tom measured each room and drew a sketch of the Mitchell's floor plan so we could piece together what might have happened on the night Bobby died. There had been a fight and a chase, clearly, but the question remained: who was chasing whom? In my gut, I felt that Noi had not deliberately killed her husband. I believed that Bobby had chased her and, sometime during the fight, had been fatally injured. If that was true, then, this was not a case of first degree murder, not at all. No one in their right mind would have made such a mess of killing someone. My client was innocent, I thought. *I know it. She has to be innocent; either that, or she is just plain nuts. But, I don't think so.* My challenge, maybe one of the biggest challenges of my life, would be to prove that.

Gaining access to the crime scene had proven to be so difficult that I was not ready to leave without going over every square foot and every piece of furniture in the place as if it were my very last chance to do so because, well, it just *might* be. "Bobby" Mack Mitchell III's father, Bobby "Mack" Mitchell, Jr., was a wealthy and influential man well-known throughout Oklahoma political circles. Not up-in-the-stratosphere wealth of the kind often found in Tulsa oil families, but, still, he had enough to secure him clout and respect. He had been appointed by the court as special administrator to control the assets owned by his son and Noi. In his tremendous rage and grief over the loss of his son, he put every legal obstacle in my way that his battery of expensive, high-powered attorneys could think of, including barring me from entering Noi and Bobby's home with a private investigator to do our own research. Mr. Mitchell had the keys to the house and had taken possession of it. His determination to keep me from entering the home was as great as my determination to do so.

When we had first inspected the house on October 20, 1982, I had arranged a shaky truce with Mr. Mitchell and Karen Shaw, one of his attorneys. To my surprise, when Tom Cook and I arrived, four officers from the Broken Arrow Police Department were waiting for us. Tom and I had wanted to video tape the scene and photograph some of the numerous blood spatters, but we were never left in peace to do so. The constant hovering and milling about by the officers both distracted and interfered with our accomplishing a thorough search.

In the master bedroom, I was sure I'd seen a jagged piece of glass about three inches long and tapered to a sharp point lying on the cushion of the green chair. When I returned to the bedroom only a few minutes later, it was gone. I didn't know if this piece of glass had anything to do with the case or not. I *did* know, however, that every piece of possible evidence in a murder case should be left alone. I was angry and began questioning everyone about it, starting with the Broken Arrow Police Officers. Each person denied taking it, until I got to Karen Shaw, one of the attorneys for Mr. Mitchell. She stared at me flatly, shrugged a little, and said, nonchalantly, "Yes, I put it on the television. I guess I'm guilty of tampering with the evidence."

Now, I was only a cub lawyer, but I was aghast at how the sanctity of criminal evidence was being handled. Even though this simple statement would, ultimately, have nothing to do with either the case or with Karen Shaw, it proved to be both prophetic and foreboding in terms of how the criminal evidence was handled. It took me a year to unravel the mess made by various law enforcement agencies and what I considered their unprofessional handling of evidence. I began to feel stubborn. *This is not the right way to perform our duties*, I thought.

A week later, I was in court attending one of the numerous hearings on this case. Mr. Mitchell was there surrounded by his cadre of expensive lawyers so I asked if I could go look inside the house to conduct a further investigation. He snapped, "If you set foot on that property, I'll have your ass thrown in jail for trespassing!"

Once again I felt stubbornness take root in me. Clearly, he felt no need to sugar-coat things or spare my feelings. In fact, it seemed Mr. Mitchell was trying to let me know he was taking charge, running the show, so to speak, and I'd better steer clear of him. He went so far as to put deadbolt locks on all the doors of the house to keep me out.

I admit to feeling pity for Mr. Mitchell at first — sympathetic toward his grief, even his rage. It was familiar to me in a raw and terrible way. Every time I saw Mr. Mitchell's gritted teeth it reminded me of losing my own son. In a rush I would remember preparing for my boy's birth. I had, essentially, seven or eight months to envision the baby and how this tiny new being's life would intertwine with mine. And I resonated with Mr. Mitchell's pain. Nancy and I had picked out the perfect name – ours was Brandon Scott Lloyd – his was Bobby Mack Mitchell III. And I had worked myself into such a frenzy of parental excitement that, by the time Brandon arrived, I felt as if I had known him, that he had been a part of our family forever. I would sing to my baby in Nancy's belly and tell him how much I loved him. Whenever I rubbed her belly he would kick my hand, like we were bonding. *He knows it's me!* Mr. Mitchell may have played that same game with Bobby before he was born. Our grief in losing them, in not having been able to protect them was real and huge. Then, I realized that this emotion of empathy I was feeling toward Mr. Mitchell was interfering with my professional duty to Noi, my client.

Further, I knew that Noi would lose *her* two girls – her babies – if she was convicted. And it would be just as permanent. Those little girls would lose both their mother *and* their father. As Noi's attorney and, as a parent, I could not let that happen.

So, I went over Mr. Mitchell's head and asked a judge in the Criminal Division for permission to inspect the house for further evidence. I was dug in now – my course of action unflinching – I would find a way into that house. The judge denied my request so I got creative. If the "normal" channels were closed to me, I had to find a new way to achieve my goal. I devised "Plan B".

Plan B was my brilliant idea of asking Noi to sign the deed to her home over to me with a Quit Claim Deed. Now, this was unorthodox in the extreme. That's probably why they didn't see it coming.

In my mind, her signing reinforced how unworldly my client was and how uneven the fight was going to be. I wasn't much, but I was all she had.

Without first getting a quit claim deed (placing the legal title in my name), it would be nearly impossible to have access to the home at all of the hours and as long as I needed. With all the pressures put on me, I was worried I wouldn't be given an emergency order.

But now, with that quit claim deed, it could be done without giving notice to Mr. Mitchell or his fleet of attorneys. Tom Cook and I could conduct an investigation at the home without being monitored. Because I now owned Noi and Bobby's home, we were free to come and go as we pleased. No matter how much they despised me, Bobby's family and the Broken Arrow Police Department could not keep me out of it.

So here Tom and I were on October 29th triumphantly investigating every square foot and every drop of blood in the crime scene by ourselves with nobody breathing down our necks. Finally, after all this time and effort, I could do my job and I was completely focused on that.

When Tom and I wrapped up our investigation, I said good-night to him and we agreed to meet back at the Mitchell home the next morning at 6 am, sharp. Then, I went out to get in my car and it was gone.

Dammit! Nancy left? How could she do that?!

I cooled off, though, when I looked at my watch and realized that my wife had been in the car with our baby for over two hours while I was in the house investigating. That probably wasn't what she envisioned when she said we were going to spend quality time together. I'm sure she got tired. She was probably bored; most likely mad at me. She had left – understandably, I guess. My heart sank.

I was on a path now with this case and it was going to interfere in what I held most precious. I may have been creative in getting access to the house and finding clues, but I had no idea how to solve this problem. I would soon learn, though, that this incident was just the precursor to how our lives would go in the coming year.

19

Jim Lloyd and Jody Seay

CHAPTER 4 – THE CASE I *ALMOST* DIDN'T TAKE

"Jim, why on earth did you ever take that case?" That's the question everyone wanted an answer to – my friends, my business associates, my fellow lawyers, my family and, particularly, my wife Nancy. It was a good question deserving a good answer, but I didn't have one of those clear-cut, easy-to-fathom reasons on hand, not even for myself.

Maybe I took the case because I had a feeling, just a *feeling*, that my client was innocent.

Perhaps I took it because I needed a challenge. I wanted some sign that would assure me that, yes, I was a great lawyer, or that I should hang up my cleats as an attorney and go learn a trade of some sort.

So much about this case reminded me of another Creek County murder case. I had gotten my first taste of reality, in terms of justice in Creek County, when I was in law school at The University of Tulsa. I was working as a legal intern then for David Young at the Creek County District Attorney's office when I went out on a homicide investigation.

The naked, tattooed body of a beautiful young girl was found just inside the Creek County line. When Luther Cowan, the Assistant District Attorney, and I arrived, the place was almost undulating with television cameramen, reporters and radio personalities. It was total chaos. Luther quickly took matters under control and ordered everyone back one hundred yards from the body. The famous Creek County Sheriff's deputies were scurrying around like Keystone Cops, but not accomplishing a thing that I could tell.

I approached the dead girl's body and looked at her face. Her eyes were still open, with a blank stare. Her left breast was punctured numerous times with what I believed to be a knife. There were deep defensive wounds on her left forearm where she attempted to fend off her attacker. Only sixteen years old, she had been a dancer at a strip club and – who knows – maybe, only a few years earlier, had been her Daddy's little darling.

The girl's clothes were neatly folded near her body and an envelope fluttered in the breeze near her right hand. She had the word L O V E tattooed on the fingers of her left hand. I noticed her rings and bracelets had been removed and were lying next to her neck.

"Aren't you going to rake this area?" I asked.

"No, we never do," replied the Deputy Sheriff.

I told the arriving Oklahoma State Bureau of Investigation (OSBI) agent what I had seen and he said, "I feel like it's a good idea to rake this crime scene."

I heard the deputy muttering something about "… never doing that before…"

When we got back to the courthouse I noticed that the deputy had missed raking up the envelope I had spotted. "It may have had the killer's name and address on it," I said.

The D.A. agreed and sent me back to get it, but it had disappeared. Maybe a gust of wind had blown it away, like the spirit of that young life. I will always wonder if that envelope might have revealed some clue to the killer's identity. Still, to this day, that case remains unsolved.

I don't know why memories of that old case kept surfacing after I read the newspaper story about the Thai woman suspected of murdering her American husband. Was it my Cherokee blood stirring and telling me to pay attention? Dissatisfaction with that old investigation was certainly rekindled – it kept nagging at me. I had an odd feeling that I'd not heard the last of the new Broken Arrow case even after I put the newspaper away. My intuition was proven right with the very next phone call I received, which was from Dick Hynd. Dick and his Thai wife, Kim, are clients and friends of mine. He told me a friend of theirs was charged with first degree murder of her husband.

Without even asking, I knew it had to be the same woman from Broken Arrow who'd dumped her husband's body in Creek County. Dick and Kim Hynd loved Noi's two little girls and wanted to hire me to help them get custody of the children. Dick told me that Mack Mitchell, Jr., the father of the murdered man, Bobby Mitchell III, was determined to keep his son's children away from them, as well as from their own mother. Noi's older daughter, Mia, was six and the younger girl, Maggie, was only eleven months old.

Very specifically, I told Dick that I would take the child custody case, but that I did not want to represent the mother in the murder case. I had already mentioned to Nancy that I wouldn't touch that case with a ten foot pole when we first heard the story. Things such as resolutions and iron-clad statements, as we know, have a way of changing, however.

Noi was friends with Dick and Kim Hynd and she wanted them to care for her children while she was in jail. In the State of Oklahoma, a non-relative, such as the Hynds, had never won a custody battle against a relative where the relative was a fit person. I could not prove that Bobby's father and step-mother were unfit. They were good people. They were also wealthy and could afford top-notch attorneys to fight for them. In fact, my only strategy was to try and prove that Mia and Maggie would be happier and better off, emotionally, in an environment where they could stay close to the Thai culture and language. "After all, it would be in the children's best interest," I argued.

I heard that Mr. Mitchell had disowned his son after Bobby III had married Noi and that he had not seen either of his granddaughters for quite some time. It would be safe to say that those little girls did not even really know their grandfather.

After a hard-fought battle, Judge Gordon McAllister finally agreed with me and the two little girls were placed in the Hynd's home. Dick and Kim, who loved children, were overjoyed at this new, instant family and probably thought they would be keeping the girls for good.

Noi was happy with the outcome, too. It was an impressive win. That's when some of Noi's friends began to suggest that she hire me to represent her in that other trial.

Among those friends were Jerry O'Brien and his Thai wife, Leigh. They were our next-door neighbors in Oklahoma City and had been our close friends for more than twelve years after both of our families moved to Tulsa. Through my association with the O'Briens and the Hynds, I knew that Noi would choose me to represent her in this murder case. Noi was a woman who did as other people suggested. She would listen to her friends about who to hire as a lawyer. *Oh boy. Lucky me.*

"I do not want to take the murder case," I reiterated again to the Hynds. "There is no way."

"Could you please just go and see Noi in jail?" Kim said looking at me with her soft brown eyes. "She's so lonely."

Dick put his arm protectively around his wife's shoulders to support her. "Noi's afraid. She doesn't know any lawyers."

"She's got no one to call for help," Kim whispered.

"Maybe you could... I don't know... steer her in the right direction?" Dick suggested gruffly.

With great reluctance, I agreed. "I'll just go see her to give her some advice. I'm *not* taking the case. I'm mainly going because I've gotten to know the kids during the custody case and they deserve some kind of effort on my part. But I'm *absolutely not* taking the case."

When I first met Noi, she was sitting in a room off the jail cells. My first impression of her was that she was pathetic, so frail-looking and terrified. The sudden sound of a car backfiring might cause her heart to stop. Her eyes were red and swollen and she acted ashamed.

Most of us are used to associating with people who have a fair degree of self-confidence. Certainly, lawyers are supposed to be confident. Until I met Noi, I'd never run across anyone who had no discernible feelings of self-worth. None. This feeling was ingrained in her every movement. She would not look at me. I might as well have been a speck of sand for all the attention she paid to me. I wondered if she found me repulsive to look at or was she afraid of me? She pulled at her hair constantly when I tried to talk to her, but, still, with all of these irritating behaviors, I found myself feeling sorry for her. She was wounded – damaged – wrecked down deep, somewhere. If I could meet her at that damaged place without judgment, maybe she would learn to trust me enough to look at me.

Now at this point I had no intention of being her lawyer, but I still needed to find out some information so I could figure out which lawyer would be the best fit for her. "What happened, Noi?" I asked her.

She began wringing her hands. Her eyes got red and glassy. She answered my question with a question. "When? What? You ask me!"

I realized she only wanted to answer with a 'Yes' or a 'No.'

It was like the childhood guessing game, Twenty Questions. Her voice had an aching, whiney quality about it that made me uncomfortable and, just feeling that made me also feel guilty. In addition, Noi would giggle at completely inappropriate times. When I asked her why she dumped the body, she looked away, then laughed and laughed.

25

Was Noi crazy? Many people thought so. Most people told me they thought Noi's only chance was to plead insanity. At first, I would probably have agreed. That would not have set her free, however, only sentenced her to a mental institution. Later on, I would piece together the evidence for using the defenses of accidental shooting and self-defense but, right at first, an insanity plea looked inviting, and that might be the only thing to save her.

So, even though I didn't believe Noi to be insane, I do think she had some psychological problems. She was partially in shock and also suffered from extremely low self-esteem. She was like an animal that had been abused so much and so often they could no longer even cry out when it happened again. Even though I conceded that Noi might have been temporarily insane when she killed Bobby, I still felt she was not a killer; that was not who she was. I did not know how to explain these feelings to other people. My own feelings built up to a strong conviction that, despite all evidence to the contrary, she was not the type of woman who could have deliberately killed her husband. The O'Briens and the Hynds did not think Noi would commit cold-blooded murder, either.

So, then, why did I take this case?

I've looked at it a thousand different ways over the years. I guess, secretly, I really did want to find an impossible case because, if I won it, I'd be the hero. If I lost, well, nobody would have expected me to have won it anyway. At the time, I was a pretty new attorney and I had no idea if I'd ever be a good one. I'd only tried one civil case up to that time, and I'd lost it. All of the other cases I'd handled had been settled out of court. So, an impossible case seemed like a good strategy.

Also, Nancy and I were solid; we had a good marriage with a young son and a new baby daughter, but we were both silently reeling from the loss of our baby son who only lived twelve hours. I was feeling pretty much like a nobody at a time when I really needed to feel like a somebody. This case, for better or worse, seemed like a

Godplop! Maybe I would be valuable if I made this happen, if I made a name for myself in the world of law.

There is also the fact that I'm not a big guy physically, not quite five feet seven. And I have been teased about that since I was in Junior High School. Maybe it really is the Napoleon Complex that makes short men drive harder. I know that, for my entire life, I have tried to compensate, in one way or another, for being short – feeling insignificant. I wanted to make my mark, to do something remarkable that would allow other people to recognize me as a great person, a great father, a great lawyer. This case, it seemed to me, could be the vehicle for that. I don't like admitting it because it makes me seem egotistical, but it's there and part of my truth in telling this story of the impossible becoming possible.

As far as impossible cases went, it would have been hard to find one more difficult than this one. Noi was accused of beating Bobby to death with a baseball bat. An Oklahoma State Bureau of Investigation agent found the baseball bat she had used – cleaned up and hidden in the attic of her home. Noi's name was engraved into the bat's handle. Later on, the prosecutor in the case would make a big deal out of that. The important thing about the bat, however, was not that her name was engraved upon it, but that she had removed the bloody tape from the handle. The Medical Examiner reported that Bobby had received five or six concussions and fractures in his skull, all of them, most likely, from being hit with that bat.

In addition to that, Noi was also accused of strangling Bobby to death. The Oklahoma Medical Examiner found fingernail markings on his neck and a fractured thyroid cartilage (the hyoid bone or Adam's apple).

Noi was also accused of shooting Bobby to death. Police skin-divers found the gun at the bottom of a lake. She had used a .38 caliber revolver. The bullet had torn through Bobby's right chest wall, ripped through his lung, and exited out his back.

Noi was accused of dumping Bobby's body in a nearby county. For this, she had an accomplice, George Rivera, a Puerto Rican man with whom she worked at a local restaurant. It was mistakenly reported that Mr. Rivera pled guilty to being an accomplice and was sentenced to two years in prison. In truth, we recently learned charges against both him and another friend of his, Wilfredo Torres, who threw the gun to the bottom of a nearby lake, were dismissed at the request of the State due to "Insufficient Evidence."

And, if all of that were not bad enough, at the Broken Arrow Police station, Noi had given a four and a half hour tape-recorded confession to the department's top interrogator, David Anderson.

The interview was divided into two segments. For three and a half hours, Noi repeatedly lied to the Police, saying that Bobby had gone to play golf with his cousin and she stuck to her story. When the Police finally asked her if she knew who had murdered Bobby, she answered, "You tell me who killed him." Noi also denied that she and Bobby had argued and fought at all the last night of his life. Given that, according to neighbors and friends, they fought almost constantly, Noi seemed to be digging herself into a deeper and deeper hole with her inconsistent stories.

The second part of the interview occurred when Noi had been left alone for a few minutes, after which she broke down and told the Police she was ready to tell them everything. Getting hysterical, falling apart, she blurted out, "I need to do it. We had fight. He want take my kids. He tell me I can't have the kid, nothing, the kid is mine!" She said she told Bobby that all of the children were hers. "He can't have none," she cried.

In her attempt to cover up Bobby's death, Noi was exhibiting all of the actions of someone who is guilty. She left her husband's body lying on its side in his red and silver Pontiac on an oil and gas lease near Kiefer, Oklahoma, then threw his car keys into the same field. His billfold she tossed into a dumpster at The Marina Apartments in Tulsa. Noi then delivered a brown bag containing a gun and six bullets as a "present" for her unfortunate Puerto Rican friend,

George Rivera. Mr. Rivera and Wilfredo Torres then tossed the gun and bullets into a lake by those same apartments.

Initially, the Broken Arrow Police Department surmised that Noi and Mr. Rivera were having an affair; therefore, they had conspired and killed Bobby together. This was not true. Noi told the Police in reference to Mr. Rivera, "Don't do anything to him. He's just a student. He don't know anything. He's a student. He's a student."

One of the officers asked Noi, "Why did you hit Bobby so many times in the head?" Her reply was that she wanted to make sure he was dead.

In trying to destroy evidence at the crime scene, Noi had used paper towels to mop up the blood but, when it turned out the mess was bigger than she'd thought, she used her good thick towels, then washed and dried them in her laundry room. As hard as I tried to look for it, there was nothing in her actions after Bobby's death that made her look innocent.

And to make matters worse, Noi was an Asian woman who had married a hometown American boy whose wealthy and well-connected father was furious about this pairing; and he wasn't alone. Many people in the community were prejudiced against Asians. Indeed, some members of my own family feel that the United States should "ship any foreigners who cause us problems back to where they came from."

And Noi's father-in-law, Mack Mitchell, Jr., was hell-bent on revenge. He wanted the death penalty for Noi, and, if he couldn't win that, then life in prison, for sure. Mr. Mitchell's wealth and status in the community meant influence with the prosecutors and the Police. He had also hired his own detectives and attorneys to help the prosecutors win the case. He was a powerful and wealthy man focused on avenging the death of his son. His grief and his rage were massive; his pockets were deep ones. The only one standing between all of this force and Noi Mitchell being executed or spending the rest of her days in prison was me, Jim Lloyd. I couldn't let them run me over.

The OSBI (the Oklahoma State Bureau of Investigation) supplied many, many gruesome pictures of Bobby's body, which was beaten, bloody, and naked. These photos would inflame the jury. Gashes in the skull, bullet wounds, and lots of scratches in vivid color made true the saying, "A picture is worth a thousand words." That may be, but, in this case, I knew, somehow, that those pictures weren't telling the whole story. Noi was an abused woman who had finally had enough. Her husband, Bobby Mitchell III, was a violent man who had died a violent death. Karma has a long memory, big teeth and a short fuse. Sometimes the Karmic Boomerang strikes fast and hard. I believe we tend to reap what we sow, and in my opinion, Bobby Mitchell had done just that.

Winning this case would be a miracle, I knew that, but I also knew that winning it would ensure I would not have to live out my life as just another obscure lawyer. I could be David slaying Goliath; I could be Rocky Balboa taking out Apollo Creed. Hell, I could be the 1980 USA Olympic hockey team, or the 1969 Mets; even the Cubs winning the World Series in 2016. If I did not take this case, I would always wonder what would have happened if I had been willing to put my entire professional and financial future on the line for the chance to become preeminent, to make a difference, to make the impossible, suddenly, possible. I could rise up from the bottom of the heap. I felt I was inconsequential at this point in my life. My only other jury trial I had lost, my tiny son I couldn't save no matter how much I loved him. And even though the Oklahoma Bar Association had voted me as one of the Outstanding Young Lawyers in Oklahoma in 1979, which was a tremendous honor, still, for me, it wasn't enough. Winning this case would take me from "the nobody I felt like" to "the somebody I was desperate to feel like" – impressive, somebody to be reckoned with and appreciated in the world of law, at least.

In law school, I had avoided all the courses trial lawyers were supposed to excel in like "Moot Court" and "Trial Practice." I was so terrified to get up and speak in front of the class that, whenever I was called upon to recite a case, I'd have to say, "I am not prepared," or I would hold my throat and whisper, "I have laryngitis."

The law school professors were so intimidating that I completely lost my nerve. I was so scared, I'd almost be vibrating. I'd find myself shaking and sweating like a bird dog crapping peach seeds. Each time I was called upon in class, it was if I'd walked through a rendering plant and had been eviscerated and castrated at the same time! So, I was more than a little apprehensive in trying a first degree murder case. In truth, I was scared to death, but the payoff seemed so big! Most people would never realize how much of a personal challenge this really was.

Lawyers specialize much like doctors do. For example, there are criminal, tax, business, oil and gas, patent, divorce, and personal injury attorneys. I was not a criminal lawyer. I had never even tried a criminal case, but I knew taking on Noi's case would force me to grow, professionally, like nothing else ever would. On the other hand, I might also get her killed or locked up for the rest of her life.

Tulsa, Oklahoma is overflowing with lawyers, so I knew the odds of my getting another first degree murder case were very small. I really wanted to feel important and to be known as the man who had won a seemingly impossible murder case. In short, I knew I had just talked myself into accepting Noi's case, as stupid as it seemed on the outside – to everybody, especially my wife. I can be very stubborn. Whether that's a good trait or not, I couldn't say, but, still, that is a big part of me.

I wish I were magnanimous enough to say that I took the case because I knew she had to be innocent and that I believe in justice. I *do* believe in justice but, then, don't we all? At that point, my client's innocence was only a hunch on my radar screen, a tiny blip landing on the scales of justice, hoping to tip it in our favor. I prayed that she was innocent, but I also believe that every person must be presumed to be innocent under our system of justice and I would defend that belief. I decided to trust my hunch that she was innocent, but I really did not know enough about the case at first to prove it.

Then there is the fact that I am a sucker for a beautiful woman. Even though I was happily married and not looking to take advantage of the situation at all, Noi's dusky beauty intrigued me. Although she was extremely hard to get to know, I understood one thing almost immediately. There are women in the world for whom people just want to do things. They are, almost unknowingly, damsels-in-distress, for whom people, usually men, will do almost anything to help. If that was Noi, she didn't know it or didn't use it. I didn't realize it, either, not back then, but there we were.

One big question my wife had was, "What about your attorney's fees?" Fiscal stability is important to Nancy. Her work as a CPA with a prestigious accounting firm brought in most of our household income at that time while I was working to grow my law practice. At that point in our marriage, I was feeling like a sack of concrete Nancy was forced to drag along through her life. I didn't have much of a law practice and her job as a CPA was bringing in more money than mine as a lawyer. I don't like admitting that it stung, but it did. Nancy comes from a long line of hardworking people. That's how she is, too. I was terrified that her Dad's notions about my not being a good provider were coming true.

That was mostly my insecurities talking. In fact, my law practice had been chugging along – growing at a slow and steady rate. It was growing well enough that I didn't feel I *needed* this case, financially speaking. In fact, I was aware that Noi had no money, so I could not get my fee up front, as lawyers like to do in criminal cases. Really, that's the only practical way to get paid at all. An old lawyer once gave me his thoughts on the subject. He said, "You can do the work and get paid, or you can do the work and not get paid; therefore, get paid in advance."

I knew this case would financially drain me; I just had no idea to what extent that would happen. It would be up to me to advance money to hire experts, arrange for testing and, eventually, to pay for my Private Investigator. And, besides, I wouldn't have a lot of time to take on other work.

Noi was concerned about my finances, too. She, along with everyone else, was questioning my motives because, it really didn't make sense for me to take her case. "I feel bad," Noi repeated almost every time she saw me, because she knew I was spending large sums of money and turning down other work due to the intense demands her case was placing on my time and energy.

Nancy also felt badly. Trained as a CPA and watching from the sidelines as our bank accounts dwindled down, she often asked, "What's going on, Jim? You're consumed by Noi's case." She was right, of course. Nancy almost always is.

On one of my visits to the jail, Noi expressed personal concern. "I worry about you and Nancy," she said.

"Why?" I asked. I really wanted to know.

"Well, you don't make any money on my case and you don't have any time to take other people's cases. I worry you might go broke trying to help me, that's all." She paused and added, "Maybe you might give up, too."

Even though I would eventually use up all my life savings in helping to defend her, I never considered – not for a moment – giving up. I am a Lloyd and we don't give up, just like I told my baby boy, Brandon.

"Noi, don't worry about the money," I told her.

"But, how can I ever repay you?" she asked innocently. "What will you want of me?" This last question exposed her concerns.

It took me aback. And I had to take a breath. Then I said as firmly as I could, "Noi, I know what some of the other women in the jail have told you about their lawyers. The sad truth is that some attorneys have sex with their clients in return for legal services. I'm not going to do that. Do you understand? I'm not going to do that."

Of course she didn't look at me, but she did say, "My friends tell me that why you spend so much time and money on my case."

At first, I was hurt because she did not trust me. Then, I tried to imagine her perception of reality. Given her experiences of men in her life, she probably thought she had reason to be suspicious. Others were suspicious, too.

"All I want is for you to trust me and be my friend," I assured her.

"Now what is it?" she asked. Because of her life experience, that term 'be my friend' confused her.

I had spent so much effort in her case, I didn't want her to fire me and get a Public Defender. I had several reasons for feeling this way. One was that I felt deeply that I was the only person in the world with the dedication to her and inclination to save her. Also, I felt that, possibly, I was on the verge of winning a million-to-one case, something that doesn't come along for everyone in a lifetime as an attorney.

After several attempts to win her trust, one day I simply said, "Noi, the only thing I want from you is all your money." We both laughed out loud and held hands.

"But I don't have any money," she volunteered.

"I know, so don't worry about it," I said, and we laughed again.

Noi slowly began talking more and opening up with me from then on. It was a struggle, however, to piece together the exact details concerning the fight between Noi and her husband and what she did to cover up his death.

She was a pathetic, confused woman-child. I could not leave her at the mercy of some over-worked, uncaring Public Defender. Certainly, no one else was stepping up to fight for her case.

Is that why I took this case?

Well, I have always rebelled against rules, regulations, and limitations. I never was a model child, student, or member in my church. Taking this case may have been my way to prove to myself to the world and to create my freedom. Maybe I was rebelling at my role as a money machine for my family, a predictable member of my church, and as an ordinary member of the legal profession. Something churned in me, though, something deeper than a yearning. I wanted to be the gladiator, the unknown who rises up to slay the giant against all odds and win the day.

With Nancy, back then, I sometimes felt like a slot machine: feed him, clothe him, give him some loving, and he puts out the money. Now the biggest part of me knew that kind of thinking wasn't fair because, as I said, at that point, Nancy was bringing in more money than me. It's just that my wife comes from a long line of hardworking people, just as she is, herself. She wasn't looking for glory; she already felt great about herself. She knew she was amazing; she had nothing she felt she had to prove. Stability was important to my wife. She did not want to rock the boat. Nancy liked what we were building and where we were going. She wanted to maintain that status quo. I wanted more than that.

If I did not take the case because of Nancy's needs, I was sure that, eventually, resentment would rise up in me, smothering our marriage and dissolving it. If I did take the case and lost it, I could lose her, too. It was a gamble either way, so I decided to roll the dice.

Jim Lloyd and Jody Seay

CHAPTER 5 – THE LOVE THAT *ALMOST* WASN'T

Nancy and I met as students at Oklahoma State University in 1969. We were taking a class together, something she excelled in far more than I did. I'd noticed her and thought she was cute – petite, dark-headed, and with soft brown eyes. She seemed a bit shy, although I could tell she had a superior intellect to most of the people in that class, myself included. *(A few years later, when she sat for her CPA Exam, she made the highest score of anybody in the State of Oklahoma, just to give you an idea of how much superior her intellect really is.)*

I am drawn to smaller women because, as I mentioned earlier, I am of a smaller stature, too. Given all of that, I knew I'd have to rely on charm more than anything else to get the attention of this tiny, beautiful girl from Ponca City, and I wasn't even sure I knew how to do that. I didn't have much money; I drove a rattle-trap car. I had to keep the radio turned up loud so I could hear the music over the sound of my right front fender. Even though I worked when I could to help ends meet, still, tuition and books were taking up all the money I had just to get by. It's the life of a college student.

Finally, mustering all the courage I could find within me, I asked her one day if she'd like to go get a Coke with me. I didn't want to spend a lot of money on a date with her unless I could find out if she liked me, especially since I didn't have a lot of spare money to spend. So, we went out to get a Coke together and, to my delight, she did seem to be enjoying my company. I could make her laugh with my dumb jokes and, with just a subtle look toward me with those brown eyes of hers, she could make my heart thunder in my chest like majestic herds of wild mustangs galloping across the Osage Prairie in Oklahoma.

There was a dance at school coming up and, finally, I asked her to go to the dance with me. When she said yes, I almost leapt up from the table; it was all I could do to keep from racing around the Hideaway Pizza joint with my arms in the air like those Mexican soccer players when they score the winning goal! I was so excited and I don't think I even slept much over the next week or so, lying awake at night, rehearsing, in my mind: what I would wear, how shiny my shoes would be, freshly polished and gleaming on the dance floor, what I would say, how she might react, how lovely she would probably look.

I wasn't disappointed. She looked gorgeous, wearing a beautiful, well-tailored, apricot-colored dress she had made herself with tiny snaps down the back. Neither Nancy nor I come from great wealth, so learning to either make something yourself or repair things are important skills passed down through our families. Besides, our parents all lived through The Great Depression, which hit Oklahoma like a blast of buckshot, just about as hard as any place in the nation, leaving most Oklahomans ragged and tattered. Learning to make or fix or make-do were good survival skills to have and we both have always been grateful we learned them.

One survival skill that wasn't passed down to me was how to "cut a rug". Fast-dancing wasn't my forte. I couldn't Boogaloo or even Bop very well. The Pony made me look like I was having a seizure. Doing The Jerk, I felt, only emphasized how much I looked like one. Slow-dancing, though, well, when a slow one came on, finally, everything in me ached to take this young, beautiful girl into my arms and hold her close to me, which I did. I could smell her hair, the cologne she wore, could feel the smallness of her waist and back, as well as the heat between us.

Toward the end of the first slow dance, I gave this girl of my dreams a squeeze. I wanted her to remember how good it felt to be close to me. When I did that, almost all of those tiny snaps on the back of her dress came undone. Panic-stricken we stared into each other's eyes. *What should we do? Could we be thrown in jail for this?* We didn't know.

Luckily, another slow song came on right away. I pulled Nancy close to me again and swayed with her, pretending to dance, grappling with her dress and fasteners, and praying we weren't about to be expelled from Oklahoma State University. I spent the remainder of that song getting her snaps back together. Bottom line is: by the end of that second song, I was in love, no two ways about it.

Nancy must have been, too, because we dated for another several months and decided to marry. My parents, both staunch, conservative Republicans, liked her very much but were concerned because Nancy was a Democrat. When she told them she'd rather run into a member of the Black Panthers in a dark alley than a member of the John Birch Society, my mother decided that her future daughter-in-law probably had some Communist tendencies. Still, my folks knew we were in love and wanted me to be happy.

Rex, my brother, was only fifteen years old then and tended to believe everything I said to him. I told him, "Nancy is the smartest woman in the world *and* the strongest woman in the world!" Rex, already a burly guy, laughed out loud, so I made them sit down and arm wrestle. Wouldn't you know it? Nancy beat him with both her right arm *and* her left one! It just goes to show you what the power of the mind can do. I looked at Rex and put my arm around Nancy. "She's small, but mighty!" I said proudly and Rex wasn't laughing any more.

The next day, Rex said, "Nancy, I've got a very important question to ask you."

"Okay," Nancy replied. "What is it?"

"What do virgins eat for breakfast?" Rex asked.

Nancy, embarrassed, leaned over to me and whispered, even though everyone there could hear her.

"Jim," she whispered, "I've forgotten what the answer is."

I shouted out, "Anything they want to!"

We all exploded into laughter and the ice was broken for all of us. My family, from then on, has always thought Nancy was just great.

Not the same could be said for how Nancy's family viewed me, however. I went with Nancy one night to her parent's home in Ponca City to ask Nancy's Dad for his daughter's hand in marriage, which seemed like the respectful thing to do. It didn't go so well.

"NO!" he yelled, pounding his fist on the table, making all of the dishes hop up into the air and clatter back onto the table, "ABSOLUTELY NOT!"

I couldn't understand why he was so against that idea, except that her Dad coached basketball and was used to being around really tall guys. Then, here I come swaggering into his home, looking like I was still in Jr. High School – maybe just finishing my paper route – and asking to marry his little girl. I looked like an adolescent, not a young, ambitious man with a future and a good career in front of him, not someone who could support a wife and family. I'm sure none of this scenario fit any of the pictures in her father's head about how this day would be.

So, we eloped. If I thought then that doing so would change Nancy's father's feelings for me, I was mistaken. Every time I saw Nancy's dad, he looked down on me and I felt small. Eventually, slowly, he got over it. Every time I passed an important milestone, he thawed a little bit. Once I graduated and started earning a living as a lawyer, then he came to see me as a responsible adult with a future.

But, way before I earned his faith and trust, on May 24, 1971, I put on my only suit, polished my best shoes and headed out to claim as mine the girl I loved. I knew she loved me, too.

Nancy wore a peach-colored suit, another outfit she'd made herself, And even though I'm sure we still looked a bit like eighth graders, we stood before the minister at a little church right across the street from the OSU campus, pledging our love for and commitment to each other.

Nancy didn't tell any of her sorority sisters of our marriage plans so she had no one she knew to share the day with. My Uncle Ted and Aunt Ruth and eight-year old cousin, Brian, were present. My best friend, Stan McGilbray, a United States Marine, stood up for me as my best man in his Marine Corps dress blues, just for the occasion. The problem was, Stan was only twenty years old so, technically, as I teased Nancy, he wasn't of legal age and our marriage wasn't legal, either! She took my teasing with a smile like she always did. Luckily, my Aunt Ruth, Nancy's matron of honor, was plenty old enough to serve as a legal witness to our union, and according to Oklahoma Common Law Marriage cases, if you hold yourself out to be a married couple, you are considered to be just that as soon as you do. So, either way, we were covered.

Our first son, James R. Lloyd II, whom we call Buddy, was born April 14, 1977. A few years later, our son, Brandon Scott Lloyd, was born on April 22, 1981, and never made it out of the hospital. A year after that, our daughter Jamie was born on August 23, 1982, giving us answered prayers as she completed our family.

I know I haven't been the perfect husband. I am a self-focused man. Although it's not a trait I am proud of, I know I tend to think of myself more than others and to go for the glory while Nancy gets the work done. I know I've made some really stupid choices over the years.

Nancy has forgiven me more times for being a dunce than I have ever deserved. After almost 50 years together, though, with two grown and successful children, five beautiful grandchildren and a thriving law practice which now includes me, my wife and our son Buddy, this much I do know: MARRYING NANCY WAS THE BEST CHOICE I HAVE EVER MADE.

Jim Lloyd and Jody Seay

CHAPTER 6 – THE BULWARK OF LIBERTY – HOW IT'S *ALMOST* PERFECT

"What constitutes the bulwark of our own liberty and independence? It is not our frowning battlements, our bristling seacoast, our Army and our Navy. Our reliance is in the love of liberty which God has planted in us. Our defense is in the spirit which prizes liberty in the heritage of all men in all lands everywhere. Destroy this spirit, and we have planted the seeds of despotism at our own doors."

– Abraham Lincoln

"Noi, you can trust the judges to protect your constitutional rights in America. This is not Thailand. In the United States, we have a written document called The Constitution which ensures every person certain rights, rights that the police and the prosecutors cannot violate. If they do, they cannot use the evidence against you and, if they do use it, the conviction can be overturned. We have safeguards for the rights of the accused in this country." I did my best to assure Noi. I was proud of our system of justice in this nation and proud to be an American.

The Fifth Amendment protects a defendant against forced confessions. The Miranda Rights are designed to warn a suspect that she has the right to remain silent, that anything she says can be used against her, that she has the right to counsel, and, if she cannot afford a lawyer, one will be appointed to represent her. Anyone who has ever watched *DRAGNET* or any other cop show, I'm sure, can quote the Miranda Rights by heart.

To me, the Fifth Amendment is probably one of the most cherished rights. The constitutional test for a suspect to give up her Fifth Amendment rights is that she understands what she is giving up. There must be a voluntary, knowing, intelligent waiver of those rights.

I wanted the Judge to throw out Noi's tape-recorded confession. For the first three and a half hours of that interrogation, she repeatedly lied to the police. I was afraid the jury would believe that, if she lied often enough, she would lie in court, too. During the next forty-five minutes of the recording, she broke down and made some very confusing and damaging statements to the police. I cringed when I heard them. Once more, I considered using an insanity defense; that's how bad it was.

I felt I had a good chance of getting the Judge at the preliminary hearing to throw Noi's confession out because it was not a voluntary, knowing statement and, therefore, in violation of Noi's constitutional rights. If not suppressed at the preliminary hearing stage, then, perhaps, the trial Judge would throw the confession out.

Oh, they Mirandized Noi, but she did not understand the Miranda warnings due to her difficulty in understanding the English language. In addition, when she gave her statement to the police, she had been without water or nourishment of any sort for over six hours and, indeed, had not slept for two days. She was haggard and exhausted. David Anderson, with the Broken Arrow Police Department, was slick in his questioning. He took her statements, then twisted them around and fired them back at her, like a hard and fast tennis volley.

"Noi," Anderson said, "turn around here and look at me. Tell me the truth."

"I have to," Noi answered.

Anderson then did his little twist. "Why did you have to?" he asked

Noi responded, "He couldn't take my kids."

"Where's the gun at?" Anderson asked.

Noi replied, "I throw it away. He try to do lots of things to me and then I kill. I'm not going to do anything..." Her voice trailed away.

Anderson continued. "Tell me..."

Noi interrupted. "I never want to do this," she said.

Anderson asked again. "What did he try to do to you?"

Noi replied, "He tell me I can't have the kid, nothing. The kid is mine."

Clearly, there were two levels of communication going on, the police interrogators' and Noi's. Her answers did not really fit the questions being asked. I wanted the Judge to hear the recording, rather than the testimony of the witnesses who were there when Noi talked to the Police, to get the real flavor of her problems with English because she was so terrible at it. The Judge, in my view, needed to hear the entire confession, not just the most damaging excerpts.

Tom Cook, the P.I., and I went to the office of Assistant District Attorney, Edward Roosevelt (Eddie) Lewis, to make a copy of the original five and one-half hour tape recording. Lewis was a twenty-eight year old lawyer, an immaculately dressed black man who graduated from Georgetown University School of Law, one of the finest in the country. On his three-piece Brooks Brothers suit, he sported a gold watch chain that was sharp-looking and stylish. He had never lost a case and was an impressive man, both as an attorney and a member of the community. I respected him for his pride, his smooth and polished courtroom appearance and for his intelligence. I also liked him because he was short, like me, although I suspect I liked him more than he liked me.

I knew I was starting to get under the skin of the prosecutors when I was in Lewis' office. Assistant D.A., Sharon Moore, pounded on the door. We shut the tape recorders off. She then barged into the office and lit into me. It was hard to keep from smiling when she began shaking her finger in my face and screaming, "WHY IN THE HELL DID YOU GO OUT TO THE MITCHELL HOUSE?? YOU'VE GOT NO RIGHT!"

That was such an absurd thing to say, it was almost funny. I was investigating the alleged crime and needed to be able to get into the house for evidence to prove Noi's case. It was imperative that my experts do their testing in Noi's house. I think she hated me even more because I did not get mad at her. I know it always makes my wife go wild as a banshee when I refuse to get mad, or – even worse – when I act like she is being ridiculous. It works because there is nothing to push against and the argument, all of a sudden, collapses.

Sharon Moore, however, was so irate that she even threatened Tom by saying, "You've got to get along with us." Tom's license as a Private Investigator was issued through the city and the prosecutor's office has a lot of pull when it comes to license renewal time. The implication was clear: Tom's livelihood was suddenly on the line. Tom, as you might imagine, did not think this was very funny. His olive skin became pale and he got a sad, disappointed expression on his face. Of course, his real concern was whether I would tell the prosecutors about the evidence we had found in Noi's home. He felt that the prosecutor might charge us with obstruction of justice, something neither of us wanted.

"Obstruction of Justice" is a serious charge, not one to be thrown around lightly. Licenses can get yanked and I could get disbarred, plus, it's a serious stain on your record if you are an attorney or a private investigator, which is why people in these professions do everything they can to stay within the rule of law.

So, as I said, Tom was worried about an obstruction of justice charge whereas I was enjoying the drama. I'm a gambling man sometimes and I was gambling that I was within the rules of law on this in how I was handling the evidence we found.

I used to try and change both Tom and Nancy but gave up when I realized they both got a certain satisfaction out of constant worry. I feel like they both see themselves as more conscientious than I am because they both fret so much more than I do. In truth, I should have been the one worried, not Tom or Nancy. I'm sure I don't worry enough, that I just trot through life with a goofy grin on my face, somehow certain that everything will turn out okay. That night, at dinner, I tried to tell my family about Sharon Moore and how mad she was. And right on cue, Nancy started worrying about how irritating Sharon Moore would affect my future career in Tulsa as an attorney. My six year old son, Buddy, did not really understand what the big deal was, but he enjoyed the turmoil I had created. He already understood the fun of a good fight. I should have known then he'd grow up to be an outstanding attorney, and he has.

Judge Shaffer was appointed to the Criminal Division a few months prior to Noi's preliminary hearing. A man in his late 40's, he had a lean, scowling look around his mouth and eyes. I knew Shaffer's reputation as a tough, no-nonsense former Assistant D.A. Even though I enjoyed a good fight, I had a feeling that this wasn't going to be a fight at all. Shaffer intimidated me and I was angry at myself for letting that happen. I walked into the courtroom and wanted to disappear through the cracks in the floor. I wanted to be anywhere else but here. It was embarrassing to me for Noi to see me so scared. I needed her to believe in my confidence and strength. Hell, I even wanted to impress her.

This preliminary hearing was important to us. Basically, I wanted to find out exactly what evidence the State would present in Noi's trial in the coming months. I knew they had more than enough evidence to press charges. I wanted the Judge to listen to the tapes of the recorded confession so he could determine if her Fifth Amendment rights had been violated. I subpoenaed all ten witnesses that the state had listed in the criminal complaint.

One of the ten witnesses was Bobby's mistress. She was very attractive, very well turned-out. I learned that Bobby had never actually given up his girlfriend Theresa, even after marrying Noi. The two of them had renewed their "intimate friendship" in the recent past, according to an OSBI agent. Theresa actually lived a few doors up and around the corner from Noi and Bobby's home, in a modest stone house on Walnut Avenue right there in Broken Arrow. If Bobby and Theresa had decided to renew their "intimate friendship," Bobby didn't have to travel very far to make that happen.

I guess my impressively detailed questioning was too much for Judge Shaffer. The judge was growing impatient and to me it sure looked like his mind was already made up to charge Noi. He acted like it was a waste of time for me to question the State's witnesses so thoroughly and kept muttering, "We'll never get done" all day long. In addition, he continuously interrupted me when I questioned the prosecutor's witnesses to discover the facts. I needed answers and I needed to learn about these people. That's why the questioning was important to our case; I could not find out what I needed to know directly from the prosecutors. The Judge reminded me that this was not a trial and I told him I knew that. I did.

Thank God, I would have more time to develop my evidence, I thought.

The first day of the preliminary trial was rough. Tom was probably one of the few people who stood by my side the entire time, and even he was a little nervous about my performance. Tom told me, "You had better get some help, Jim!" He meant that I should refer this case to an experienced trial lawyer. If I did that, however, I knew I would lose control of the case and I would also lose my chance to grow as well as my chance to be the hero. I also felt, as conceited as this may sound, that I was the only one who cared enough to see it through. Most people I ran into already had their minds made up that Noi was guilty as sin and they were in a rush to punish her. I needed to slow things down so everyone could get a good look at what was really happening – including me.

I felt so badly about my cowardly performance by backing down when the Judge kept interrupting me that I never mentioned my frustration to my wife. I was silent on the subject to several lawyer friends, too; quite the opposite of asking for help. I really wanted to talk to somebody about this, but I was too proud to let them know how I did not stand up for my client against the Judge when he had no right to keep interrupting my questioning. With every interruption, my hands got cold and clammy. Even my voice turned into a squeak. I felt insignificant and sweaty and squeaky and I knew I was not being effective as Noi's attorney.

I am a short man, but I was deathly afraid I was becoming a *little* man.

The second day of the preliminary hearing was even worse, if you can imagine. Chances are, you can't. I really didn't know it could go so badly. All I needed to accomplish was for the Judge to hear the tape of the confession. Detective David Anderson was the officer who questioned Noi. He refused to authenticate the tape because it stopped when Sharon Moore, the Assistant D.A., had burst in to Lewis's office, interrupting us as we were making our copy of the tape. To introduce a tape or any other physical evidence in court, the person wanting it admitted must prove that the evidence is what he says it is. I had to show that the tape recorded copy was a fair and accurate copy of the tape made the night of Oct. 7, 1982 in the Police Station.

I asked Anderson to authenticate the tape. This meant all he had to do was say it was an accurate copy of the official tape and identify the voices. Anderson refused to help me. He said it was not the same because there was a *gap*. This "gap" was created when we erased Sharon Moore's interruption. Only one word was affected – the word "the" was slightly broken up and garbled. Although this would normally be acceptable, Anderson refused to authenticate the copy.

And Lewis refused to furnish his original tape of the confession. I caught Lewis and Anderson exchanging all-knowing nods and winking eye movements. *They think they have figured out how to shut me down*, I thought. "Your Honor," I kept fighting, "I'd like Tom Cook to authenticate the tape; he was there." But the Judge refused to admit it since Tom had only been there for the tape's reproduction, not during the original interrogation. I was so upset over being treated this way that I forgot to call forward any of the witnesses I had subpoenaed to testify. Noi was now charged with murder and the preliminary hearing was over.

I noticed that Lewis looked down at his stack of file folders as I left the room. *I figure he can't look me in the eye because of his actions in the courtroom,* I complained to myself. *I have never felt so frustrated and boxed into a corner before. I swear to God this will be the last time.* But I also knew that Lewis was strategically clever and so quick on his feet in the courtroom that all the swearing I just did might turn out to be an empty promise.

Noi asked me, "What happen?"

As ignorant as she was about the law, she knew things were not going as I'd hoped they would. I told her that Judge Shaffer did not want to consider her constitutional rights but that Judge Dalton might. Shaffer had transferred the case to Judge Dalton for arraignment and trial.

I was encouraged that, unlike Judge Shaffer, Judge Dalton had *not* been an Assistant D.A. before he became a judge. Dalton was in his late 40's with an abundance of gray hair to show for his wisdom. Some of my lawyer buddies had mentioned to me that Dalton had been a staunch defender of people's constitutional rights until about five years prior to this time when his whole personality seemed to change. It had happened during the particularly gruesome "Steak House Cooler" double murder cases. Shortly after that trial, it was said that Dalton became more and more like a hanging judge. I think something inside him must have snapped under the pressure of those multiple murder cases. His recent record seemed to indicate that he had acquired a mistrust of defendants.

But this seemed obvious: before Noi could consent to a search of her home, especially when the Police did not have a search warrant and before she could confess to a crime, she was supposed to understand – completely – what rights she was giving up. Based on how much difficulty I was having in trying to pry Noi's story from her, I knew she really did not have command of the English language. She could give common responses like "Yes" and "No" and "What you say?" and she could take orders from a menu in the Mexican restaurant where she worked, but she was a long way from understanding the meanings of words, especially when they related to abstract principles, like constitutional rights.

Now, it was clear that the Broken Arrow Police recognized this problem because they brought in an interpreter to explain her rights to her. Unfortunately, they selected one who understood neither English nor Thai very well. Kao Vue, the interpreter, was from Laos and was fluent only in Laotian. Laos is a tiny country northeast of Thailand and, although Kao spoke a little Thai, the Laotian language is distinctly different. To law enforcement, however, this, apparently, was close enough for government work. It would be like bringing a Russian person in to interpret for a French national who was in trouble in a small Greek town. It would be impossible to convey abstract principles.

Tom Cook managed to find a Thai translator, Kosin Ponpayuhakiri, who knew the Thai language well, having lived his first twenty years in Thailand. He went on to get his degree in Pharmacy at the University of Oklahoma and was currently working at a drugstore in Tulsa. He wasn't that hard to find. We asked Kosin to attend the upcoming suppression hearing.

The purpose of a suppression hearing is to weed out any evidence that should not be presented to a jury. For the suppression hearing before Judge Dalton, I had subpoenaed the original tape of Noi's confession from the District Attorney's office. I wanted Kosin to translate what Kao Vue had said to Noi in mixed Laotian and Thai when he got her to sign a consent form for a complete search of her home *before* she was given her Miranda rights.

I tried to play a five to ten minute portion of that tape on which Kao Vue translated, from English to a mixture of Laotian and Thai, first the *"Consent to Search"* form and then the *"Miranda Rights"* form for Noi.

"Your Honor," I said, "we would like to play the first few minutes concerning the rights as they were given to my client, first in English by the Police, and then as they were given to her in Kao Vue's mixed Thai and Laotian."

Lewis jumped up. "I object, Your Honor," he said, "She speaks English and it is immaterial what the interpreter translated."

"We have a transcript of that," the Judge muttered as he thumbed through the transcript of the interview. A secretary for the Broken Arrow Police Department had transcribed Noi's interview with Detective Anderson. Whenever Noi or Detective Anderson requested assistance from Kao Vue in translating, the transcript read, *"Interpreter to her in her native language."* Hardly an exact quote, if you ask me, and certainly not a factual description.

"Well, the transcript does not give the interpretation of what Kao Vue told Noi and what her response was." I stood as I spoke. The judge stared grimly at me, but I doggedly continued to plead my point, "Kosin can listen to the tape and translate what Kao Vue told Noi in Thai and Laotian and what her response was. It just covers the first five to ten minutes of the tape."

"I wouldn't understand it if you told it to me in Thai," the Judge said, perfectly straight-faced.

I was shocked silent for a moment. *Perhaps Dalton heard the beat of a different drummer; perhaps one far, far away.* I thought to myself. Out loud I asked, "Pardon?" Maybe I wanted to give him another chance at courtroom humor, even though I didn't see anything funny about this at all. I couldn't believe what my ears had just heard. "Pardon?" I asked again.

The Judge repeated, "I wouldn't understand if he did tell it to me in Thai."

I was beginning to get irritated. Obviously, Lewis didn't want the Judge to hear what Kao Vue had interpreted to Noi. And, perhaps, the judge was confused. Using all the restraint I could muster to keep the irritation out of my voice, I said, slowly but emphatically, "We would like for Mr. Kosin to listen to the tape and translate what Kao Vue said to Noi. That way, we can determine exactly how Kao Vue explained Noi's consent to search her home and then how he explained her Miranda rights to her."

I slid a sideways glance at Lewis. His face was set with determination. I could tell he was not going to let my interpreter, Kosin, translate what Kao Vue had said. At this point in our careers, Lewis seemed like a shark to me and I felt him chomping around in my minnow pool. *I can feel the water churning faster and faster,* the narrator in my mind was telling the story, *until, during this frenzy, the little fish will be devoured.* It seemed like I was standing in waist-deep water with a bull's eye target on my ass and the theme from *JAWS* pounding in my head.

But, I persisted. I was beginning to learn that tenaciousness in the face of fear just took focus. So, we finally got Kosin to give his interpretation but only after having Lewis object nearly all morning. I was getting exhausted from having to side-step Lewis' objections for over three hours. This bickering between Lewis and me was starting to wear on Judge Dalton, too, like Chinese Water Torture. Drip… drip… drip… Excruciating to both of us.

First, Kosin wrote down, word for word, using the Thai alphabet, what Kao Vue had said to Noi about the *"Consent to Search"* form and then he verbally translated that into English. This Thai translation was marked "EXHIBIT A."

Here's Kosin's translated (into English) version of Kao Vue's explanation of the *"Consent to Search"* form: "The way the official bring you here, before you will be interviewed and to ask you several questions, to ask you questions, you have to allow, permit it. You have to write down the consent and you allow it, permit it, just print (your signature) before it can be done. You print it."

Noi asked him, "One more time?"

Kao Vue then said, "I shall ask you questions. There are several questions, but before we can ask you questions, you have to write down, allow us to ask you questions."

Then Noi had responded to her translator by saying, "Oh! Let (inaudible) Noi to be (inaudible)."

To which "Kao Vue said, "Permit us to, allow to interview you about this morning, about the accident, you allow, permit us and ready to be asked and you print it."

Kosin had written that Noi's response to this was, "Oh! To be interviewed?"

Kao Vue answered Noi with, "It mean I will go to your house to examine about everything which happen (inaudible). Do you have any questions to ask officials? If not, print it."

"Noi answer, 'No, don't have anything.' " Kosin added, "Means she has no questions."

Then, Kosin wrote down, word for word, using the Thai alphabet, what Kao Vue said to Noi about her Miranda rights and, then, he verbally translated that into English. This Thai translation was then marked Defendant's "EXHIBIT B."

Kao Vue's explanation of the Miranda rights to Noi were as follows. "Kao Vue say, 'The way things go, before you will give any statement to answer every question, you have to understand, which you might not. You don't have to answer. If you think you can answer, you answer it. It involve about a matter involving the court case this morning, and (inaudible) to go to court. And, if you need a lawyer, if you think not necessary to answer, don't answer. Do you understand? Because you have to go to court.' "

"Noi say, 'You think I should answer?' "

"Kao Vue say, 'The thing you know, you answer.' "

"Noi say, 'I tell them what I know. The things I can answer, I answer. Things I don't know, I cannot answer.' "

The judge admitted Kosin's Thai translations into evidence as Exhibits "A" and "B" and strongly suggested to Lewis that he bring Kao Vue to court to hear his side of the translation problem. I was feeling a little feisty and asked the court to issue a bench warrant for Kao Vue's arrest since I had subpoenaed him and he hadn't shown up for court.

"I'll take the bench warrant under advisement," the judge said and then he passed the case for a week so Lewis would have time to get Kao Vue there.

Of course, Lewis protested, saying, "I don't think we need Kao Vue here. I think, after listening to the tape, you will understand that the use of the interpreter was only a safeguard and not a necessity. I feel like an interpreter was not necessary. Noi understood English well enough to waive her rights." But, it was a no-go. Lewis was to bring his interpreter to court.

However, when Kao Vue finally did appear in court, it took me an unbelievable three days to get him to translate what he said to Noi during the five to ten minute conversation with her.

I gave Kao Vue the copy of Kosin's Thai translation; Exhibits "A" and "B." and I asked him, "Would you please translate into English what you believe you said to Noi on October 7th?"

Kao Vue looked at me with a blank stare, like he'd suddenly been rendered deaf and mute. I rephrased my question in simpler language. "I want you to say – translate it for us into English and tell us in English what you told her."

"While looking at Exhibit A?" Kao Vue asked, "Read this thing and translate?"

"Yes," I said.

"No, I cannot do that," Kao Vue responded.

"Why not?" I asked.

"Because, it is different from my words," Kao Vue replied.

"Well, you've had a chance to listen to your words from the tape, haven't you? You have listened to your words several times, haven't you?"

"Yes, but, see, if I look at this thing and translate here, even though correct like the tape…"

I was feeling punch-drunk by now, but I tried to keep my balance. The room had begun to spin in slow motion. I anchored my feet to the floor, pushing down through the soles of my shoes. I felt the tibialis anterior muscles on each of my shins harden like steel. "Tell me," I said softly but with steely determination to Kao Vue, "what were your words, your first question to this first statement?"

"To who?"

It was too much, like being trapped in a vapor of stupidity and willful ignorance. I lost my temper with Kao Vue. I didn't mean to; it just happened. I raised my voice and roared at him, "THAT LADY OVER THERE, NOI MITCHELL, WHO IS THE DEFENDANT IN A FIRST DEGREE MURDER CASE! THAT IS WHY WE ARE IN COURT! WHAT DID YOU TELL HER – IN ENGLISH, PLEASE?"

He jerked back in his chair and just sat there with that irritating blank look on his face. I began to feel guilty for having yelled at the poor man because he looked so frightened. *What was the matter with him, anyway?*

Judge Dalton offered a solution. "Why don't we do it this way? You have gone over these Exhibits 'A' and 'B'. Is there any way you can tell us how they are different from your translation of what was said on the day in question? That is the simple way to get to it, I think."

Kao Vue studied my Exhibits 'A' and 'B' and said, "Okay. The translation here, the first word here is different from what I explained in my translation, and, also, hers is different, and this is Noi, and here the whole word is different, and this word, here, and…"

I remember thinking, *DEAR LORD, WHY COULDN'T I HAVE BEEN BORN SMART ENOUGH TO BE A BRAIN SURGEON?? WHY JUST BARELY SMART ENOUGH TO BE A LAWYER??*

Dalton broke in and exclaimed, "My God, why can't we get this done? You can do that, can't you? You can listen to the tape and listen to what she responded and just write down what you said to her in Thai…?"

"Yes, sir," Kao Vue interrupted.

"And, what she responded to you in Thai?" the Judge anxiously queried.

"Yes," Kao Vue responded.

"That's what the defense, the State, and the court wants, and to save us all a bunch of time. I don't think anyone will make any sense out of the way we are going about this." He looked at Lewis, for some reason, at this point. "Is it agreeable with both attorneys?"

I quickly agreed, "Yes, Your Honor." But, Lewis didn't agree or say anything in response to the Judge's question.

I then added, "With the understanding that we want his ENGLISH translation."

"This is the only way I'll be able to know what the translation is," the judge replied, with a shrug and a grin that seemed to say, *YOU DUMMY*.

But the way things had been going thus far in the suppression hearing, for the first time, I didn't feel like I was the dummy in this courtroom.

Lewis took Kao Vue by the arm and escorted him to the jury room to listen to the ten minute segment. Kao Vue spent forty-five minutes laboriously playing the tape back and forth and was wiping sweat from his forehead between scribbles on a legal pad. If my law professors had intimidated me when I was a student, Kao Vue, in his nervousness and terror, had me beat by miles. I was afraid the poor guy might have a stroke or a seizure of some sort before he was done.

Lewis finally told Judge Dalton the translation was finished and Kao Vue resumed his place on the witness stand.

I proceeded, "Let the record reflect that we are now back from a forty-five minute recess taken so Mr. Kao Vue could listen to the tape and translate into English what he said in Thai to Noi and her responses in Thai on October 7, 1982. Mr. Kao Vue, would you please tell the court what you told Noi?"

Kao Vue responded in a strange tongue I knew to be Thai. Judge Dalton's eyes got wide and he said, "I can't understand that." His voice was strained, like he couldn't believe the absurdity of this whole mess. His face turned bright red. There was laughter in the audience; even the Thais sitting in the gallery broke out laughing.

Lewis seemed to want to tear his own hair out; Kao Vue looked like he might die. I found out later that the reason for his unusual behavior and his reluctance to appear in court was that he was terrified of being executed for mistakes he had made in his translations. Apparently, life in Laos is tougher than in the USA. In my mind, this reinforces my case of how terrified Noi was during her interrogation. *Why wasn't anyone else noticing this?*

Despite the moments of levity we had, trying to understand what Kao Vue told Noi about constitutional rights, it was at an end. I am a Rat Terrier when it comes to research – digging and digging and digging until I find what I need. I had thoroughly researched Supreme Court cases about violations of constitutional rights and had enough ammunition to argue for days. I counted and listed some half-dozen violations of her constitutional rights and there were probably more I had missed.

One of the big constitutional violations was that the police had her sign a *"Consent to Search"* form before they had given her the Miranda rights. The police had also unwittingly used Kao Vue to misstate her constitutional right to remain silent in a clearly improper manner by telling her she had to answer the questions if she knew the answers.

Dalton gave me only fifteen minutes of legal argument and then he ruled against me. I was stunned – angry. *Now, only a jury would stand between Noi and prison* I fumed to myself. *I had found many, many constitutional violations, but no one seems to care that Noi's rights had been shredded and stomped on.*

I did, however, gain a momentary whiff of satisfaction when Lewis, the opposing counsel, looked right at me and said, "Something tells me this case is going to be a real dog fight."

He seems upset, I thought smugly, *He spent weeks in these hearings when he probably thought this was an open and shut case. I'll bet he thinks all of this is a waste of time.* Then I mused, *Did Lewis even study constitutional law while attending Georgetown University Law School?*

Everyone filed out of the courtroom but I sat in my chair, shoulders slumped, head down, and reflected on what had just happened to Noi's constitutional rights and the events in the courtroom.

This was not the law that I knew and loved. This was not even the justice system that I believed in. Instead, it seemed like a very sad joke had just been played on this fragile and helpless young woman.

Jim Lloyd and Jody Seay

CHAPTER 7 – *ALMOST* A FAMILY

I got home early that night, which, surely, was a sign that something had gone badly wrong. Since I had taken Noi's case, I'd been motivated to work until 12:30 or 1 am. On this night, I was home by 9:30 pm and Nancy was shocked to see me walk in the door.

I had been fighting all day long and the last thing I wanted when I got home was another fight – of any sort. I wanted someone to talk to and someone to give me comfort, someone who would hold my hand or stroke my head or lay an arm of understanding across my shoulders.

But as I walked in the door, Nancy wasted no time starting right in on me. Clearly, from the pressures I had inflicted on myself and my family, I would have to wait until Noi's trial was over for my simple pleasures.

It's not like I didn't know the fights by heart. We had two we fought over and over again: money or attention. Tonight it was the same old line of aggravation, namely, my lack of attention to her and the children.

Nancy said, "You know how babies change so fast and that's especially true if you only see them when they are asleep."

Children? I thought to myself. *My infant daughter does not even look familiar to me.*

And at the same time that I was thinking, *"You think I don't realize that I'm losing out on getting to know her as a baby?"* Nancy was saying it out loud. "I don't think you realize that you are losing out on getting to know Jamie as a baby."

I felt scared about that ... and guilty, which made me mad, so I said something stupid and defensive – I don't remember what exactly.

Nancy countered with, "And you are completely ignoring Buddy."

She was probably right about that, too.

"You know he's acting out at school. That's what happens when you're never around. He loves you. He's trying to get your attention." Nancy was in all-out blame mode now, her voice rising in volume and pitch.

In retrospect, Nancy was most likely right about Buddy trying to cause me to interact with him, although I couldn't see it at the time. Even negative attention is attention in the mind of a child, and if Buddy was acting out, the negative attention he was getting was almost making up for the absence of his father from his life.

When Buddy was born, I considered him to be my child – *My Child* – he bonded to me, not Nancy because she had to go back to work as a CPA less than a month after he was born and I had the time to nurture him. Back then, I had barely started my law practice so there was time to spare in my life. I had been the most important person in the world to Buddy and now, six years later, here I was rejecting him.

I'm not sure why – perhaps, my own guilt – but suddenly my son did not seem so cute to me anymore. Whenever I saw him, he was usually causing problems and, in my view, he was becoming sneaky and spiteful. I found myself avoiding him. Nancy surmised that my rejection was causing Buddy's personality changes.

I blundered, at that moment in our fight, one of the worst blunders I've ever made, "Honestly, Nancy," I said trying to share my feelings with my wife in an open and frank way, "I've sort of lost interest in Buddy because he's no longer cute, like a baby."

My confession caused Nancy to break down into horrible sobs and she left the room. I stood there frustrated and stupid. She came back, still crying but quieter, and she moved me to the sofa to sleep.

Most of the night on that sofa I kept telling myself that I would make it up to them after this trial was over, but I wasn't even sure the seams of our family unit would hold together that long. And I kept beating myself up for the truly stupid things I said to the mother of my children.

In the years since, doing some arm-chair psychoanalysis of myself, I can see that out of my own guilt over allowing Noi's case to overtake my life and the lives of my family, perhaps what I was doing was building a wall between myself and them so my time would be free to get the things done I needed to do.

We were in a mess, as a family, and it was of my own making. The love we all shared was dying right before my eyes, it seemed, flickering like a melted candle, and I had no one to blame but myself, no one to turn to in order to make it better.

I thought back on better days when Nancy and I met as students at Oklahoma State University. I felt again the instant pull of attraction for Nancy when I met her. I could lose myself in those velvety brown eyes of hers and I loved her figure. She was always eager to please me, as I was her.

Nancy had always been a team player and we made a good one. There were so many times when she just plain bailed me out. I think I mentioned earlier how much smarter Nancy is than I am. Also, there is an air of pragmatism about her that I've never shared. I tend to fly by the seat of my pants; Nancy figures out the right path, ducks her head and plows forward to get the job done. Those traits, being so different, rather than pushing us apart, made us complement each other, and I was grateful to have won the heart of someone who could be so many things I knew I wasn't.

Back then, in college, we were always excited to do things together and had so many good times at concerts, picnics, football games, wrestling matches, even study breaks. You name it, we did it together. While we were still single, everyone teased us, "You two are always chumming around together. When are you getting married?" And, when we finally did, that aspect of togetherness just got stronger. I longed for those sweet times of closeness with her. God, how I missed my Nancy!

I was miserable reliving these memories but if I couldn't hold on to her, at least I could hold on to the memories of her – of us.

When Buddy arrived six years later, he was our little prince. He had his mother's beautiful brown eyes and luscious olive skin. He was a gorgeous baby and a joyful toddler. I would even wake up my little Buddy to play on nights when I got home late. It would have been hard to imagine a family with more love running through it than ours had been.

Looking back, the first crack in our relationship appeared after our tiny, newborn son, Brandon, died just hours after his birth. The hurt was so raw we wanted to crawl out of our skins. Nancy and I both felt almost desperate to fill the void he left behind.

We worked so hard to get Jamie, our miracle baby. Nancy's pregnancy was difficult and fraught with complications, causing her doctor to order bed rest from the third month on. In addition, there were several surgeries and hospital stays, which meant blood tests every hour. Black and blue marks ran up and down each of her arms from so many needle sticks – poor Nancy!

As a family unit, during Nancy's pregnancy with Jamie, we were all on edge. The alarm clock fired off every two hours so Nancy could take the medication to keep her from going into labor. The medicine made her shake and feel miserable. But once Jamie arrived, we were both ready to relax and enjoy the pleasures and wonder of a new, healthy baby.

Jamie had a firecracker type of spunk, my almond-shaped green eyes, and a captivating, yet, ornery smile. She was so much wilder in temperament than Buddy. It was shocking sometimes to realize that they were brother and sister. Our theory was that the medication Nancy had taken while she was pregnant made Jamie colicky, loud and demanding. Were we right? We didn't know. What we *did* know, however, was that our family suddenly had to stretch our love to include a distinctly new personality.

Tonight when I had come home early so severely depressed, I thought that somehow I could get some sort of comfort. I couldn't help feeling disappointed again at our short explosion and Nancy's tears and her going to bed alone and me here, in my spot on the sofa without even bothering to fold out the hideaway bed. My mind was reeling; my heart was heavy. *What had happened to our good ol' days?*

It was the case; this case that was causing the problems. We used to do everything together. Now Nancy and I had stopped communicating with each other except for our fights. *Maybe*, I thought as I shifted my hip out of the crack between the sofa cushions, *it's because our interests and our focus have become so different. Nancy wants help with the children, someone to be a full partner with her in this marriage. I want help with this case; at least, someone to understand how difficult and frustrating it all is. I want acknowledgement that I'm trying to do something monumental.*

I shifted again, more uncomfortable with my thoughts than the state of the sofa. *When I am home, my wife wants me to actually be here, involved in the lives of our children and being a good Dad to them – and a good husband if there is any time left.* I winced. *And what am I?* I thought. *I am mostly absent, or absorbed in papers and files or boxes of evidence. Nancy is fighting just as hard as I am. She just wants respect, something I'm not giving her. I'm only paying attention to what I want and need, not my wife. Why is that? Why is that?* I knew I could keep myself up all night asking questions like this.

Nancy and I were operating on different planes. It was not a comfortable feeling knowing I've taken a case that could further divide us and our whole family. I have always believed in the sanctity of marriage but, here I was, doing something I also knew might tear my marriage apart. Perhaps what I really wanted, in the final analysis, was for Nancy to choose my happiness by helping my career over her need for financial security. That's what I told myself, as self-absorbed and oafish as that sounds; it was the only way I could drift off to sleep that night feeling so sad and lonely.

Sunlight burning through the cathedral windows above the doorway woke me, hitting me as I stretched out on the sofa. Today, I felt uncomfortable with this untimely, sparkling dawn. It was too bright for my dark mood. I wanted a warm, comforting, dark bed and someone to cuddle up to. I began my search in Buddy's room.

I considered crawling into bed with my son, in his twin bed with the bright blue Pac-Man bedspread. Buddy's skin was covered with a fine sheen of perspiration and he was squirming around in his sleep. Even though he was six years old, he still slept with his bottom up in the air at a slight angle, like a baby. He looked like he was right in the middle of a dream. I watched his eyelashes flutter slightly. I did not have the heart to wake him up, so I moved on.

Next, I peeked in on Jamie, such a gorgeous little baby girl. She was sleeping on her back, sprawled out, with her mouth open. Her nose had been stuffy the night before, so I thought she must be getting a cold. She was snoring, so I did not lie down on her bed. I noticed her blonde hair was starting to get curly like Nancy's hair and that it had grown much longer. I tried to remember the last time I had really looked at Jamie. She had thrown her covers off so I covered her back up, patted her cool arms and left the room.

I went on down the hallway to my own bedroom and decided to check in on Nancy. She was lying on her side with her dark hair spread out and softly curling on the pillow. I like her curly hair because I think it makes her look so feminine.

Back in our college days, Nancy was self-conscious about her curly hair. Curly hair was not cool back then, unless you were Arlo Guthrie. Nowadays, everyone is spending lots and lots of money for permanents to give themselves curls and Nancy is happy with her head of lush, naturally springy and wavy hair. I think it makes her feel like she won something and maybe she did.

On this day, Nancy is thirty-two, one year younger than I am. She looks much younger in her sleep; her features and skin tone are so smooth, like every wrinkle and every worry has been ironed away. She looks so inviting. I curl up next to her and cuddle. We can, at least, still remember how to do that.

For the moment, all the bad stuff drifts away and I relax. It feels good to know that my family is here with me — and safe — despite what, I hope, are temporary differences.

Jim Lloyd and Jody Seay

CHAPTER 8 – *ALMOST* NATIVE AMERICAN

My family is between one-quarter and one-third Cherokee Indian, depending on whom in the family you can find to admit to having any Native American blood at all. Personally, I am proud of this heritage. It is as much a part of me as being from Oklahoma and I have always been proud of both of those things. That's how I have raised my children, too.

The Cherokee believe that visions are sacred and their leaders were chosen from those visions. They believe that dreams are based upon thoughts you hold just prior to drifting off to sleep and that reality is created from those dreams.

My own version of this understanding is much more simplistic and, consequently, I refer to each of them as a *Godplop!* They are those moments of insight or luck which seem to have just dropped from the sky – or from the hand of God, which has just slapped me in the head. Either way, I have learned to not question them, but to just be grateful for them.

Even with all of that in mind; even with my respect for my Cherokee heritage so firmly entrenched in me, still, I was skeptical as Noi held up a piece of paper. "Wait," she said, "before talk about case. Friend give me this."

"What is it?" I asked.

"What does this mean?" she whispered. She placed her cold, clammy hands around mine and slipped me a note. I slowly unfolded it and read:

"Dear Sir:

My name is Madeline. I am full-blooded Cherokee Indian. In my spirit, I have been very concerned for Noi Kanchana. For what it's worth, my spirit keeps revealing the number three (3). The significance of this is not clear. Could be a combination to equal three; i.e., two years suspended, less time served. I don't know, but it still gives me three. I have been in constant prayer since I met her."

Noi explained, "She's in a cell near me, and all of the girls say I better listen to her. What does she say?"

Noi was so tense I could see her fingernails beginning to turn white so I told her I had never heard such hogwash in all my life. "Never mind," I reassured her, "she doesn't know what she's talking about. Just relax."

"What does this mean?" Noi pressed for an answer.

Something in my Cherokee Spirit perked up and this thought came into my brain from somewhere I couldn't name: *three trials.* The message was clear, even though, at the time, I did not want to believe in the prophecy and couldn't even wrap my mind around the idea of three trials.

"It seems preposterous," I said, slightly flustered, so I spoke without thinking, "but maybe it means that you will have three trials." I noticed Noi's eyes looked panicked so I hurried to explain, "No, no, it's a crazy idea because after the jury comes back, it is all over."

I must not have been as reassuring as I intended to be because Noi was flushed with anxiety. "No more trials, no more courtrooms?" she fretted.

"Just one trial," I reassured her. She looked relieved.

I was still uneasy about Madeline's message, though, which I suspect Noi could sense because every once in a while she would reaffirm under her breath, "One trial."

I think we both braced ourselves as we waited for her first trial to begin.

The Tulsa County Courthouse was built in 1954, a kind of an art deco type of design. Although it was built almost thirty years prior to this trial, many people consider it to be modern, especially compared to some of the rural Oklahoma Courthouses which aren't even air-conditioned. The rural courthouses have the old wooden framed windows which open up to catch the summer breeze. However, compared to other modern buildings, the county courthouse is old. In the bathroom, visitors still have to turn one water faucet for hot and a different one for cold water.

It was during law school, just about 1973, when I first became acquainted with the Tulsa County Courthouse, but the memory of it is through my nose. They say that smell is the sense most closely associated with memory and I, for one, can attest to that.

I noticed such a foul smell on the bottom floors of the courthouse that I know I will never forget it. For example, in the Men's Room on the bottom floor there were three urinals placed entirely too close together. The wall behind those urinals is covered in dark orange tiles and made of granite. I doubt they've ever been polished or even cleaned thoroughly, for that matter. Everybody knows that men aren't the best shots in a bathroom of any sort, and almost thirty years of urine being sprayed hither and yon in a small space left it smelling like a very unkempt nursing home. I imagined hundreds of lawyers over the years dashing to the bathroom, peeing as fast as they could, trying to stuff Little Willie back in the barn without splashing on the shoes of the guys beside them, then dashing out to get back into the courtroom in time. I understand — perfectly — the urgency of all of it, but *jeepers! What a smell!* All the Pine-Sol in the world wouldn't eliminate that miasma. When the ammonia-like odor hits my nostrils and feeds right up into my olfactory bulbs, I have a knee-jerk reaction and want to bolt out of there like a race horse. I always wondered where they had hidden the sewer plant or the nursing home, the smell is that distinct – and that bad.

Judge Dalton's court was on the fifth floor. There was a large silver '5' imbedded in the granite floor right in front of the elevator door as you exited. The gray carpeting in Dalton's courtroom looked like it had never been replaced. The walls were covered with one-quarter inch imitation marble plywood; sort of a green, marbled, Formica kind-of material. The Judge's bench was elevated by two feet. Behind the bench was the door to his office which blended in with the modern-looking teak woodwork. High above that was a large, Official Seal of The State of Oklahoma.

The courtroom space itself was roughly 30 feet by 40 feet, smaller than what you might see in movies or on TV. Still, when a case is a big one – and this one was – it was possible to cram fifty to sixty people into the gallery. The air could be stifling, though, with that many people and that much emotion pounding through all those in attendance. Unrest, upset, insecurity and rage leaked out of everybody in there like a virus, like we were contaminating each other with our emotions. I welcomed the moments when I could race out into the hall just to get a deep breath, or to breathe air that felt like it still had some oxygen left in it.

On the right hand side of the Judge's bench was the witness chair. To the right of that was the juror's box. Facing the Judge were two counsel tables with four chairs, each separated by a small aisle. The prosecutor's table was closest to the juror's box. Behind the prosecutor's table was a wooden railing or "bar" which separates the courtroom from the gallery. Behind the bar were four rows of hard, light-colored wooden benches for the audience. This was a pretty common setup for most courtrooms in the country.

The District Attorney's Office decided to beef things up and had brought in another prosecutor, Jeff Carson, to help Lewis. Carson had a nasty sneer and quick temper which I was able to ignite easily.

I could just look at the guy with a big, syrupy smile on my face and know he was wondering what I was up to. It reminded me of my favorite April Fool's joke, which was to let someone think I had a big, nasty trick to play on them and then do nothing at all.

Carson was about thirty years old, had blue eyes and black hair with a thatch of white in it. He was a big guy, well over six feet tall and had a disconcerting habit of jumping to his feet when I was trying to speak to the jury. He was always leaning in towards me in a domineering manner, trying to intimidate me, I assume.

These two guys, Lewis and Carson, apparently, decided to set themselves up as sort of a "tag-team," like wrestlers do. When one would finish up, the other would jump into the ring. They used the "good guy, bad guy" trial strategy, also known as the "Beauty and the Beast" approach. In this method, the bad guy tears the witness apart, and the good guy charms the jury.

Behind the prosecutor's table sat members of the Mitchell clan and some of their friends. Mr. Mitchell was heavy-set and probably in his late sixties. His face was etched with lines pointing downward around his mouth, setting it into a permanent frown edged with bitterness. His wife looked unhappy, too. She was always dressed elegantly and expensively, even overdressed, to my way of thinking, especially during the summer months. When the air conditioning worked only sporadically and struggled to cool the building, Mrs. Mitchell dressed in layers as though it were still cold. She looked to be about the same age as her husband, although much slimmer. My overall feeling when I looked at Mrs. Mitchell was one of sadness. Despair dripped from her like East Texas rain off of Cypress leaves.

An aunt and uncle of Bobby's were present, a couple just a little younger than Mr. and Mrs. Mitchell. The uncle was nearly bald and his hard, black eyes burrowed into me from his pale face. It was hard to ignore the hatred I felt he had for me. His wife was softer-looking. She was thin, wearing elegant jewelry, yet her poorly-fitting clothes hung on her, making her appear unkempt. I guessed she had lost quite a bit of weight recently. She seemed subdued and her eyes had a glassy quality that was a little bit unnerving.

Bobby's grandmother came when she could; she was quite elderly and frail. I noticed that she always sat next to Bobby's Dad and never next to her daughter-in-law. Her hair was so thin on her head she almost appeared to be bald. She might have been tall and regal-looking at one point, but, by this time, was nearly bent completely over with age and, most likely, osteoporosis. A strong wind might actually snap her in two. I could see blue veins in her neck and around her nose and I guessed her age to be around eighty, maybe a little older.

I also recognized several friends of the Mitchells. The men would often pat Mr. Mitchell on the back whenever they thought the prosecutor had scored a point against me, like coaches at a football game. To see them do that was unsettling to me and I could feel the sweat run down my back every time I witnessed it, making me mad at myself that I let it get to me.

Buck up, Jim, I gave myself a pep talk. *You are going to be despised and have everyone rooting against you.* "Look at them," I muttered under my breath, "they're all so familiar with each other, easy, neighborly." But then I thought, *That's how I usually am — neighborly, well regarded — now I'm the outcast.* And I was rattled at how much of a pariah I was becoming. *It's unsettling,* I fretted, *for a whole social group to decide you are not acceptable, not like them.* That's when I noticed I really was not like them. I realized the average age of the Mitchell side of the room must have been at least sixty years. *Huh?* I thought. *That's interesting. None of Bobby's friends are in attendance at this trial.* He was only thirty-nine years old when he died. *Did he not have any friends? If so, where are they? If not, why was that? Could it be that Bobby's temper and overbearing attitude that he displayed in his marriage had leaked into other areas of his life as well?* I filed this bit of observation and inquiry away in my brain in case I needed to use it later on in the trial. My mind was back in the fight.

In contrast to the Mitchell side was the Thai side, those "rooting" for Noi. They sat behind the table where Noi was. I would look their way and notice a sea of Asian faces, mostly female. There were usually between six and nine Thai women who came to support Noi. They huddled together closely, whispering and gesturing and occasionally I could detect a Thai accent in the air. At times, I was even surprised at the dedication with which these Thai ladies rallied around Noi and it made me feel good to know she had that kind of support. Sometimes, Americans can be too self-sufficient and lonely.

The audience was seated as Deputy Sheriff Ray Manning led Noi into the courtroom. Of course, I stood out of respect for her. And then, we were seated. The door swung open and the jury panel entered in single file. Noi suddenly got a wild, wide-eyed look on her face and jumped to her feet. I thought she might try to dash out of the courtroom and run away. I felt the same razor-sharp pain of fear race to the pit of my stomach as I watched her but then, just as suddenly, she calmed and sat down. I felt the knot in my stomach ease up and I took a deep breath.

It was now time for the first phase of the trial, jury selection. Jury selection is, in the world of law, called *voir dire*, a French phrase meaning, "to speak the truth." There are twelve persons who must be qualified for cause in a capital murder case. "Excused for cause" is the standard phrase used to excuse a juror if there is some extreme personal situation or other reason which would prevent that person from following the law to reach a correct verdict. An example would be if a person had already made up his or her mind from having read newspaper articles about the case. Another example would be if a juror was somehow involved as a witness or knew the parties from either side of the case.

After jurors are accepted by the lawyers for cause on each side, the defendant and the prosecution get to strike nine jurors each and these strikes can be used for any reason. This way, a lawyer tries his best to get a jury that will be sympathetic to his side.

Selecting a jury is really a process of de-selection. I would throw out the nine worst jurors and the prosecutors would throw out the nine best jurors. A lawyer can also use *voir dire* to educate the jury as well as to eliminate prospective jurors who may be biased against the defendant.

Each juror has his or her name dropped into a hopper when they report for jury duty. Then, the bailiff draws a name out of drum like a lottery drawing and the prospective juror comes to the front of the room and is seated in the jury box.

Some lawyers select the jury by following certain rules of thumb mostly based on stereotypes and past experience. There are many, many books on ways in which to categorize people. For example, the famous San Francisco attorney, Melvin Belli, recommended that if you represent a defendant in a criminal case, you strike engineers and accountants from the jury because they are, as a group, very authority-conscious and fairly narrow-minded. Blacks are supposed to be good on a jury and Asians are bad news when it comes to showing compassion for a citizen accused of wrong-doing. I'm assuming that's because of the fear they have of government authorities in the places where they grew up.

I was excited about the prospect of picking the jury and I was well-prepared. I had written down a list of questions in my lucky orange OSU three-ring binder that I wanted to ask each juror. I made each prospective juror promise that he or she would not be prejudiced against Noi. I wanted to tell them all the weaknesses in the case and see how they would react to the worst facts.

I choked out the question, "Would the fact that Noi is accused of beating, strangling and shooting her husband to death automatically make you think she was guilty?"

The first few times I asked that question, I could see the surprise on each juror's face. My thinking was that I might as well get the weaknesses in her case out into the open first by conditioning the jurors to some of the shocking facts. None of these facts made Noi look anything close to innocent, I knew that, but I wanted to lay it all out on the table. It all looked so bad, in fact, that, surely, some of them must have been thinking that there was more to the story than just this – because there was, and I intended to prove that. I also wanted the jury to know I would give them all of the bad facts before the prosecutors did because I wanted their trust. Each juror promised me he or she would wait until they had enough facts to make a decision concerning Noi's guilt or innocence. I felt like this fairness was all I could ask from any juror.

Under Oklahoma law, I could remove nine of the jurors without giving any reasons. I accepted the jury after my questions and used only three of my nine strikes, which was highly unusual. Generally, even nine strikes are not enough.

The prosecutors used their strikes to remove people they thought would feel sorry for Noi. Several of their strikes seemed to be founded on studies of how to classify people based on their age, sex, occupation and other traits indicating a tendency to acquit. Whether we know it or not, or like it or not, we all tend to be judgment-and-evaluation machines, sizing each other up constantly from a wide variety of factors. Basically, I decided to ignore all of these studies and used my theory of trusting everyone to be fair.

I tried to convey a message with my eyes to each juror that I trusted them. Years before, back in my college days before I met and fell in love with Nancy, I had read a book similar to the one entitled *HOW TO PICK UP WOMEN* by Eric Weber. I can't remember the title of it, but the idea was that you could build instant rapport with women, but you must first forget that your physical attributes may not be what you'd like, or even what you think a woman would like. For example, I would try to forget that I am short, with a slight build, that my hair is beginning to thin on top and that I still have an occasional out-cropping of teenage pimples, even though I am a grown man with an impressive nest of dark chest hair.

After the formal jury selection is over, a lawyer cannot talk individually with the jurors. Therefore, now – *this moment* – was my chance to make an individual connection. With my eyes, I tried to convey to each female on the jury that she was special and important to me. The key to building rapport is to start from a foundation of mutual trust. To make a friend, you must first be a friend. I was trying my darnedest to be the nicest guy in the courtroom, without being cloying about it and without appearing to be weak. My fear was that, rather than building rapport with the jury members, I would seem more like a sappy little puppy, desperate for friendship and attention. It's a skinny line to walk and I didn't know if I managed to toe that mark.

After I used my third strike, I announced that I would accept the jury as is. The Judge called a recess and I walked through the hallway, relieved to be out of that space packed with too many people and too much emotion.

Rex, my brother, had come to help with the case, but was upset with me. He did not buy into my theory of accepting the jurors on trust alone. There were several older women on the jury and Rex felt sure that they would turn out to be bad news for our case. These women were wealthy and successful and had probably been loved by their husbands all their married lives. Rex didn't think these women would be able to understand the degrading experiences with which Noi had lived.

In particular, Rex did not like one young woman's harsh facial expressions. She was one of the two single women on the jury who were both well past what would be considered prime marriageable age. Rex thought that many white women, especially those who had never been married, would feel that Asian women should keep their hands off white men and leave them for the women here in this country. He did not think these women would be naturally sympathetic to an Asian woman like Noi, one who had permanently depleted the marriage pool. I thought Rex was being silly in his paranoia about this matter and that he had been watching too many World War II movies. I also didn't feel that the hallway outside the courtroom was the best place to try to explain to my brother why I was confident that I'd already won two of the jurors over to Noi's side.

One of those jurors was Martha Diller, a reporter from *The Tulsa Tribune*, the evening newspaper in Tulsa. She was in her late twenties with a wholesome look. She was married and had a small son. Martha seemed to be friendly, well-adjusted, and not the type of person to judge other people unfairly. I was aware of the half-dozen articles she had written about the murder case. She had interviewed me earlier and asked what Noi's defense was going to be. Of course, I told her that these types of questions would be answered only at the trial.

Ironically, I had tried to cheer Martha up the week before she was summoned for jury duty. She dreaded it; almost everybody does. She told me she was always the first one bumped. I said, "Martha, don't worry. Some lawyer will surely trust you to be on his jury." When Martha and I had talked, we had no idea that the following Monday she would be sitting in Judge Dalton's courtroom waiting for her name to be called.

It is funny how a person will moan and whine and use every reason in the world to get excused from jury duty. However, if the judge does not excuse him and his name is drawn, he will do almost anything to be accepted on that jury. Many times, a juror will lie, or smile their most dazzling smile at the attorney, or do anything to keep from getting bumped off. Some people just take a strike off a jury as a personal rejection, I guess.

Martha was the seventh juror called to the front. From studies I had done in metaphysics and ancient cultures, I knew the number "seven" was a Hebrew way of symbolizing "Godliness," and it is considered to be the perfect number. I took that as a significant sign and knew I should keep her on the jury. I looked at her as she sat there in the box with her mouth open just a little bit and her head slightly cocked to the side. She was poised to listen to every question, which I trusted her to do, just like the thorough and competent reporter I knew her to be. Carson and I both questioned Martha about whether or not she'd made any decisions or had any knowledge about the case that she felt would prejudice her one way or the other. She expected the prosecutor or me to strike her from the jury, but it didn't happen.

I wanted to keep her on the jury because I felt she would be fair and thought it wouldn't hurt to have more publicity about the case. I knew having a reporter right there on the jury every minute would assure me of some attention in the newspapers. Regardless of the outcome, having Martha on my jury would ensure close coverage of the case and some interesting articles about the trial from a juror's perspective.

I also trusted Martha Diller's professionalism and sense of fairness to keep an open mind, which is what good reporters are trained to do. So-called "facts" can be misleading when a person knows only part of a story. And, who would know that better than a newspaper reporter? I liked Martha like a sister and I wanted her on the jury because she had always been so receptive to me. Surprisingly, the prosecutors wanted her on the jury, as well. They loved her. I believe they thought that Martha knew facts which would convince her of Noi's guilt. After all, in Martha's interviews with several Broken Arrow Police Officers, they had given her shocking and gruesome details about the night of Bobby Mitchell's death.

The other juror I felt to be on my side was a Cuban man, Mr. "Bermudez" (not his real name), who had been in the Cuban Secret Service before Castro overthrew the Bautista regime in 1958. He now worked as a bailiff in the city court and was almost too good to be true. Here we had a man who had been questioned by Castro's forces and threatened with death. Mr. "Bermudez" said he had personally witnessed brutalities which, he confirmed, were not pleasant.

I was betting that Mr. "Bermudez" had a real distaste for authority. I was certain he knew fear firsthand. Flashes of torture appeared in my mind. He would know what it was like to suffer. He could also understand that police officers were not always good men. He had been forced to leave Cuba, his homeland, when Castro took over. When I asked him what would have happened to him if he had stayed in Cuba, he made a dramatic slicing movement across his throat. The courtroom became hushed after he said that several of his family members were unable to get out of Cuba in time to escape Castro's revenge. He whispered that his little sister was still there on the island somewhere. It was good to have someone on the jury who would surely be able to relate to the fear Noi felt the night Bobby died. Yet, I was a little uneasy about my feelings because I could not quite figure out why the prosecutors wanted to keep Mr. "Bermudez" on the jury, too. I shook off this feeling the best I could because I believe that whatever a person expects to happen *will* happen and I didn't want to create that as part of my reality. I didn't want to direct my energy in that way.

I almost danced to my car as I thought about these two jurors. I celebrated with Rex that night by drinking a beer while relaxing and putting the final touches on my opening statements set for the next day. I had a strong feeling that, with my Cuban friend as my ace in the hole, I could not lose this case.

When I got to the courthouse the next morning, though, my bubble burst like soap suds. There was a young and pretty attorney on the public defender's office staff who had always been friendly toward me and honest with me. I could tell it irked her when lawyers would talk down to her, thinking her to be too young and too pretty to be an attorney. I, on the other hand, treated her like an equal and I could tell she really appreciated that.

She asked me if there was a Cuban on the jury and I said there was. She confided that this Cuban man had told another judge he had been the interpreter for the Puerto Rican man charged with being Noi's accomplice by helping her get rid of Bobby's body. This accomplice was Jorge "George" Rivera who had worked with Noi at Monterey House Mexican Restaurant. I was told by an Assistant D.A. that Mr. Rivera received a two-year suspended sentence when he confessed, but then fled the country.

(It turns out that Mr. "Bermudez" was the interpreter for the two men charged as "Accessory After the Fact", but the State had actually dismissed all charges against the men as of November 17, 1982, according to the Official Criminal Docket Sheet Jody Seay and I found in an old warehouse in north Tulsa in June of 2016.)

If a public defender knew about this strange coincidence, I was sure Carson and Lewis knew it, too. There was no telling what Rivera had told the prosecutors and the Broken Arrow Police in order to get off the hook for covering up a crime. The only thing I knew for sure was that the Cuban man, Mr. "Bermudez", had heard exactly what George Rivera had said about Noi and that I had not.

Crap. My ace in the hole had just turned into a joker. I walked into the law library in the courthouse next to the Court Clerk's office and just sat there. This strange twist of events affected me more adversely than I wanted others to realize. I felt like a giant rug had just been yanked out from under me and that I'd fallen flat on my back, slamming onto the concrete like a fifty pound bag of pinto beans dropped from a second story building. The wind had been knocked out of me; I couldn't catch my breath. I felt I must be white as a ghost and glanced at my hands. I was right – they looked whitewashed, like they'd been soaked in bleach. I was sure, at least, at that moment, the only thing that kept me from looking like a corpse was the fact that I was sitting upright, my eyes were still open, and that I was sweating hard. Without a doubt, any moment now, sweat would begin squirting out of the top of my head like Moby Dick, I just knew it. I was a mess.

As I sat there, trying to regain some sense of composure, I realized it was almost time for Judge Dalton to start the trial. I also had a premonition that I would be dealt even more surprises before this day was over. I am rarely ever wrong when that feeling hits me.

When Dalton asked me to join him in his chambers, I almost groaned out loud. This day was not turning out like I had planned, not at all. The Judge then told me that Mr. "Bermudez" had called in sick. He had checked into a hospital one hundred and twenty miles away in Oklahoma City with a stomach ache. I guess "Bermudez" wanted to be out of the case that badly and I didn't blame him. I knew how he felt. My stomach ached, too, and my throat had so many lumps in it, I felt like I was suffocating; like I'd managed to swallow two or three pairs of balled-up sweat socks.

I told the Judge that I'd discovered "Bermudez" to be the interpreter for Noi's accomplice, George Rivera. "I do not understand how in the world Mr. "Bermudez" could have forgotten such an important thing as having been the Spanish interpreter for the Puerto Rican accused of helping Noi dispose of Bobby's body," I said.

Judge Dalton looked a little puzzle, "Yes, it's strange I'll admit. I don't know how anyone could forget something like that. But, there is no evidence of harm being done to your client so I want to go back to the courtroom and try this case." We went out of his offices and took our seats and Judge Dalton questioned the jurors to reassure himself that "Bermudez" had not discussed any part of the case with them.

The Judge was pleased with their answers and proceeded to use the alternate juror I had only barely questioned because I was so sure we would not need her. This was another junior mistake that I have never made again.

All I could remember about the alternate was that she was a housewife who appeared to be about middle-aged and that she had worked some years earlier as a bank teller. She had a kind look, reminding me of my aunt who was also about that same age and had also worked at a bank. My aunt certainly was understanding and it was my hope that this woman would turn out to be that way, too. I tried to concentrate on how to make the best of being so knocked off center. It was a bad situation. I knew I needed some kind of push to get myself together enough to make the kind of opening statement I wanted to make.

The jury was in the courtroom and eager for the trial to begin. Carson went first. He began by calmly reading the criminal charge against Noi. He told the jury that Noi had reason to kill Bobby and that she had ambushed him. Carson promised to share with the jury her motive for and methods of killing him. He then went on to describe where Bobby's naked body was found abandoned in Creek County.

Carson strode back and forth in front of the jurors confidently, "The defendant lied to the Police many times. She is an admitted liar," he continued. "I promise to bring in both the bat and the gun so you can see for yourselves what Noi used to kill Bobby." His voice built up to a crescendo as he loudly proclaimed, "Even though the defendant looks sweet enough to melt your heart, she is a cold-blooded killer." Carson pointed his index finger at her, stating sarcastically, "She looks like she could never even say a curse word, she looks so sweet." As if that was a fault. Carson was convincing, I'll give him that. It was a stirring opening statement.

The reference to a curse word, though, deeply disturbed me. I could hardly believe what my ears had just heard. Perhaps I was just being a little paranoid, but Tom and I both looked at each other. We were both thinking that this reference to a curse word was too much of a coincidence to be an accident.

Earlier in this whole process, Noi had spoken with me and Tom in a private interview room provided by the Tulsa jail for these purposes. Just the week before the trial, Noi refused to say the 'bad words' Bobby used during their fight. She said she would write them down, but she would not say them. Now, Tom and I both seemed to be wondering if that room had been bugged. I would not have put it past the prosecutors to have listened in on our private interviews. *No, you're just being paranoid,* I thought, but I broke out in a cold sweat – again – just thinking about Carson and Lewis laughing as they listened to our interviews with Noi. *They may know everything Noi had said,* even my thoughts were shaky. *They might also know the strategy I planned to use that I had confided to Noi.*

Judge Dalton swiveled in his chair and asked me if I was ready to give my opening statements. I jumped and squeaked out that I was and, trembling, walked in front of the jurors and then committed a trial lawyer's biggest sin: I stared down at my notes and read my opening statement, totally ignoring the jury.

I was so nervous my body shook and my voice quivered to the point of almost disappearing, like my vocal cords were vaporizing inside my throat. I read to them a story about a beautiful little dark-skinned girl who had not had the privileges most of us in America take for granted. Noi loved Bobby Mitchell enough to leave all her friends and family to come to a foreign land. Yet, she did not know him. Bobby and Noi's marriage, never much more than a shaky arrangement between the two of them, was rocky from the start due to his drinking and his anger. It grew progressively worse until finally, they had such a violent fight one night that he died from the wounds she inflicted.

I admitted that Noi killed Bobby, but she had not meant to. The gunshot was an accident which happened when Bobby pulled on Noi's hand as they wrestled for the gun. Noi fractured Bobby's skull with her bat – but only because she was so frightened of his rage and he was scrambling for the gun they had both dropped on the floor. She was terrified that if he got hold of his gun again, he would shoot her and their children. In fact, even after she hit him, Bobby did grab the gun and did manage to get up and did follow her out of the house with gun in hand. "She was acting in self-defense," I managed to squeak out. My voice sounded like somebody big and mean had me by the throat, someone determined to squeeze the life out of me.

By the time I got to the end of my opening statement, I was nearly out of breath from reading my notes so quickly. I had raced through that opening statement so fast I'm sure some of the jurors thought I had a plane to catch, or that prior to having become an attorney I'd been a calf roper on the rodeo circuit and was trying to get my job done in the shortest amount of time. I'm betting they almost expected me to throw both hands into the air like ropers do when the calf is finally tied up. I had, however, practiced my last sentence so many times in front of a mirror that I dared to look up from my notes at the jurors one row at a time and conclude,

"Ladies and gentlemen, after you have heard all of the testimony and seen all of the evidence and after we have discovered all of the truth together, I am going to ask you to return a verdict of 'Not Guilty'." At least, I was able to get my last sentence out with some power in my voice and without falling over in a faint. *Phew!*

I sat down, wishing for another chance to deliver the entire opening statement with the same kind of power and intention I had used in that last sentence. I prayed the jurors would not hold my shaking and weak delivery against Noi. I quickly glanced down the two rows of jurors, but was unable to detect any clues from their facial expressions about what they were thinking.

Dalton called a lunch recess and Deputy Sheriff Ray Manning escorted Noi back to her cell. Deputy Manning shook his head slightly back and forth and warned Noi that he had never in his entire life heard an opening statement like that. He was dismayed that any lawyer would actually read his opening remarks to the jury. He told Noi she would get convicted in a New York minute.

When I returned to court after lunch, Noi whispered to me, "Ray say you not very strong, that D.A. is beating you. He say I will lose case. What does 'New York Minute' mean?"

"Hey, Noi, the trial has just started," I reassured her. "Just wait 'til he sees the evidence that we have prepared." I reminded her that it was not up to Deputy Manning to decide her future; it was up to the jury. Noi did not answer and looked down like she didn't believe me. That was brave talk I was spouting – that's all – she knew it as well as I did. However, there was no use in letting her know that I felt the prosecutors were overwhelming me. I also tried to remember that Ray Manning was a friend of mine.

Lewis presented his first witness that afternoon. A leathery-faced man in his mid-fifties sat down in the witness chair. He described his morning work routine of checking oil tanks out by Keifer, Oklahoma in Creek County, about forty minutes outside of Tulsa, when he noticed a silver Pontiac parked under a tree off the road. "I didn't think much of it," he said, "not at first. I just continued doing my job." He continued to explain the situation. "Teenagers and other lovers often make their way out to those oil lease fields and park among the thick, dark green leaves of the burr oak trees to make out. Sometimes, someone is too drunk or stoned to drive home and gets a lift from someone, leaving a car behind, so it's not entirely uncommon to see an abandoned car out there. By mid-morning, however, someone has usually come back to collect the car and leave, but this one, the silver Pontiac, just sat there." He paused to take a breath.

"Go on," Lewis urged him, lending an air of urgency to the story.

"On my way out, I began to wonder why the car was still there so I walked over and peeked in the window on the driver's side." He gulped.

"What did you see? Lewis asked.

"I spied a person's legs and then noticed dried, caked streams of blood on them. I ran to my truck," he said, "drove into town and called the Creek County Sheriff's Office on a pay phone. The body," he told the jury "was partially hidden from view by the hatchback seat pulled over it."

My cross-examination of this witness was short. I asked him if he had taken off work to testify and he said that he had. I thanked him for his time and efforts and I told him that Noi and I both appreciated his doing his civic duties. The way I see it is that there's no need to holler unless you are hurt and he had not hurt us.

Judge Jay Dalton dismissed us early, about 4 pm that day. The air conditioner in the courthouse was not working well and July is sweltering in Oklahoma. Besides, Judge Dalton probably needed to throw back some whiskey. Most people in the judicial system had heard rumors about his severe alcoholic condition. When he wasn't having jury trials, he would always take off at noon. He would only schedule hearings in the mornings. Hence, he earned his nick name "Half-a-Day-Jay". But by the next morning he was always lucid and cold sober. By all accounts, he was a good judge and up to this point in the trial, I respected him.

I dragged home that night like a whipped pup. The date was July 7, 1983 and I had never had such a devastating day in court in my short career. My opening statement had been as weak as thin soup and I felt like Carson and Lewis had complete control of the case. When I crept into the house, Rex was planted in a kitchen chair, ready to blast me with both barrels. "You acted like a wimp!" he accused me. "Noi is paying you what you are worth – NOTHING!" Rex continued to hurl insults at me, ranting and raving for another five minutes or so.

Our Dad owns his own chemical company in Texas and Rex is his number two man on board. Dad graciously loaned Rex to me to help with the case but, at this point, I felt like phoning Dad and asking him to take Rex back. I could not return my brother, though, because I needed his help too much; I just didn't need this kind of criticism. The last thing I wanted was another person ragging on me over something I'd done wrong or hadn't done right. I began to explain to him that I was trying to get the jury to trust me by trusting them. Rex exploded at me.

"Forget that sentimental crap and get your act together!" he shouted.

My brother had a knack for cutting through the bull and I didn't offer to him any more excuses. Still, I thought my philosophies would ultimately prevail, somehow.

The ruckus in the kitchen between Rex and me brought Buddy and Nancy running. They both seemed excited to see me and wanted to know how the trial went. Honestly, I didn't want to talk about it, so I put them both off with, "It was really great. Noi did not get convicted today, anyway." That's when Rex piped in with, "Yeah, just because the jury did not vote today."

I could not take it anymore. This discussion was more stressful than being in the courtroom. To avoid further questions about my performance – and to keep from slugging this brother of mine in the nose – I rushed out of the kitchen and laid down on my comfortable sofa. I closed my eyes, hoping the world would fade to black, just for a while.

Our Fourth of July weekend really sucked. Nancy had little to say to me. When Dalton set the trial date for July 5, 1983, he had wiped out our holiday for that year, and Nancy refused to understand why I had no choice in the matter. We had been invited to a party at some friends' house for the Saturday night before the trial and we had always, from the time we met in college, been delighted to celebrate together the birthday of this nation we both loved. Parties, picnics and barbecues had all been part of our family life for years to honor and acknowledge our country's beginning. We loved those gatherings. We loved the feeling that we were woven into the tapestry making up the fabric of America and knowing that millions of other Americans were doing just what we were doing – honoring, with pride, the distinct privilege of being part of the USA. Because of Noi's trial date, however, a Fourth of July celebration wasn't in the cards for us this year. Nancy could not see that this was disappointing to me, too, especially when I insisted that she call her girlfriend and cancel our previous commitment to attend. This case, already having overtaken our family and work lives, had now managed to drain any fun out of our lives, too. Needless to say, Nancy was pretty upset with me. Well, I'll just say it: she was pissed. And, Nancy being pissed is not something you ever really want to witness in person, especially as her husband. For such a tiny person, her anger can be massive, even in its silence, *especially* in its silence. I was not the most popular guy on the block that summer.

As I lay on the couch thinking about all of this, I knew it was too late in the case to get another lawyer to help, something Tom Cook had been suggesting I do again and again. I couldn't afford to hire another lawyer anyway; my money was draining away as fast as my confidence, like both were being sucked into a pneumatic tube and whisked away forever. I knew I had to find some inner reservoir of strength to pull through this trial and continue with my life, which was, at the moment anyway, entwined with Noi's future whether I liked it or not. Somehow I drifted off into a dreamless sleep.

When I awoke, I felt angry at myself, my wife, my brother, at Tom, Noi, the prosecutors, the Judge, and at the legal system in general. The rage inside me made the coffee cups rattle as I yanked the cupboard door open. I was furious at everyone:

I was furious with myself because I had taken a case I was not prepared to handle and that, no matter how hard I tried, it seemed like I was just digging my own grave deeper and deeper. I felt like I was humiliating myself every time I opened my mouth.

Oh, I was mad at my wife because she stayed concerned about finances and our children getting to see their daddy when grave events were unfolding.

My brother kept needling me about my performance and that angered me, too.

I was mad at Tom because he kept after me to associate with a "real" attorney to try this case. Like I wasn't real; and I was afraid he was right.

And after all this time and all my efforts Noi still did not fully trust me and that hurt and made me furious.

I was mad, so mad, at the prosecutors because I felt they kept stooping to low tactics. They had made it extremely difficult to obtain evidence they were just supposed to hand over to me and, generally, gave me the run-around and a bad time in all my dealings with them. It was so frustrating. *Surely, they would never take advantage of my inexperience in handling criminal cases by bugging Noi's interview room – would they?* That's something I would have only expected in some sort of hackneyed spy movie. I let the anger rise in me; then forced it higher, but I didn't feel any better. It wasn't the least bit satisfying to accuse the other lawyers of doing something unethical. I knew they were young, ambitious and determined – just like I was – and that winning this case was as important to both of them as it was to me. I couldn't even discuss this with Nancy because she would probably say I was being paranoid and this was only a far-fetched theory of mine. And she would point out that I couldn't prove it. But I was still flip-flaming-mad at both of them. I really had no idea which tactics were 'over the line' of professionalism, never having tried a criminal case before. All I could go by was what I was seeing and hearing and, of course, my own gut response, but, even with that, I wasn't sure I could trust that to be true. I did not yet have that kind of experience.

And, I was furious at Judge Dalton this morning because he ruled against me every time – with or without legal justification.

Everything was going wrong, both in my personal life and in my professional life; and, when I really looked at it, taking responsibility for it, I knew I had no one to blame but myself. As mad as I wanted to be at everyone else – and I was, plenty – still, I knew that I had made the choice to take this case on. Whatever cascading series of horrible consequences dropped onto my shoulders because of that one choice were, ultimately, of my own doing. I could see the leaves on the trees outside rustling in the warm summer breeze and I knew this was my perfect opportunity to back out. This was it – *RIGHT NOW!*

Still, I couldn't do it. Neither my feelings for Noi nor my own over-sized ego were keeping me on this case; it was something even bigger than that.

I did not realize until that very moment how deeply a poem I had once read affected me. I must have really taken it to heart because it turned out to be the essence of what was to keep me going with this case. I slinked out of the kitchen, made my way over to my favorite bookshelf, and reached for a thin, black notebook I'd not touched in more than six years. This is what I read:

> *Until one is committed, there is hesitancy, the chance to draw back,*
> *always ineffectiveness.*
> *Concerning all acts of initiative (and creation)*
> *there is one element of truth,*

the ignorance of which kills countless ideas
and splendid plans:
that the moment one definitely commits oneself,
then, Providence moves, too.
All sorts of things occur to help one
that would never have, otherwise, occurred.
A whole stream of events issues from the decision,
raising in one's favor all manner
of unforeseen incidents and meetings
and material assistance,
which no man could have dreamt
would have come his way.
I have learned a deep respect
for one of Goethe's couplets:
'Whatever you can do, or dream you can, begin it.
Boldness has genius, power and magic in it.
Begin it now.' "
– From the Scottish Himalayan Expedition

I have visions sometimes of things I don't speak of. Occasionally, I can see what is going to happen right before it actually does. And, when I was a boy, I made friends with a dragon, mostly in my dreams, but not exclusively. Now and again he just came into my mind, like a breeze blowing in through the window. He didn't show up often, but just often enough for me to know he was real. His whole job, it seemed to me, was to ask me questions and to make sure I asked them, too. I dubbed him "Quizzer" in honor of his pop quizzes; but mainly I called him "Quiz."

"Always question, Jimmy," he'd whisper to me, "and question yourself most of all. Ask yourself this rhyme: IS IT GOOD? IS IT TRUE? IS THIS PATHWAY RIGHT FOR YOU? Your heart will tell you the truth, always."

As I grew up, Quiz showed up less and less, but when he did, his voice wasn't as kind as it had been when I was young. He seemed impatient with me, even mad. By then, as I was watching Perry Mason on TV and thinking about law school for myself, I sometimes thought of "Quiz" as "The Cross Examiner" or sometimes just "Cross" since he always seemed so angry at me. I think my indecisiveness and lack of confidence made him a little crazy.

"You try my patience, Young Jim," he would say, "when all you really have to do is look inside and ask yourself this rhyme: IS IT GOOD? IS IT TRUE? IS THIS PATHWAY RIGHT FOR YOU?"

Taking advice from a dragon is not an easy thing to admit or explain so, mostly, I don't. I haven't. I have wondered, though, if it was God speaking to me in a way a young boy might understand and be more receptive to. I have also wondered if I was nuts. Nonetheless, as I grew into a man, Quiz slipped further away. Sometimes, he might show up in a dream, but he was usually far away and I could only catch a glimpse of him. His lesson, though, has stayed with me, and I question everything – all the time – especially myself.

So this morning, even though I was so furious at everyone, I looked inside myself to find the power of my intention and commitment in all of this situation. I just asked myself Quiz's rhyme: IS IT GOOD? IS IT TRUE? IS THIS PATHWAY RIGHT FOR YOU? I took it as my talisman, my touchstone, that advice of his.

Besides, you never really want to piss off a dragon.

CHAPTER 9 – *ALMOST* PERSUADED

The next morning, the prosecutors threw everything they had at us in an avalanche of evidence, witnesses and experts. At times, it felt as if Noi and I were being blasted by Gatlin guns, all of them aimed at us from different directions and all of them firing at once. They continued, on and on, to introduce their evidence against Noi.

The Broken Arrow Police Department turned out in full force, or so it seemed. They were everywhere I looked in the courtroom. The interrogating officer described how Noi had given a two-part, four and a half hour tape-recorded confession in which she had lied and then admitted to having lied for the first three and a half hours of it. She was also caught lying again several times during the second part of her confession after she had promised to tell all of the truth. Clearly, it was the aim of the prosecutors to paint Noi as a pathological liar who could not be trusted to speak the truth. She also made some extremely damaging statements that she killed Bobby because he wanted to take her children; and, when I say damaging, I mean that in terms of being able to say that Noi killed her husband in self-defense. Nobody would fault a mother for wanting to keep custody of children, but even that kind of fierce mother-love would not warrant the taking a life, not legally, not even in the state of Oklahoma. I had to be able to prove that Noi feared for her own life and that, when she killed Bobby, she was acting out of her fear of him and in self-defense.

Another police officer introduced pictures of a bloody mattress, the intention of which was to spur the jury toward drawing the conclusion that Noi had murdered Bobby when he laid down to sleep. This same officer also introduced pictures of the bedroom in which Bobby had suffered his wounds, as well as part of the bullet found in the bedroom. A police skin diver brought forth to the court the actual water-logged bullets and gun that he'd found submerged at the bottom of Marina Lake.

The OSBI had been working in tandem with the Broken Arrow investigative team. One of their agents introduced the bat into evidence that Noi had used to fracture Bobby's skull several times. Bobby Mitchell was a slender man, but he towered over his wife by at least a foot. When he was drunk and enraged – which, according to Noi's account, he seemed often to be – I'm sure he looked even taller and more menacing. Because of how I now knew her, I could understand Noi's fear that Bobby would suddenly spring back to life after she shot him. I could understand the terror and urgency she must have felt that night to race and get the bat and make sure her snarling demon of a husband was not only dead, but good and dead, so there was no way he could get up and kill her and their two small daughters. Blamming her wounded husband in the head with a bat enough times and with enough force to crack his skull five or six times... I knew, that was going to be a hard thing to defend. Such an action on Noi's part didn't make her look scared; it made her look vengeful. I still felt, though, that I could make the jury understand who Noi was and the terror with which she lived constantly in her marriage to Bobby. If I could do that thoroughly, I was *almost* certain I could trust those twelve people enough to serve the cause of justice well.

The ballistics expert testified that the bullets found in the wall and dresser had been fired from Bobby's gun. More importantly, he stated that the tests he performed showed the bullet entered the decedent's chest at a downward angle.

The woman who lived across the street from the Mitchells testified she had seen a man standing in the garage the night after Bobby's death. At the time, she thought it was Bobby.

Next, Bobby's father testified that Noi had called him two days after she killed Bobby to ask if he knew where his son was. Mr. Mitchell then recalled a time when Bobby told him Noi had attacked him with a kitchen knife. He said, "Bobby told me Noi was dangerous." Certainly, this was also damaging testimony for our side. I felt something deep inside me start to curl up; I hoped I'd not just magically grown a tail and now I was tucking it under me.

Next, Bobby's cousin testified that he and Bobby were very close – closer than brothers – and Bobby had confided that he had finally decided to leave Noi that day, the day of Bobby's death. Together, Bobby and the cousin packed Bobby's clothes and loaded them up in Bobby's car. As they were about to leave, Bobby decided to stay one more night to discuss his problems with Noi since he couldn't bear to lose the children. I cringed when he said that because, even if it was true, which I doubted, I didn't want the jury to start thinking Bobby had a soft side. Certainly, if he did, it was only toward the little girls and not toward his own wife.

The prosecutors saved their most damaging witness, though, for last. The information this guy had to share threw a spear right into the heart of our defense. The medical examiner, Dr. Omar J. Masood, who performed the autopsy introduced photographs of Bobby's mutilated body and testified as to how brutal his wounds were. He stated Bobby had been shot in the chest and his right lung filled with blood. He said Bobby also had several concussions, fractures in his skull, a black eye, and numerous bruises from his beating with the baseball bat. He then stated that Bobby had a cracked hyoid bone or Adam's apple and gouges in his neck caused by manual strangulation. He concluded that the cause of death was a gunshot wound, fractures to the skull, and strangulation. All of these acting together or singly killed Bobby.

During cross examination, I had the opportunity to confront the prosecution's witnesses and to discredit their testimony while presenting Noi's side of the story. I wanted to show the jury that the Broken Arrow Police Department had botched the investigation. I wanted them to see that the Officer in Charge had made up his mind immediately when Noi made her confession. I had to make the jury understand that the police did not even care about Noi's side of the story and had decided she was guilty before they even tried to decipher her broken English. I wanted to show the jury, in as many ways possible, that the police had operated to convict Noi, rather than conduct an investigation of discovery. Basically, the Broken Arrow Police Department thought they had an open and shut case – a slam-dunk – and did everything in their power to prove themselves right, regardless of the accused person's constitutional rights.

I was able to point out that the police had asked Noi loaded questions in the interview, did not let her explain what happened, then twisted what little she did say. They did not ask her any details about her fight with Bobby, nor did they ask her to re-enact the scene of the killing. I stressed that the Police Department did not ask her about the bullet hole embedded almost eight feet high up on the bedroom wall which Tom Cook and I discovered during our investigation. They did not ask her about the blood on the carpet, the mirror, in the hallway, on the front porch, and in the garage. They did not ask her about the towels she was washing and drying. They did not ask her where she and Bobby were struggling when the gun fired. No, none of these very pertinent questions were asked of my client at all. In my mind, this was a pretty piss-poor way to conduct an investigation, especially in what would turn into a murder case. From my point of view, these guys weren't interested in understanding the truth of what had happened. The questions of the interrogator were designed to trap Noi. There were no questions designed to discover the facts. Just thinking about this made me mad enough to throw something, but I knew I had to maintain my cool, so, (a) I wouldn't get tossed out of the courtroom; (b) I could do the best job that I could for my client, and (c) I could blow a hole in the prosecution's case and really nail these cocky bastards. I steeled myself for the fight.

Because I felt the law enforcement officers ran a biased, incomplete investigation, *that's all there was to it*, my job was to challenge their tests and their tactics. I began by hammering away at some of the obvious tests the Police Department and the OSBI failed to make. I asked if they tried to determine the trajectory of the bullet which had probably killed Bobby.

No, they had not.

I asked each officer if he had tested for blood on the front porch of the house.

None had.

I asked if they had run tests for blood on the carpet in front of the dresser in the bedroom. I asked if they had run tests to determine if there was any gunpowder on Bobby's hands. I asked if they remembered to take pictures of Bobby's hands to see if there were scratches, gunpowder soot, or a pinched web between his thumb and forefinger. All of these tests, pictures and so forth are standard investigative procedures in a murder case if – and that's a big *IF* – interrogators are actually trying to discover the truth in such a case.

To each of these questions I asked, the answer was "No."

It was my hope that the jury was seeing what I did.

My next job was to focus on the bloody mattress. I had asked to see the mattress the police department had whisked away during the investigation, only to find out that the Broken Arrow Police had buried it forty feet under ground at the Broken Arrow dump. My questions were aimed at reminding the jury of the fact that the police may have been hiding something.

The police witnesses were quick to introduce a picture of a postage-stamp size cut-out of the mattress which showed blood on it.

I asked if they had run tests to determine how old the blood was. I asked if they had run tests to determine if it was menstrual blood, as Noi had claimed.

No, they said, they had only tested to determine the blood type (Bobby's) and to verify that it was human blood.

They did not tell the jury that Noi and Bobby shared the same blood type, but I was quick to bring that up. Anything I could do, any chance I got, to make them appear to be incompetent weasels, I decided, I was going to take it.

Carson struck back hard when he asked the OSBI agent if "Jimmy Lloyd" could have requested that the lab run the blood tests on the mattress.

The agent said there was a procedure for ordering tests and that the agency had always complied with requests by defense counsel. He politely pointed out that this service was free of charge.

What this meant, clearly, was that the defense counsel, namely, ME, had dropped the ball here rather than the police department. Carson' determination to refer to me as "Jimmy Lloyd" seemed to me to be, of course, not only a jab at my small stature, but also a way of diminishing me in front of the jury, like I was too young, too new, too much of a greenhorn to know what I was doing in the courtroom. Naturally, because I was embarrassed, my ears were bright red and burning when I discovered at the same time the jury did that it was partly my responsibility to make sure all of the proper tests were run, too. At this point, I was fairly certain I would be spontaneously combusting at any moment.

Carson turned to me with eyebrows raised in mock surprise when the OSBI agent explained the proper procedure. Of course, this disclosure unnerved me, but I remembered *"Boldness has genius, power and magic in it"* and I was determined to go on from there.

So I looked around and I could see I was upsetting the police officers by attacking their sloppy investigative procedures. My nerves began to calm down. The officers were extremely sensitive about their lack of thoroughness and did not take kindly to this type of questioning. Their bristling manner and extreme defensiveness clearly indicated to the jury that they had conducted a sloppy investigation. That was my hope, anyway. I did not win any friends in the police department, but that was not a new feeling for me.

I had a knack for making people dislike me. Maybe it's a gift. I had grown up with a little brother and sister to practice on. The words

100

most often heard in my childhood were "Jimmy, quit. Jimmy, quit." My Mom always said I would have made a good *only* child. She was tactful about it, because one of my strongest character traits was the ability to stir up trouble. I was gradually gaining confidence in the trial by using my ability to make people blow up in the courtroom.

I went after the investigating officers with everything I had, blasting away with both barrels at their incompetence and lack of thoroughness, even hinting at a severe lack of professionalism, which I knew would sting them badly. It was easy to see how much they hated everything I insinuated about them, too, their faces glaring with rage at me from various points in the courtroom, including the witness stand.

It felt great to me watching them lose their "in control" attitude, although, I knew if some of those guys got me alone in an alley they'd beat the holy crap out of me and never think twice about it.

This badgering style of questioning really is a dangerous tightrope to walk with a jury because, no matter what, no matter whose side a jury is leaning toward, nobody likes a bully, and I didn't want to appear as one. It speaks to the basic goodness in all of us that we tend to side with the one being bullied, that we will want to step in and help in some way. Still, I had to keep hammering through layer after layer of "BS" the police department and the prosecutors had thrown up. *They won't keep me from doing my job*, I kept telling myself.

I was slowly starting to win this fight – I could feel it. Like rocking a car out of snow bank, however, it was a slow go at first.

"You are finally starting to hold up your end," Rex murmured during one of the recesses.

"Oh yes," Tom Cook agreed, "The trial is beginning to get more even."

"I'm not making any friends in this scuffle," I replied, darting my eyes around the hallway then hastily added, "But that's not the point. I'm leading this jury toward the light of truth."

Tom winked at me and Rex slugged me in the arm, which was my bother's way of telling me he liked what I was doing. Rex would also sneak into the courtroom after a recess to signal to me that the wimp who had begun the trial was starting to toughen up. Our secret signal was for him to put his hand in his back pocket which meant "kick butt".

In between our times in the courtroom I was obsessed with this case, prioritizing it over everything else in my life. I spoke of it constantly, endlessly. I couldn't stop myself. I badgered people, actually to the point of pestering everyone. I tried to convey my excitement with several of my colleagues, even though Nancy told me I was boring everyone with the details of Noi's case. The previous summer, I had taken the Dale Carnegie course, "How to Win Friends and Influence People". The guiding principle was to make the other person with whom you were interacting feel important and to be interested in them and their problems. I knew I was not doing that *at all*, not with anybody, but I could not seem to stop myself. A bore talks about himself. I knew I was being a bore, but I did not care. I also knew, on some deep and shameful level, that if I was still getting my ass kicked in the courtroom, like I had been at first, I wouldn't be shooting my boring mouth off about all of this like I was; but I was starting to feel like a winner..

One weekend at a bridge party, I questioned all of the players there about what they would have to hear to determine if Noi was not guilty. I was relentless about this, even though I knew Nancy was getting more and more aggravated with me for it. I directed the conversation around to Noi and the trial case all evening, trying to stir up some admiration for myself in the process. My behavior was rather like the actor John Barrymore's – or at lease like something I'd read about him saying, "Well, enough about me. How did *you* like my performance?" I'm sure most people just wanted to get away from me, and I know Nancy may have been right about me being a bore, because we have never seen or heard from any of those people since. It became a test of friendship. I felt if people liked me enough, they would want to hear about this case that was so important to me. Looking back, I can see that I should have listened to my wife and kept my big, boring yap shut.

My friends in the Thai community, I'm sure, had mixed feelings about Noi's case. Thai women are raised in a culture where the man is supreme. They could not understand a Thai woman who actually killed her husband. But they appreciated that I had won a bitter custody battle for Dick and Kim Hynd, which allowed them to keep Noi's little girls in their home while Noi was in jail. The Hynds loved these little girls and provided a much more stable home environment for them than Noi really ever had – or ever could have (in my opinion). The discord between Noi and Bobby was just too great for a stable and loving environment. That seemed clear to a lot of us. Unlike Bobby, Dick was a model father. He was always patient and kind with the small girls who now called him "Daddy", which he loved.

The Hynds were well-liked by the people in the Thai community, whereas Noi was practically unknown to them. Bobby rarely permitted Noi to go to the Thai parties and she only knew one other Thai person in the community, which was Kim Hynd. Noi seemed aloof and hard to get to know; she seldom tried to carry a conversation. The Thai women, for the most part, wanted the Hynds to permanently keep Noi's little girls, Mia and Maggie. I knew for that to happen, I would have to lose Noi's case.

I was certain the Hynds were good people and I liked them so much that I was concerned for their mental health if they should have to give the children back to Noi. Taking in a foster child would be so difficult, I think, because just when you have learned to love the child, to take it into your heart, to laugh and to play and cry with the child, you would have to give it up. For people as kind and good as the Hynds, I knew this would be a devastating heartbreak.

After realizing I was boring everybody in my world with my constant yammering about this case, I decided to hone my focus on the jury. Right now, the most important people I wanted to persuade about Noi were my jurors. Rex turned out to be very helpful to me, not because he was a hard worker, which he was and is, but because he had plenty of common sense about getting along with people. I had Rex sit in the courtroom and observe the juror's facial expressions and body language and give me impressions on what was occurring. I was too focused and too involved in the case to tell what was really going on around me without his help. I've always felt a person cannot tell if he is living in a zoo if he is sitting on top of the cage.

This testimony and cross-examination of police officers and OSBI agents took the rest of the week and the first two days of the following week. On the third day of the third week of the first trial, I asked Lewis to give me the tapes of Noi's confession. I wanted the jury to hear Noi's exact words so the police could not take them out of context and make them appear worse than they already were. Carson and Lewis both fought me ferociously on introducing the tapes, but, since there was no procedural rule that would keep them out, the Judge let the tapes be introduced as evidence. So, the jury heard all of the tapes that day. After my battle to get them into evidence, I had a day where I could sit back, relax, and watch the reaction of the jurors as they listened.

What they heard was a pathetic attempt by a young, terrified woman to cover up a killing, followed by a series of broken sentences. Noi sounded hysterical and confused by the police questions. Personally, I didn't think her confession did much damage to our case. In fact, it might even have helped her because the jurors would get to know her better. It is hard for members of a jury to identify with a young, foreign girl who has no experiences in common with them. It is even harder for a juror to send to prison someone they think they now know or, at least, understand a little better.

At home that evening, I did not say much to anyone because I had to go and prepare Noi for her time on the witness stand. I went to the jail to review what I was going to ask her the next day. When I arrived, I noticed Noi had the look of a captured animal cornered for the first time. She was cowered in the corner of the hallway not far from her jail cell all alone with her head resting in her hands. Tears streamed down her face in great rivers. Her lips were swollen and she sniffed constantly. She looked a mess.

My work was cut out for me. I sat next to her on the wooden bench and began by telling her to just relax and tell the truth. I held her hands, hoping she would trust me and feel safer. We sat there quietly together. I had asked Rex to teach me a little Thai he had learned when he was stationed in Bangkok some years earlier with the Air Force. I wanted to speak Thai to break the ice with Noi and I wanted her to trust me. I wanted Rex to teach me to say, "I care about you very much and I think you are very pretty." Rex told me that was easy to say and gave me the words. I practiced for several minutes and then Rex tested my accent because, as we all know, an Oklahoma twang does not translate easily into Thai. I decided to surprise Noi that night to take her mind off the next day's ordeal.

"Noi?" I began.

"Yes," she replied between sniffs.

Then, I said to her exactly what Rex had taught me, or so I thought. Noi began laughing and laughing. Her dark eyes got really wide. "You know what you say?" she asked.

Before I could answer her that I thought I did, she asked, "Who tell you this?"

I told her it was my brother, Rex, and she began laughing again. She laughed as long and as hard as she physically could, out loud, then she fell silent. But her shoulders shook and her mouth would continue to laugh, even though no sound was emerging. It was unsettling.

"What's so funny?" I finally asked.

"Go ask brother," she replied.

Noi relaxed with me after that. I also never spoke Thai to her again. Instead, I concentrated on trying to clean up her English so the jurors would not lose interest in listening to her because she was so difficult to understand. People tend to get impatient if they have to work at understanding what the witness has to say. There was still a great deal of work ahead of me. By 10 pm, as Noi continued to butcher the English language, I tried to convince myself that her foreign accent was charming instead of irritating and we called it a night. We were both exhausted.

The next morning at breakfast, Rex was laughing and slapping his sides. I asked him what was going on; I wanted to know what he had taught me to say in Thai. Clearly, whatever he'd taught me to say was the funniest thing he or Noi had ever heard.

"Just that you like her a lot and want to make a baby with her," Rex said, laughing hysterically. I choked and sprayed orange juice across the table.

That day, when Noi testified, she held up better than I did because I was so nervous for her. Overall, she behaved like a pro. When the prosecutors tried to trick her, she got confused and they could not get an answer. The language barrier actually helped her in that regard. She kept to her story. I was almost doubled over with exhaustion by the end of the day. I felt tired, looked tired, even *smelled* tired, I'm sure. My feet ached; my *clothes* felt tired and hung on me like threads on a sick and skinny, elderly man. The trial was winding down and the pressure was weighing on me badly. I had lost about twenty pounds in the past three to four months and I was looking more and more like a corpse. I'd been living on orange sherbet shakes and soups. My allergies also flared up and my nose needed honking often, which was distracting to everyone and embarrassing to me. My eyes felt swollen into tiny slits.

I introduced several other witnesses later in the week, but my case centered on Noi's testimony. If the jury believed her story, they would find her not guilty. If they didn't, I expected a conviction. It really was that simple.

The next afternoon, I got what turned out to be the biggest break of the trial – another *Godplop!* Carson and Lewis requested that three jurors be questioned about possible misconduct. They turned the names of the three jurors over to the Judge. Dalton summoned the jurors to his office and questioned each one about having been overheard discussing Noi's case with someone else. He had warned the jurors to never discuss the case with anyone until it was over. To do so would be serious misconduct.

The prosecutors had accused my courthouse friend Martha Diller and two other women of discussing Noi's case. Carson had heard Martha whisper, "Dr. Masood" to a fellow reporter. Dr. Masood was the State Medical Examiner and was still testifying in Noi's trial. Martha explained that she had simply told her friend that the Medical Examiner was still on the witness stand and she would not be able to pick up her child at the babysitters so she needed her to tell Martha's husband to pick up the child.

The second juror was seen talking to her son across the railing during recess. It turned out they had been speculating as to what time the trial would be over that day so they could work out between the two of them just who would have the car keys that afternoon.

The third juror said she had asked another juror if the case could continue on a Saturday.

I told Judge Dalton I did not see a problem with any of these discussions. Both prosecutors stood there, stone-faced and cold. Dalton held that these explanations were adequate and all three of the women jurors glared first at Carson and then at Lewis. Not many things are worse than being falsely accused and now these three women understood the underlying principle of my defense of Noi better than ever. Carson and Lewis slinked out of the room.

We adjourned for the day. I knew I had three people on my side now who would find any reasonable excuse they could to believe Noi's story. However, I did not have time to gloat over this fact because I had to go home and prepare closing arguments for the following day.

When I arrived the next morning, there was a buzz in the courtroom. I was a little nervous because my wife and several of her close friends, as well as about a dozen of my relatives, came to the courtroom to see me in action. They were ready to see me as The Gladiator. I was prepared, of course, but I was still nervous and, even that early in the day, could feel drops of sweat slide down the middle of my back, reminding me that, no matter how together I seemed to look, I was still facing the strong possibility of falling apart or dropping the ball and I couldn't let that happen, not after all we had been through, not after having come this far.

This time, I did not read from flash cards, as I had my opening statements, but I also had not made an outline of my closing arguments. Thus, I rambled somewhat …for three and a half hours to be exact, but I bet nobody accused me of being in a hurry with this presentation. It's a wonder nobody dozed off in the courtroom while I just yammered on and on, but I never saw that happen. Murder cases can be very intriguing, I guess. Despite my worries over having bored everyone by talking so long, I still felt proud that I was able to speak that long without notes.

My throat was dry – no, it was *parched*, like I'd been standing in the middle of an Oklahoma dust storm all day. I stepped out into the hallway to get a drink of water and was stunned to see a close friend of mine sitting all alone on the bench. She said she felt sick to her stomach and needed a rest. I asked her how she liked my closing statement. She said it was good, but I could tell she was only being polite, so I pressed her, asking her more questions. I really needed to know the truth of what she thought. Finally, reluctantly, she blurted out that she could not accept the way Noi had dumped Bobby's naked body into the car, left the car out in a field and then just driven off with her accomplice, like Bobby was not even worth burying. She said she did not think she could bear it if this had happened to one of her three little boys. Her reaction let me know I had generated too much feeling for Bobby.

I now know why I did that, something I did not understand then. Years of introspection and little splashes of wisdom have shown me things I'm not sure I could have understood at the time. Whenever I spoke of Bobby's death, it reminded me of the death of my son, Brandon. I would get a little misty-eyed and think about the sadness of Brandon's death. I would see his little blue blanket and his dark blue eyes, still open and looking at me, even in death. I thought of kissing and hugging him, of holding his tiny head against my cheek, praying that he would come back to life. I saw those images of my son when I talked to the jury about Bobby's death. I now know I should have not let myself become so emotional and that I should have done everything in my power to keep those images of Brandon out of my mind.

I should have stepped on my own foot, if that would have worked, or stabbed my hand with a fountain pen – *anything* – to keep from seeing those pictures of my tiny son's face in my head. Of course, as they say, hindsight is 20/20. At the time, I could barely get a handle on the consequences of my empathy.

In contrast, one of the most effective tools I used in my closing arguments was the use of charts showing the jury some forty reasonable doubts I had accumulated during the trial. Many of those doubts concerned the incompetence and bias of the police investigation. When the jurors saw those doubts listed on a chart and heard my explanation for each of them, it made more of a lasting imprint in their minds.

At the end of my closing arguments, I vividly remember Carson lurching to his feet, like he couldn't wait to tattle to the jury about something bad I had done. He was almost gleeful about it. He looked at the jury and said, "Weren't you getting as tired as I was of hearing little Jimmy Lloyd whimper and cry? Didn't you just want to throw up?" He then launched into a personal attack on me, rather than Noi's guilt.

I know what you're thinking – what a jackass – but, in truth, every time Carson came after me in that diminishing way, the jury became more sympathetic toward me and, by extension, toward my client. So, to my mind, he could go after me all he wanted. Then, almost as an afterthought, Carson finished with a blistering account of Noi's sins. He concentrated on her actions after Bobby's death in an attempt to prove her guilt.

Then, we were done. It was 3:05 pm when the bailiff and jury retired for deliberations. Now, the hard part began – the waiting. My life and my career were interwoven with Noi's fate and I knew that if I lost this case, I would be losing part of myself, too. Several concerned friends had called Nancy to let her know how worried they were about my mental health. They thought I would never recover if I lost this case.

My family and I waited until 8 pm at my office, then they went to get me some pizza from the restaurant next door. The baby was cranky, so Nancy took her home to put her to bed. I had mixed feelings when she packed the family up and left because I dreaded being by myself to continue the wait. On another level, though, I was relieved to be left alone with my own thoughts. It was too difficult to be polite when I was about to implode from the anxiety. I felt like I was beginning to unravel like an old rope and nobody, nothing – not even the love and support of my family – could keep me from flying apart.

I laid down on the couch in my office and stared at the degrees and certificates, framed in gold and black, hanging on the wall. They were impressive, certainly, as were all of my law books resting on their shelves. I knew those books and degrees had little meaning when compared to Noi's future, or even my own future. I refused to dwell on the consequences, if we lost; I also refused to think about a victory. I just focused, instead, on the myriad of little details which occurred during the trial, and ran over and over in my mind the thousands of split-second decisions every trial lawyer has to make.

The grandfather clock in my office chimed twelve times. It was now midnight and I still had not heard a word. When a jury takes this long to make a decision, it usually means there has been a problem.

If it were a "not guilty" verdict, it should not take this long. Gradually, I began to give up hope of a victory as the hours dragged by. Just as I began dozing off, the phone blasted out its ring at exactly 2:10 am. I jerked awake and grabbed the call. The Clerk ordered me back to court. I scampered out the door, practically sprinting the four blocks from my office to the courthouse.

In those days, Tulsa did not have what would be considered a cosmopolitan downtown. Nancy and I used to kid about getting out of the downtown area by 8 pm so we wouldn't get rolled up in the sidewalks at 8:15 pm, even on the weekends. It seemed weird to be racing along empty sidewalks which are usually filled with crowds of all kinds of people during the day. I did not wait for lights to turn green; jaywalking was the least of my concerns. It was a lazy night in downtown Tulsa and I was the only frantic blur around. The moon was just a toenail sliver in the night sky and there was no breeze on this evening of July 22, 1983.

When I arrived, out of breath and sweating, Noi was seated at the table in her prison blue sack dress (the blue color generally indicates a low risk detainee). She looked tiny and rigid, like a statue. Her face held no expression and her eyes looked completely blank. Lewis and Carson were also there, but neither of them even looked at me when I blasted in the door. Judge Dalton arrived and unfolded the note the bailiff handed him announcing the jury's dilemma. It said, "We are deadlocked at eight to four."

Oklahoma law requires all twelve jurors to agree to either convict a person or to let her go. If the jurors cannot agree on a final decision, the Judge declares a mistrial. What this meant was that we would have to retry the case before a new jury.

I later discovered that the jury took its initial vote by secret ballot. The first vote was six for First Degree Murder and six for Not Guilty. Finally, after hours and hours of deliberations, two jurors changed their votes. The final verdict was eight for First Degree Manslaughter and four for Not Guilty. Nobody would budge from this compromise, even though they were all exhausted from eleven and a half hours of deliberating. Changing enough votes to make it unanimous would get all of them off the hook and out of there, I knew that, so it made my heart feel good to know these jurors were principled enough not to cave just for comfort or convenience. I found out that three of the four Not Guilty votes were from jurors Carson and Lewis had accused of misconduct, something I had hoped would jump up later and bite the prosecutors' right in the ass. It had, and I thanked God for giving me another chance. However, for me to actually win an acquittal, I would have to become a real trial lawyer and not rely on the prosecutors' missteps.

Dalton looked disappointed. He sighed and offered to give the jury more time to reach a unanimous verdict. He even offered to put them all up in Tulsa's finest hotel if they would please continue trying to reach a verdict. He gave them fifteen minutes to take him up on his offer.

If the jury remained deadlocked, the four jurors who voted "Not Guilty" would be giving Noi a new chance. They would also be giving me a chance to obtain trial experience without getting anyone hurt or killed. It is similar, in some ways, to a surgeon's training. They first let the surgeon-to-be operate on cadavers because he can't hurt a dead person. In actual practice, something I've learned as a Personal Injury Attorney, most negligent doctors or surgeons bury their mistakes. A trial lawyer's mistakes live with him or her forever, riding around on our upper backs like some foul-breathed ape ready to do us in. It's awful. At least, my glaring mistakes would not show up in a law book with law professors and fellow attorneys noting them in a "How NOT to Do It" lecture, or so I hoped.

On the other hand, statistics show that whenever a first trial ends in a mistrial, the prosecutor manages to tie up any loose ends or problems in his case and usually gets a conviction in the second go-around. It happens all the time. The prosecutor can become terribly effective once he learns what the defendant's testimony or defense is going to be.

All of this suspense was giving me a ripping headache. I was exhausted and in desperate need of a shower, a shave, and a vacation. I was so tired my mind began drifting off to Hawaii, which is not a bad place to think about. Just as I was beginning to relax, I heard a knock at the jury door and the bailiff slowly walked over and let the jury out. Judge Dalton asked the foreman, "What have you decided?" The foreman answered quietly, "It just wouldn't do any good, Your Honor. We are still deadlocked."

I heaved a sigh of relief. Once again, I was limp with gratitude, and thanked God for throwing this giant cog in the wheels of justice, as everything screeched to a halt. I was overwhelmed at the redemption just laid at my feet, and thrilled that I would have another chance, *one more time.*

Jim Lloyd and Jody Seay

CHAPTER 10 – *ALMOST* BROKE BUT, STILL, UNBROKEN

I felt like a thief, a cheat, even an adulterer. How in the world would I ever explain to Nancy that I'd just withdrawn another $1,000 from our personal savings account – this time, for two criminal defense seminars?

Nancy and I hardly talked about anything these days except money; more specifically, she talked to me about how much money was going out and how nothing was coming in, as if I didn't already know that, as if I didn't already feel guilty as an embezzler about it. I think every time she looked at me all she could see was someone who continually took funds away from her family and threatened everyone's financial security. Because Nancy was an in-demand CPA, most of our savings was money she had put into our accounts. She handled our financial books … and saw our funds disappearing daily, so I could understand her feelings, but, still, I took out money again and again, hoping either that she wouldn't notice, or, that she would let it slide.

Thus far, my accepting Noi's case had cost us somewhere between $45,000 and $50,000. This included my office overhead costs, since I had taken no new cases in the past nine months. Of course, my wife was always quick to point out that this number did not include my loss of revenue. I was spending an unbelievably large amount of money with negligible income. There was simply no time left, after handling everything I needed to do for Noi's case, for me to pursue other cases.

Not having enough money had put a terrible strain on our marriage, like we didn't even know each other anymore, something I never would have imagined happening to us as a couple. I had just about stopped making love to her because she was shutting me out and so angry at me most of the time. I didn't blame her for that, I really didn't, but it was hard to get excited about a nagging wife. I mean, we were both young and both with healthy sex drives, so our physical needs were occasionally being met but, emotionally, we were miles and miles apart. I missed that connection and I missed my Nancy, the woman I loved.

One of the hallmarks of a successful marriage is feeling that your partner has your back, no matter what, and I know neither of us was feeling that about the other during that time. I wanted her to understand how hard I was working and to comfort and encourage me. I needed her to understand how much it meant to me to win this case, but all I was seeing was a woman mad enough to strangle me most of the time, not the woman I thought would be crazy in love with me forever.

I'm sure Nancy was wondering who had kidnapped me, as well. I was hardly ever at home and when I was, I was withdrawn and distant or busy and submerged in papers I needed to review for Noi's case. I wasn't being a good husband to my wife or a good father to our children. Time, the most precious commodity we have to offer to those we love, was gobbled up with my search for whatever I could find to use in fighting this case. I, literally, had no spare time at the end of those incredibly long days to devote to the ones I loved most in the world. Nancy felt that she alone was shouldering the responsibility for the sailing of this ship that was our family and that all I was doing was throwing all the life jackets overboard.

In truth, I had been more forgiving of her attitude when our sex life was steamier. Now, it seemed, even the sex had become a chore, and, for both of us. *Is this going to feel wonderful? Or, is it just going to feel like work?* That's what I found myself thinking when it came to sex with my wife during that time. I'm sure Nancy was thinking those same thoughts.

As chickenshit as it sounds — as it *was* — I handled the expense of the $1000 worth of training seminars by not mentioning it to her until much later. I knew it would make Nancy's head explode, but I thought these seminars were worth every cent.

By attending them, I felt I was taking Tom Cook's advice on getting some help. I was wrong. That's not what Tom meant at all. What Tom really meant was for me to associate with an experienced criminal lawyer as co-counsel, but I was too stubborn for that. The thought of trying to explain to a competent attorney all the specifics of this case, the uphill battle we would have to fight to defend a client with no money, no hope, and no way to look innocent in front of a jury, well, it was daunting. I couldn't bear the thought of being laughed at by another attorney who would have his act together better than I did. Besides, after what the prosecutors and their friends had done to me, I wanted more than anything to strike back.

My birthday is November 23rd; I am a Sagittarius on the cusp with Scorpio, yet seem to have more Scorpio traits than those of Sagittarius, the "Hunter". The three hallmarks of the Scorpio zodiac sign are the high-flying, soaring eagle, the gray lizard, and, of course, the scorpion. At various times in my life, I have seen all three of those icons in myself. When I am happy and on top of my game, there is nobody more excited about life than I am. I soar like an eagle. If I am down in the dumps, or, if things in my world are going poorly, I can feel that gray veil of the lizard settle over me as I burrow down into the mud. When I have been wronged; particularly, if I have been made to appear foolish, the scorpion in me wants to strike back, sting 'em fast and hard, make them remember who they're dealing with. I wanted a little personal vengeance. These seminars and additional training, I felt — I hoped — would give me the edge I wanted.

Clearly, I needed help, but didn't know where to turn. Then, I remembered a Bible passage my mother had hammered into my thick skull when I was a boy. *How could I ever have forgotten?* It was Matthew 7:7: "Ask and it will be given to you; seek and you will find; knock and the door will be opened to you." I decided to swing for the fences and seek out counsel from world-famous criminal defense attorney, Gerry Spence, a man admired by so many in my profession.

After checking with the National College of Criminal Defense for the best criminal defense training courses to enroll in, I chose two. The one in Lake Tahoe, Nevada offered a three-day course in cross-examination techniques. The other, in Jackson, Wyoming, offered a three-day course in closing arguments in his home town. Plus, I wanted to see his law office built inside a Fort. I chose these two trainings specifically because Gerry Spence would be at both of them. He and a dozen other nationally-known lawyers were scheduled to be on hand to help coach fledgling attorneys. By this time in my career, I was certainly not what anyone would call a "fledgling" attorney. I had already been running a moderately successful law practice. Still, in terms of being a criminal defense attorney, nobody could have been more inexperienced or scared shitless than I was. I knew in my heart that getting advice from world-class attorneys like Gerry Spence and others at these workshops could only make me better. That was my hope, anyway.

I knew of Gerry Spence because he had won the famous Karen Silkwood nuclear contamination case. This case was especially well-known in Oklahoma because Karen Silkwood's estate successfully sued Kerr-McGee, a corporation operating a nuclear facility out of Crescent, Oklahoma, where my grandmother lived. It was a David versus Goliath kind of case I was sure would not have been won without the expertise of Gerry Spence. He had also won dozens of other seemingly impossible cases. He was, and remains, to this day, a hero and inspiration to lawyers.

Gerry Spence is a big man, probably two hundred pounds or so and well over six feet tall, even without the cowboy boots he always wears. He was the most prominent speaker at the Lake Tahoe event and it took over ten minutes just to list all of his accomplishments in the introduction. His is a commanding presence and the trademark look he has created for himself is that of a flamboyant yet rugged cowboy. He looks perfectly at home in the gold-fringed buckskin jacket and cowboy boots which are his trademark. His face is tan, almost leathery-looking, as if he's spent a lot of time outdoors. To me, the most outstanding feature about Gerry, though, is his deep, melodious voice. He starts out in a quiet, almost halting pace and then his voice grows deeper, louder, and faster as he goes on. I sat back and noticed the effectiveness of his language. He uses clear, precise, simple words to eloquently persuade his listeners. Spence is hypnotic, spellbinding, a magical speaker, and is well-loved by his audience.

Gerry showed us how to link our feelings with the jury and how to transfer the common bond to our clients. Sharing common experiences and emotions such as fear is the key to building a bridge to the jury. We all have certain fears, fears we mostly try to hide from others and often, even from ourselves.

Some of the jurors are afraid to come into the courtroom and sit on a jury. Gerry Spence described how intimidating a courtroom can be to some people. A courtroom is an arena or stage where even a child would feel out of place – an austere place with a no-nonsense feel to it where there are no living plants or animals. He said the courtroom is a place where the judge wearing a black robe, the color we most associate with death, stares down at the other people. Gerry instructed us to bond the twelve jurors' fear of the courtroom with the defendant's fears as he stands alone. This way, Gerry told us, we could "get inside the juror's hides".

It had taken me a long time to understand Noi's irrational behavior after Bobby's death and I finally came to believe that she had acted out of fear, not insanity. I believed, also, that if a juror really got to know Noi and understand her fears, he would begin to care about her, just as I had.

As long as the defendant is unknown to the jury and all they know about her are the facts of the case, the elements of the crime, and the facts associated with the charges against the defendant, the jury will not care about her. If that's all they get to see and understand, there is no room for them to care.

In short, Mr. Spence teaches that the lawyer must bond the jury to the defendant. In teaching this, Gerry uses simple stories and analogies, even metaphors to get everyone involved and make it easy for them to understand the point he is trying to get across.

One of the examples Gerry Spence used was a segment in Antoine de Saint-Exupery's book, "The *Little Prince*". The boy wanted to play with the fox.

> *"I cannot play with you," the fox said, "I am not tame."*
>
> *"What does that mean — 'tame'?" the prince asked.*
>
> *"It is an act too often neglected," said the fox. "It means to establish ties."*
>
> *"To establish ties?" the prince asked.*
>
> *"Just that," said the fox. "To me, you are still nothing more than a little boy who is just like a hundred thousand other little boys. And I have no need of you. And you, on your part, have no need of me. To you, I am nothing more than a fox, like a hundred thousand other foxes. But, if you tame me, then we shall each need each other. To me, you will be unique in all the world. To you, I shall be unique in all the world..."*
>
> *So, the little prince tamed the fox. And, when the hour of his departure drew near...*
>
> *"Ah," said the fox. "I shall cry."*
>
> *"It is your own fault," said the little prince, "I never wished you any sort of harm, but you wanted me to tame you..."*
>
> *"You become responsible, forever," the fox replied, "for what you have tamed."*

Gerry shared with us his observations about courtroom psychology. He said, "If the fox is not tamed, when he runs through the courtroom grinning and snarling at the jury because he is afraid, the jury will then be afraid of him and they will destroy him. But, if this same fox is tamed, he can run about the courtroom, still grinning and snarling at the jury because he is afraid, and the jury could not destroy or kill its own pet fox. People fight for what they love and, if they don't care, they won't lift a finger to save it."

I went up to Gerry Spence that evening to congratulate him on his mesmerizing talk, and I asked if I could take a few minutes of his time to answer questions about a case I had in Tulsa, Oklahoma.

Gerry agreed and we talked next to the podium. He is a big man, even bigger in person than I had imagined. He towers over me even as I wear my "elevator" shoes. As he towered over me, his presence was both powerful and gentle at the same time. I kept thinking we must look like the Jolly Green Giant and Sprout; I'll leave it up to you to figure out who was who in my mind.

After I described Noi's case, Gerry sighed, laid his giant slab of an arm around my shoulder and said, "Son, you're in big trouble."

No kidding, I thought. Nobody could have been in bigger trouble than I was.

He then encouraged me by saying, "I can tell you are a sensitive and warm person. To have the jury trust you, you also have to trust the jury. Feel yourself becoming one with them," he told me. "Love in your heart will conquer all."

I explained to him how I trusted the jury in the first trial and that is where I might have gone wrong. Gerry analyzed the first trial and advised me that I still needed to weed out the jurors who were unreceptive to trust and love. He also said I had to prepare the jury for Noi and Noi for the jury by helping them to get to know and trust each other. This, he assured me, would make the difference. This, he said, would enable me to "get inside their hides."

At first, I was disappointed with this advice because it was so simple and I couldn't imagine how it would work. I kept thinking, on the flight to Tahoe, that Gerry Spence would save the day by giving me a legal formula that would, miraculously, turn me into a super-lawyer.

Now, after having mulled over in my head the advice he gave me, it seemed that it would only make me vulnerable. I wanted to get even with the judges and the prosecutors and I did not – in any way – want to be seen by them as lovable. I wanted them to see me as a warrior, a fierce attorney about as cuddly as a badger on methamphetamines. My plan was to be somebody to be feared in the courtroom with no doubt about it. I wanted to kick someone's ass, I sure did! *And Gerry Spence wanted me to be loving and kind and warm and sensitive – huh?* I was ranting to myself. *Was that big Wyoming cowboy lawyer just loco?? I couldn't see how this would work, not now, not EVER!*

Questions swirled and roared through my mind like a tornado spiraling and crashing across the Oklahoma plains. *What if the jury just thought I was being sneaky and manipulative? Would the jury be able to pick up on this kind of lawyering? And, if I made a mistake, would they hold it against my client?*

My professional style, my professional world – how I saw myself – was about to be flipped upside down.

CHAPTER 11 – A SPECIAL SOUVENIR: *ALMOST* LOST

Forgive me, here. Humor me for just a little bit. I'm going to fast-forward in my story several years, making a few big time-related leaps here, to better explain the effects of my learning from master trial attorney, Gerry Spence. Because of what he taught me, everything in my professional life changed, including how I reacted in the story I am about to share with you. We will be back in the courtroom soon enough, I promise, but it's important that you understand the significance of my surrendering to his advice and adopting it.

My first time leap is forward to when my son Buddy was a teenager. He worked on President Clinton's election in 1992 while attending Union High School in Tulsa. Because of his work and dedication, he received an official invitation to attend the Presidential Inauguration. He was thrilled, of course, and went to Washington, D.C. on the bus with a friend. Upon his return, he gave me an American flag silk tie he bought for me while he was in D.C. I was so proud of this thoughtful gift that I wore it everywhere – to meetings, jury trials, church, almost everywhere. I darned near wore the thing out.

My second big time leap is to when America was so brutally attacked on September 11, 2001. Nancy was my law partner, by then, as well as my wife. We were booked to fly to New York for a short Thursday through Monday vacation with Jerry and Leigh O'Brien. We were to see some musicals and museums, but cancelled our trip due to the tragedy in New York. We then received a last-minute invitation to attend a charity auction for the

Traumatic Brain-Injured Children's Foundation held on Friday, Sept. 14, 2001 in Tulsa, Oklahoma.

Although America was still raw and reeling from the devastation of the attack in New York, the hotel ballroom was packed that Friday night for the Tulsa fundraiser. With doctors in black tuxedos and their wives in sparkly, luxurious ball gowns filling up one half of the room; equally elegantly-dressed lawyers and their spouses filled up the other half; that is, except for *me*. I wasn't wearing a tux, but a dark suit and the American flag tie Buddy had given me almost a decade earlier. Of all times, this time, this moment, seemed the best to be wearing this favorite tie of mine. As the volunteers were carrying in more and more items to be auctioned off, I got caught up in the moment and walked up to the stage where I asked the auctioneer if I could auction off my special tie. He agreed and handed me the microphone. He then motioned to someone who directed a spotlight toward me. Suddenly, I could no longer see the crowd, only a blinding white light. It was like watching a train come at me in the darkness.

"Ladies and gentlemen," I said, "the next item to be auctioned tonight is this tie I am wearing right here." Before loosening the triangle-shaped, single-Windsor slip knot, I held the star-studded red, white and blue tie up with my right hand while also keeping it held close to my heart. "Please know," I continued, "that it's not just any tie, it is a very special tie. My son went to a Presidential Inauguration and purchased it for me there many years ago. As you can see, it's a little thread-bare and a little bit stained." Even though I can't see them at this point, I can feel members of the audience leaning in closer to get a better look at my tie. There was no sound in the room, like everyone there was holding their breath. "So, what makes this tie so special, you might ask," I said. I paused for just a few seconds. "Well, I'll tell you – it's the colors! Ladies and gentlemen, look carefully. These colors are not made of Madras…because these colors will never, ever run. We will *FIGHT* for justice! We will *FIGHT* for those who died this week in New York and we will win. We *WILL* win!" By this time, I was loosening the knot and slipping the tie from around my neck, then holding it high in front of me, and then I lowered it and held it gently in cupped hands. I began speaking in low tones, asking the audience, slowly, "Now, what am I bid for this old, tired, silk tie?"

Turning back to the auctioneer, I handed the tie to him, walked down the stairs and off the stage. Trying to make my way back to our table, I kept getting distracted by people shaking my hand and patting my back, so I could not tell who was bidding. There were whistles and commotion and a stirring in the crowd. I could see flashes of light and hands waving at the auctioneer by people making bids. The room seemed to sway this way and that, almost swirling, as I tried to find my table. I felt light-headed, but not from being ill; I felt as if I were floating on a giant, golden wave of love and camaraderie, as if I were being held aloft by the spirit and patriotism of two hundred other Americans who loved this great nation just as much as my family and I did.

The bidding sounded spirited with the doctors' side of the ballroom bidding and then the trial lawyers' side bidding. It was all very fast – shouting went back and forth across the room like a ping-pong match of words and numbers, but all in good humor and lively. Suddenly, the gavel fell while I was still standing and turning back to look at the auctioneer. He pointed, but I could not tell who the buyer was because of all the commotion. People were standing and applauding as I wound my way back to our table, all the while being stopped by well-wishers. My old, nearly worn-out, nine year old, five dollar tie brought in an astonishing $650.^{00}! It was one of my proudest moments.

My third time leap is to my birthday, November 23rd - just a couple of months later. Nancy invited two couples over as a surprise for me. As I opened a small gift box, there it was – you guessed it – my old silk tie. A close friend, Pat Carr of Carr & Carr Lawyers and his wife, Carolyn, were the mystery high-bidders at the auction and they gave my tie back to me for my birthday. Tears puddled up in my eyes, welling over and spilling down my cheeks. "Thank you," was all I could muster as I wiped my eyes. We all embraced. I couldn't say anymore because I was all choked up. Words fail me at times like these, believe it or not and suddenly, I found myself feeling a little thread-bare and worn, much like my old silk tie.

There was a time when I could not have parted with my prized trophy of a tie; and, being, basically, terrified of public speaking, I surely would not have sought out a big stage if it were not for the influence of someone else. There was a time when this man I want to tell you about gave me a priceless gift. He gave me his time and helped to shape my way of trying cases and understanding people, how to think with my heart, how to love and how to forgive. His name? Gerry Spence, truth teller and master trial lawyer.

During the several Gerry Spence seminars I attended, I also peppered him with numerous questions about many technical and practical issues involving Noi's first degree murder case. I felt so utterly lost and helpless in not knowing what to do to protect the rights and the life of this young woman accused of murder. So after a substantial amount of hounding, Gerry took me aside after one of his seminars and asked me more about my case. His last question to me was: "What is it that you're afraid of?"

Well, the floodgates opened and I don't doubt that Gerry, on some level, had to be wishing he'd not asked me that question. I began by telling him that I'd only ever tried one case and had lost it. Then I explained my fear of public speaking. I shared with him my issue of stage fright and even told him of my client's botched confession tape.

He shook his head he and his former law partner, Bob Rose, Jr., Chief Justice of the Wyoming Supreme Court, extended me an invitation to Jackson, Wyoming to attend a seminar they were hosting. Once there, they spent extra time getting me up to speed. They opened my eyes and mind to trusting jurors, respecting others, and learning to love others whole-heartedly. These two men taught me Biblical things, metaphysical teachings and more; things like: you must first give a person your trust before they will trust you; you must respect the other person before they will respect you; and, you must love another person before they will love you. These two men taught me things never heard of in law school, lessons so far beyond the practical ways of handling law cases that it made my jaw drop.

This, Gerry Spence said, was how I should work in not only Noi's case, but every law case to come across my desk from now on. He gave me new insights into my own fears and how to master those deep-seated fears so that I can own them and not be possessed by those things I fear the most. What a gift Gerry Spence and Justice Rose gave me – in time, knowledge and friendship. I will be forever grateful.

And, so, on that night in September of 2001, with my country and countrymen still reeling with the shock and horror of our nation just having been attacked, it was time for me to give back and give back with things that matter. For me, stepping up and presenting my tie for auction was, in part, symbolic of the great gift another American had given to me. I must pass it on in any way that I can. That's what happens when you are given a great truth, a great principle, a great gift – you must pass it on in ways large or small.

Some people would view this chapter as homage of deepest respect and gratitude from me to Gerry Spence. Others would call it a love letter. I'm okay with that. Actually, so much of my career as a successful attorney, I owe to Gerry Spence and what he taught me. His work and his life have been nothing short of phenomenal and I am grateful to him each day. Gerry Spence continues to inspire lawyers all over our country to better serve others and to serve justice. I am honored to know him. He was the inspiration for me in making my impromptu tie presentation and – who knows? – in looking back, maybe I even sounded a little bit like him on that one unforgettable evening.

Jim Lloyd and Jody Seay

CHAPTER 12 – *ALMOST* A TRIAL

The storm raging outside the courtroom seemed, to me, a bad omen. Another Oklahoma thunderstorm had been brewing all morning and had finally broken and unleashed its fury on us right before the second trial began, after lunch, on Tuesday, September 20, 1983.

There was a real "hanging" jury in the courtroom on that day. I could tell this when I looked at the jury pool with their eyes squinted and their lips pursed. Just looking at the jury, it seemed to me that Noi could only win this trial if the prosecutors really dropped the ball and screwed up, and I mean, screwed up badly! I have never been so sure of predicting a jury before in my life.

By mid-afternoon, Carson was still asking questions of prospective jurors. It was exactly 3:15 pm when I heard him ask, "If a person was charged with first degree murder, and if the murder weapon was found at the bottom of a lake, wouldn't you expect the defendant to explain that she did not commit..."

"Objection, Your Honor!" I jumped to my feet and interrupted. "The prosecutor cannot comment on the defendant's right not to testify, and, it is also misleading the jury about which party has the burden of proof. The burden of proof is on the prosecution, not on the defense. I move for a mistrial."

Just to be clear about what kind of shaky ground I was walking on here, I had requested that Judge Dalton declare a mistrial four other times since lunch and he had never granted one; never even reacted as if that should be in the realm of possibility. This time was different, though. Dalton was concerned that there was a serious problem.

The prosecutor had made similar errors three or four times earlier in the afternoon. Judge Dalton must have begun to feel Noi's right to a fair trial had already been compromised, and indeed, it had. The U.S. Supreme Court had already ruled that the prosecutor in a case was not allowed to make any comment about a defendant's failure to testify in his or her defense. The Supreme Court felt that a comment would, in effect, force the defendant to testify, to take the stand and answer the charge.

This time, Dalton called a recess and asked Carson, Lewis and me to join him in his chambers for a conference. His office was familiar to me by now. It was a small but elegantly furnished room. Dalton always sat behind a large brown desk, scowling. I was relieved this time to see that he actually looked resigned to doing what he and I both knew he needed to do. He began to puff on a cigarette and blew out the smoke with a loud and drawn-out sigh. He looked like the embodiment of authority itself.

Judge Dalton tensely asked me if I would like the court reporter to make a record. Of course, he knew that I would, so we waited for her to come in and to take her seat across from the Judge.

I explained to Dalton why I was entitled to a mistrial. He was a judge who believed in law and order in his courtroom; a man proud of his reputation for having the lowest rate of reversals of any Oklahoma criminal judge. He and I both knew that Carson had flagrantly misstated the law and Noi's constitutional rights. He also knew there was no way around this but to declare a mistrial.

The Constitution of the United States was about to get in the way of Noi's being convicted during the second trial. Of course, Carson argued that his comments were not made in error. He said that, even if they were, that these comments were harmless and would make no difference because Noi would still have a fair trial. When this argument did not sway Judge Dalton, Carson weakly explained that he did not mean for a mistrial to happen. This was the only time I ever saw him actually embarrassed by his blatant misconduct. Even though I didn't much like him for how disrespectfully he treated me in the courtroom, still, I had to take my hat off to him in this instance for taking responsibility for his actions on this day.

I loved it when Judge Dalton made this decision; adored it, actually. He looked directly at Carson and told him that this time he had gone too far. Dalton believed it was better to shut the trial down now, after an investment of only several hours, rather than going on for two or three weeks only to have the Oklahoma Court of Criminal Appeals reversing a conviction due to errors at the beginning of the trial. The judge made it clear that he wanted a conviction and that he wanted this conviction to stick. "I just don't want it to get thrown out due to an error this early in the trial," he said.

I had to applaud Judge Dalton's decision on this, even though it really had more to do with his own sense of practicality than anything else. Almost all murder convictions are appealed and, he was right, certainly the Court of Appeals would turn this conviction over because of the prosecutor's error. I have to say that I wasn't exactly surprised by Judge Dalton's decision, though. I thought about what I had interpreted from the Cherokee woman's psychic prediction: *three trials. When Noi first slipped that note to me, I didn't really believe this would come to pass. After the first mistrial, however, I gotta admit, I began to believe in and to trust my own Cherokee sense more. I also trust myself as an attorney more. My expectations are coming true – I am becoming better; therefore, everything I touch will become better. Now that I honestly believe in my dreams, they are becoming self-fulfilling. For some reason, I have never really gotten myself psyched up for the second trial. It was as if I knew, on some deep level I could not yet name, that the second trial would fizzle and it had just done exactly that.*

I was not keen on using any of the jury pool sitting in the courtroom, even if we had to start over with another group of fifty people. Everyone in the courtroom had already heard Carson' comments and, therefore, might already be unfairly prejudiced against my client. Judge Dalton agreed with me and set the third trial for September 26, 1983. When he said that, I leapt up into the air, swinging my fist in an imaginary knock-out punch. Dalton raised his eyebrows in surprise, reminding me to respect his office and to calm down.

Dalton's announcement of a mistrial sent the Mitchell family and the prosecutors storming out of the courtroom. The air of disgruntlement and anger made the wind whoosh behind them as they made their exit. I was both relieved and elated; Noi, however, was not exhilarated in any way at all. She looked at me as if I had gone insane. I guess she thought I was near the breaking point and, in some ways, she was actually right about that. I had lost twenty-two pounds since July, a loss which made me look gaunt and almost frail, rather than fit and trim. My family's finances were running dangerously low and I was worried.

I tried to explain to Noi what had happened, but she just stared at me like a startled fawn. She could not understand how in the world I could be so thrilled about another trial. As far as she was concerned, she was worn out and the last thing she wanted to see in her life was another courtroom. I tried to explain to her that a delay could mean a victory, but I don't think she understood or believed me. She just looked confused and helpless as the Deputy Sheriff led her back to her cell.

Buddy was waiting for me in his usual spot next to the garage door when I got home that night. I said, "Guess what, Little Buddy, the prosecutor made a bad move today." Buddy and I used to play checkers together when I had more time to spend with him and I still talked "checker talk" to him. Buddy was my most loyal fan. Even though I had not spent the time with him that I knew he needed to have with me, he was always eager to win my approval, like a little puppy. My son had not given up on me and that felt good in my heart.

Nancy, on the other hand, could not hide her disappointment that the Judge had declared a mistrial. Fury shot out of her eyes at me, like lava. I kept thinking that, if she'd had a heavy skillet in her hand, she would have smacked me right in the head with it. My wife, understandably, just wanted the whole thing to be over with so I could get back to earning a living and she wouldn't have to continually worry about her family facing financial ruin. I understood her feelings; really, I did, but I resented that she didn't understand, or wouldn't acknowledge, how hard I was working on this case.

"Grow up and stop chasing an impossible dream," Nancy snapped at me and I resented that even more.

I told her, "I didn't think the timing was right for a win in this second trial, anyway, and we're forging ahead for all the chips to fall for a win in the third trial."

She didn't even answer me. I went into the other room and called my parents and told them what had happened. They both had always believed in the Cherokee woman's psychic prediction, too. *Could this have been because they are both part Cherokee?* I thought as they talked excitedly about this new development.

At any rate, the Cherokee woman's prediction was hard to refute at this point, and I allowed myself to settle into it. I realized something: MY JOURNEY WAS CLEAR, APPEARING AHEAD OF ME, LIKE A LIT PATH AS NEVER BEFORE. I could not help but hear that rhyme in my head one more time: *IS IT GOOD? IS IT TRUE? IS THIS PATHWAY RIGHT FOR YOU?*

Like a Cherokee warrior, I was trusting in my heritage to lead me now.

Jim Lloyd and Jody Seay

CHAPTER 13 – MY OPENING STATEMENT: *ALMOST* PERFECT

"There is something different and special about the trial lawyer. When his time comes to stand up and speak on behalf of his client, something happens that is unlike anything else on earth; it is like the touch of Midas that turns dust into gold, or the miracle of electricity. There's a touch of everything wonderful in the advocacy of a lawyer for his client, in his effort to defend the right. There is a dash of love in it, and there is a little of the effect of bourbon whiskey; there is a little sex appeal, and more than a little magic. There must be a source of this transformation of personality and power that touches an ordinary man with the Pentecostal fire of an advocate."

– Frances H. Ware, Dean of the American Trial Bar

We began the third trial on September 26, 1983 and Noi had been in jail for almost a year at this point. She was locked up on the eighth floor of the Tulsa City-County Jail, a bleak and depressing place with no windows, not even windows with bars. There were no exercise yards. The overriding gray, the darkness, and the stench of the place made it deplorable – so bad, in fact, that a federal lawsuit was filed against the Sheriff of Tulsa County while Noi was incarcerated there. The suit against the Sheriff claimed that the constitutional rights of the inmates were being violated by having to live in such a place, that it was cruel and unusual punishment to have to do so. All three of the federal judges would later agree that the living conditions violated the prisoners' rights. The federal lawsuit and the decision, however, came too late to help Noi in any way.

As we left the jail to go upstairs to the courtroom, I remembered picking the jury for the first trial and how much I had learned from Gerry Spence and others since that trial. Those learned men believe that a case is not won by scorching cross-examinations nor even by brilliant opening or closing statements. They believe that a trial is won, essentially, in the jury selection. Knowing what I know now – what they had recently taught me – I couldn't agree more.

One of the biggest mistakes I made in the first trial was leaving a minister on the jury. When Carson asked the minister if she believed in the law in the Scriptures that said, "… take an eye for an eye," she responded, "Yes, I do."

The minister must have missed the day in church which covered the teachings of Jesus, because, in the New Testament, He changed that law. Jesus said that, if a person strikes you, you must turn the other cheek. I thought that Christians were supposed to be forgiving, as Christ taught them to be, so leaving the minister on the jury turned out to be my mistake; one I regretted.

Since then, I had learned from master trial lawyers that, in most instances, overly religious people turn out to be the *least* forgiving jurors. They also attempt to extract the most punishment and they don't seem to empathize with other people's suffering as much as you would expect. The minister's looks may also have blinded me, I have to admit. She was an exceptionally beautiful twenty-seven year old woman.

Melvin Belli, a pioneer of the modern trial lawyer, used to advise that a woman who appears to have a "well-regulated sex life" would make an excellent juror. I took Melvin's advice in this case and it was a blunder. This woman minister had married at the age of seventeen and had three children. I figured that *for sure*, she had plenty of practice at making babies and must be sexually "well-regulated". All of this figuring on my part proved wrong, though,

136

because I later discovered that she had voted guilty on every vote taken.

I decided to go beyond stereotypes and get a good psychological profile of the jurors this time.

As we approached the courtroom door, I remembered the Cherokee woman's prophecy about the number three – THE THIRD TRIAL. This would be the last battle and when the smoke cleared, only one side would be left standing.

Looking about the courtroom, it felt a little like a high school reunion. I saw many familiar faces there. Carson and Lewis sat at the prosecutor's table, both of them with looks of anticipation on their faces. They were whispering to each other and neither of them looked at or acknowledged me when I came into the courtroom. *No skin off my nose.* I thought. *We're not friends, anyway.*

Noi and I were at the table closest to the doors with Ray Manning, the armed Deputy Sheriff, sitting behind us.

As attorney and client, Noi and I seemed a little more relaxed this time around. I was more exhausted than scared this time and Noi seemed more calm this time, too. At least, she did not have the look of someone who was about to bolt out of her chair and run away.

I noticed how much Noi had changed during her past year in jail. She had been lonely and eager to make friends and had done so while incarcerated. She seemed to be well-liked by her friends in the jail; they helped her by giving her English lessons. These friendships were important to her and she felt more secure than ever before.

Physically, Noi had changed, as well. Her skin was now bleached almost white because she had not been out in the sun for a year. Her black hair, which had been so shiny and vibrant-looking, now hung on her head like a dark, dull rag. She had gained some weight, so Nancy's clothes, loaned to Noi by my gracious wife for this purpose, now fit her better than before when they just bagged on her as if Noi was a skeleton.

Nancy may never understand how touched I was by her willingness to lend some decent-looking clothes to Noi for the trials. Sometimes, stepping out beyond our anger to do the right thing is also the kindest thing.

On this day, because September is still a rather warm month in Oklahoma, Noi was wearing an attractive beige linen suit with a light blue blouse. Until now, I had not noticed how the beige color brought out the sallow tones in her skin. I was hoping that sallowness would not make the jury think that Noi was ill or that we were trying to gain sympathy from that kind of move, because we weren't. In truth, we were just shooting for respectable *and* respectful by having Noi dress in this particular way. Every detail counts in a courtroom setting, I had learned, and how your client appears to the jury is a big part of that.

Sometimes, I think, if we drew a giant pie chart and really looked at it, this is what we would see: one skinny slice of it would be WHAT WE KNOW; another skinny slice of it would be WHAT WE DON'T KNOW. All the rest of that entire pie would be called WHAT WE DON'T EVEN *KNOW* THAT WE DON'T KNOW. The things I had learned from Gerry Spence, especially in terms of jury selection, were helping me to figure out more and more of those things which I didn't even know that I didn't know.

I will always be grateful, Gerry, I thought, *for those lessons learned.*

Carson began the first day of trial, making the jurors promise that they would not hesitate to convict a woman if they found her guilty. Lots of times, it is more difficult for a jury to convict a woman of a terrible crime, especially if that woman is a mother of small children, and Carson was trying to cover that base right from the start. Strangely however, on a national level, women accused of killing their husbands tend to be convicted much more often than if the husband kills the wife. Maybe that's a twisted "hold-over" way of thinking stemming from how women were seen for so long as the "property" of their husbands in this country.

He asked the jurors if they had any preconceived notion of what someone accused of murder would look like. "They could come in all shapes and sizes – isn't that right?" Carson asked. Then he added, "They could even look like your next door neighbor, couldn't they?" He wanted to plant that seed so the jurors would be open to the possibility that Noi was a murderer, even as lovely and as petite as she was.

Carson then explained to the jury the term "circumstantial evidence," a chain of facts which tends to prove the charge against the defendant without direct evidence. Circumstantial evidence is a link in a chain of evidence which the jury can use to infer guilt, such as Noi's lying to the police and then hiding Bobby's body. He asked the jury, "Could you just have faith?"

I couldn't believe it. Here he was, asking the jury if he couldn't prove his case completely, would they go ahead and convict her on blind faith. I should have objected and explained to Judge Dalton that he was asking the jury to guess her into prison based on blind faith. I didn't object, though; I was too shocked.

The next day, I began the search for my jury – a jury that I could love and trust and one that could love and trust me.

"Ladies and gentlemen and Your Honor, as I mentioned yesterday, I'm Jim Lloyd. I represent Noi Kanchana Mitchell. I call her Noi. That is her nickname. I'm here to see that Noi gets a fair trial. How do I go about doing that? To begin with, I need twelve people who will feel comfortable with both Noi and me. We all need friends. Sometimes, I take my friends out to lunch and even pick up the tab. It's not much, mind you, but we all really need friends. I guess what I'm trying to say is, we need twelve folks who will listen to all of the evidence and who will be just, who will be honest and courageous and make a decision in this case based on the evidence or *lack of evidence.*

"Of course," I continued, "I'm trying to get twelve citizens who actually believe Noi Mitchell is innocent and I'm going to give you the so-called 'hard facts' to prove her innocence."

I looked over at the prosecutor's table. Carson and Lewis both leaned forward in their chairs, restless as a basket of rattlesnakes, ready to object.

"You know, by law, Noi doesn't have to come into court and say or prove anything. A defendant is presumed innocent just by sitting there. She can just sit there and look pretty and not have to do anything and she is still presumed innocent. Now, just because she is sweet and innocent-looking, could you still leave room in your mind that she *really is innocent?* Could you folks do that? I glanced around and saw a few people nod their heads *yes.* And, you wouldn't hold it against her, the way she looks, would you?" I noticed a few more folks shaking their heads *no.*

"All right, I'm not going to ask you folks to have *faith*, just to *believe* she is innocent. I'm not going to do that. I'm going to come into court and give you evidence – cold, hard facts."

Carson sprang to his feet. "Judge," he shouted out, "I'm going to object. This is more like an opening statement."

Judge Dalton looked down at me and sternly said, "Sustained." He sustained the objection because he felt I should be asking only questions which touched upon the jurors' qualifications.

Why is it, I wondered, *the prosecutor squeals whenever the defense attorney tries to get his case back in balance?* After all, Carson had questioned them earlier about not having any pre-conceived notions of what someone accused of murder would look like. He tried to get them thinking that, under Noi's veneer of beauty, there lived a monster; one that strangles a victim; one that coldly shoots a victim; one that beats a victim until his skull caves in, just to make sure he is dead.

"I want you good folks, you *citizens*, to promise me," I said, "that you will hold the State to their burden and not just convict Noi because they think you should. Can you folks do that?" I saw a few more folks nodding *yes.*

"In selecting jurors," I continued, "the lawyers ask questions which touch upon your qualifications and some of these seem to be personal, I know. Please don't be embarrassed or feel like we are prying into your personal lives. We don't mean to do that. We're looking at your qualifications to see how you could, at this time, judge this case and judge my client."

"Now," I said, "I would like to talk to you about prejudice. You know, that is one thing I'm kind of afraid to talk about. Talking about it gives me butterflies in my stomach and I haven't taught them to fly in formation yet." I paused, waiting for, at least, a bit of a laugh, but nobody even smiled or chuckled and I quickly assumed they probably felt sorry for me. I kept going, "Sometimes, my client might act differently from you or me in the courtroom, but I want you to promise me that you're not going to convict her if she turns her head to the right or left or if she cries or laughs inappropriately." During my lengthy jailhouse interviews with Noi, she would often talk to me in a laughing, self-conscious manner and I wanted to prepare the jury for that possibility. "Some people act differently and inappropriately. Mrs. Mellon, would you agree?"

"Yes, sir," said Mrs. Mellon in a pleasant and musical voice.

I chose Mrs. Mellon because she was a member of a minority. Her dark, broad features were Native American. Her dark brown eyes were moist with understanding when I spoke of prejudice. She was about fifty pounds overweight and had a warm smile. Her whole presence was one of kindness and acceptance.

"Prejudice," I said, "is an emotional term some people are kind of embarrassed or shy or feel uncomfortable talking about. Have you ever known someone to say, 'Oh, I'm not prejudiced?' But, when you knew them well, you could tell that they really were. Have you ever known anybody like that?" I waited for her silent response then continued. "I have thought long and hard and found that I could equate my prejudices with likes and dislikes. Would you, perhaps, be more willing to open up with me here in the courtroom today?" She nodded yes. "Well, one thing I'm afraid about is that

141

Noi is Asian. She is from Thailand, a place most Oklahomans have never been to or know much about. I'm afraid some people may have feelings based upon their experiences with Asian people. She was born and raised in Thailand. Does anybody know any Thai people or had any experience with Thais?"

Gerry Spence had put the words in my mouth, I just realized; all I had to do was say them with sincerity and feeling.

"I have had experiences with many minorities," piped Mrs. Mellon. "I was the leader of my daughter's Girl Scout Troop for three years. There were several little Vietnamese girls in the group."

"Are you Cherokee?" I asked her. I have always asked this question whenever I find out someone is Native American, probably because I am also part Cherokee. The Cherokee have a reputation for being very stubborn, although it would be more truthful to say they have a strong will to live. Early in the nineteenth-century, the United States government forced the Cherokee people to leave their homes. Suddenly, in the dead of winter, without supplies to sustain them, the army marched them westward, on foot, out of Tennessee, Alabama and Georgia to resettle in Oklahoma, a distance of around five hundred miles. This proud people buried hundreds of its men, women and children along the way, which is why this death march has always been known as the "Trail of Tears."

"No," Mrs. Mellon replied, "I am half Choctaw."

"What I'm hearing you say, then, is that you know how it feels to be a minority member, is that right?"

"Definitely."

"Could you tell us about some of those personal experiences you have had as a minority?"

"Objection!" Carson shouted, "I don't see how it is relevant whether she can sit here properly and listen to the evidence fairly unless it is narrowed down a little bit." He was complaining now, almost whining, and turned slightly toward me to stare me down.

The prosecutor and the Judge didn't feel comfortable with a juror talking about how the white man had hurt her feelings. It might generate too much sympathy for Noi. But, I continued on anyway, in the interest of justice, of course.

"Do you sometimes feel like you are treated differently?" I asked Mrs. Mellon.

"Sir," she replied, "I am often treated differently. It's not a matter of *feeling*. It is true."

"Could you tell us how that affects you by being treated differently?"

"Well," Mrs. Mellon replied, "when you are young, it makes you very insecure, somewhat hostile."

"And, yet, you seem to be able to cope very well with being a minority. Could you leave room for the possibility that Noi is not as strong as you?"

"Certainly."

"Could you leave room for the possibility that her reactions to being a minority for certain situations would be different than yours based on her experience in life?"

"Yes."

"How would you feel about, say, if you had a son who married a Thai lady, a divorcee, who had a small child, aged two, whose father was a poor rice and banana farmer?"

Carson shot to his feet, exclaiming, "Objection, Your Honor! This has no relevancy. This is opening or closing statements and it's appealing to the passion of the jury. It's incredible!"

Judge Dalton said, "I think the proper question is: Would this influence or prejudice her?"

"Yes, Your Honor," I agreed, "I'm trying to stay away from prejudices. I'm trying to use likes and dislikes so the jury would feel free to open up to me and relate to me and Noi."

Mrs. Mellon added that she had a twenty year old son and she would not be prejudiced due to a person's race.

"Would it affect you because she is a Thai citizen and not an American citizen? How do you feel about that?"

"The only way I can answer that is to say, if we were in a room, other than a courtroom, and I saw her sitting in the room with all of these people and I had one person I would want to go up and talk to first, she would be the person."

I could tell Mrs. Mellon was telling the truth, and I could also tell she was pleased at how well she had described her lack of prejudice. I said, "Well, thank you, Mrs. Mellon. I appreciate that candid answer. However, I'm afraid the District Attorney will strike you from the jury."

Everyone in the jury box laughed and so did all the other people in the courtroom, *except* Carson, Lewis and Judge Dalton. The Judge was stone-faced, but Carson, who was still on his feet from his previous objection, simply stepped forward and bellowed, "I OBJECT!!" The fierceness of his voice made a few people in the courtroom jump in their seats. Carson looked like he might suddenly catch fire or explode at any second. His face was red and the skin around his tight mouth was white. He clenched his fists as though he wanted to have a fist fight with me right there in the courtroom. He probably did. He was taking everything I said in a personal way, but it felt good to know I was getting under his skin. I had become his own irritating little saddle burr.

Dalton's eyes had been about half-closed until now. Suddenly, he raised his bushy eyebrows, as though he was awakening, sprang forward in his chair and barked, "Sustained!"

Carson wanted more, though, and began whining, "He knows better than that, Judge. I admonish counsel not to make those types of statements." He was indignant, huffy. It was almost funny; I tried hard not to smile.

What Carson wanted, of course, was to make it impossible for me to tell the jury that, if they presume Noi to be innocent, the prosecutor will strike them from the jury. And, since it is the job of the jury to presume someone innocent until proven otherwise, in essence, what he wanted was to keep the jury from doing its job. Rather than trying to argue that very obvious point, though, I chose another route.

Next, I explained that one of Noi's defenses was that the shooting had been accidental. Then, I asked another prospective juror, "I expect that there will be evidence, testimony and exhibits of the accidental shooting and proof that Bobby jerked on the gun causing it to fire twice. Now, many people, including some lawyers and even some judges, are confused by the burden of proof required here." I looked at Carson and then up at the Judge who frowned at me. I continued, "If the judge instructs you that it is the burden of the State to prove beyond a reasonable doubt that the homicide was not accidental, what verdict will you bring if the State *fails* to prove that his death was not accidental?"

"Objection, Your Honor!" Carson exclaimed, "This is a blatant misstatement of the law and counsel is deliberately misleading the jurors." In the first trial, Carson had convinced Dalton that Noi had to prove that the shooting was an accident, which is not really how the law is supposed to work. Clearly, I embarrassed him. Now, he was almost shouting at me as he clenched his fists. It felt good to know I'd made that snake so mad.

Dalton was mad, too, though. It was 11:45 am and he called an early lunch recess. From the way he was barking at me, everyone assumed I was going to be severely disciplined. I thought so, too. As the entire jury panel exited the courtroom, they all heard him shout to me, "Counselor, I'll see you in my chambers NOW!"

The prosecutors and Judge Dalton thought if Noi were claiming an accidental homicide as a defense, then she must prove that it was, in fact, an accident. On this point, I had thoroughly researched Oklahoma law. Like the rat terrier I resembled, I had dug deep in law precedence to come up with the information I needed just for this. If Noi produces any evidence that the death was accidental, then the burden shifts to the State. The State must then prove that the death was *not* an accident by proof beyond a reasonable doubt. I had photocopied cases with me and I dutifully marched back to the Judge's chambers. When I handed the stack of cases to him, he ordered, "Let's research this over the noon hour and be back here at 1:30."

After lunch, when I returned to the Judge's chambers, Carson and Lewis were in there, too, and quite subdued. They both hung their heads and looked down at their feet like fifth graders who'd been called on the carpet by the Principal.

"Jim," Judge Dalton began, in a polite and respectful tone.

"Yes sir," I replied.

"That's always been the law and it always will be the law," he told me. "I just don't want you saying that some lawyers and *some judges* are confused by it."

"Yes, sir," I replied, trying very hard not to show how good it felt to be right for once. This was the first time I had gotten Dalton's attention and I was thoroughly enjoying myself. When we walked back into the courtroom, even though I tried not to strut, I'm sure I did, just a little. Admittedly, I didn't really try all that hard *not* to. The jury panel was already seated and waiting for us. I began right away.

"As I was saying, Ladies and Gentlemen, before the lunch recess, some people feel that Noi should have to prove that this death was accidental, even though that's not the law. Do you think it's fair, however, to make the State prove beyond a reasonable doubt that his death was *not* accidental?"

After I visited with each juror about this, I then asked, "If the Judge instructs you that it is the burden of the State to prove beyond a reasonable doubt that Noi did *not* act in self-defense, what verdict will you bring if the State *fails to prove* that she did *not* act in self-defense?"

"Some people feel that Noi should have to prove that she, in fact, *did* act in self-defense, even though that is not the law. Do you think it is fair, however, to make the State prove beyond a reasonable doubt that she did *not* act in self-defense to the charge of murder?" I noticed how Carson grimaced every time I asked each juror. He had the strangest habit of twisting his mouth in an exaggerated look of surprise which made him look strange and a little creepy.

Now, I was satisfied. I had gathered enough information to determine who I would strike from the jury pool. The jury members had promised me they would be fair and that they wanted to be on the jury. I told Judge Dalton I was ready. The prosecutors got the first strike.

Of course, they got rid of the nice Native American lady, my friend, Mrs. Mellon. That's the problem with asking too many questions, it seems. I had tried to use her innate compassion in the most effective way I knew how, the purpose of which was to educate the remaining members of the jury pool. I kept thinking during the trial about how I wished I could look at the jury and see Mrs. Mellon sitting there smiling at me. She had those kind eyes which warmed my heart. I missed seeing her face.

The most striking juror was a woman who was chosen, originally, as the "thirteenth juror." She'd had to fill in on the jury when an old man had called in sick. One week earlier, my brother, Rex, had been out in the hallway smoking a cigarette when he spotted an old man wearing a black and white juror's button leave Dalton's courtroom and walk up to the Mitchell family gathered in the hallway. He called both Mr. Mitchell's wife and niece by name and asked them about a mutual friend. Rex quietly listened to the friendly conversation without arousing suspicion. The Mitchells had not yet connected Rex with me. Rex doesn't look like my kid brother, but more like a blonde-haired Indian, one with brown eyes that disappear when he smiles. I have green eyes and had dark hair, back then, and the only way my Cherokee heritage shows up in me is in my high cheekbones. Rex is also larger and heavier than I am. He was my man behind the scenes and the Mitchells had never seen us together in the courtroom.

I leaned heavily on Rex, though, for many things. He drove my witnesses around, ran errands, babysat in emergencies, and did all of the odd jobs and running around that were necessary to pull this production together.

The next day, I sent Tom Cook to watch the old man. This time, the old guy was talking to Mr. Mitchell, Bobby's dad. Mr. Mitchell recognized Tom from the courtroom and signaled with his eyes for the old man to stop talking. The old juror did not recognize this as a signal, however, and continued talking.

I knew, somehow, I was going to have to bring this misconduct to the attention of the court since this was a serious offense. At the beginning of the trial, one of the first questions Judge Dalton had asked the jurors was, "Do any of the jurors know the parties or families of either the victim or the accused?" No one had raised their hand. The old man had lied. I wanted him to know that I was having him investigated. I waited until he was out in the hallway and Tom and I were standing about eight feet away from him. I whispered loudly to Tom, "Investigate that guy," while nodding toward the old man with my head and staring into his terrified blue eyes.

The next morning, this same juror decided he was too sick to come in. He called Dalton and said he had "the flu." Dalton offered to wait a day for him to get well, but he said it would be a long time before he would be up and around again. So, the Judge excused him and called in the "alternate juror" to use instead.

When Noi discovered the alternate would be on the jury, she laid her head down on the table in the courtroom and cried, saying the woman looked like Bobby's mistress. She did, too. She was tall and thin, yet buxom. She wore her reddish-brown hair in a sophisticated French roll. She appeared to be in her mid-thirties, but already had a hard look about her. Her eyes were cold and unfeeling as she left the courtroom and she would not maintain eye contact with me, no matter what I did. And, when I tried to look at her, I wound up staring at her large breasts, which was more my own fault than hers, even though she always seemed to have on a tight sweater, so, it seemed to me, she really wanted them to be looked at. Of course, Nancy would have slapped me for having those sexist thoughts, but it was in the early 1980's, and men, myself included, were not as enlightened then as we need to be – and should be – these days.

The juror seated next to the alternate was a man who was in his forties. He had the air of a man used to being the one in charge of things. I counted nine other men who were on Noi's jury, so ten men in all. Two of the men were black. I liked that, although several of the Thai people did not want blacks on the jury. Asians are often prejudiced against blacks I have noticed, although I'm not sure why. All of the men, except the one in the red flannel shirt, looked at me. This man did not smile. He kept his eyes trained to the floor or on a point ahead of the door. During a recess, they all filed out in what looked like a military procession, it was so formal.

There were eight women and four men on the jury for the first trial. Noi wanted a jury of all women because she felt a woman could understand another woman's problems better than a man would. For this third trial, though, I followed my instincts which told me that men would tend to be more protective of a beautiful, young woman. I still think that women tend to be harder on other women, especially pretty ones. My wife is, I know that. Nancy can be downright cynical when it comes to evaluating other women. She thinks I am a sucker for a pretty face and she's probably right about that, too. But I know men better than she does.

The last juror we questioned was a very large, barrel-shaped black woman with very short-cropped hair – only about an inch in length – all over her head. She dressed like a man. When I questioned her, I found out she had eleven children, so, it seemed to me, she would certainly know what it was like to suffer. Many people think that suffering either makes a person bitter or better. I looked at the smile lines etched into her dark face and determined that she was a better person for her suffering.

Carson had run out of strikes, but he did not want this woman on the jury. To get her excused, he had to get her excused for cause. Dalton asked if there was anyone on the jury who could not serve due to personal reasons. This woman raised her hand and requested a private interview. We all went into the Judge's chambers.

Dalton sat at his desk in his office. The woman and I were sitting on opposite ends of the Judge's couch. Lewis sat in a chair and Carson stood next to Judge's desk by the window.

The woman stated that she had gotten a call from the Principal and that her oldest boy was in trouble at his high school.

Dalton frowned, "I don't think this is so pressing a problem that you need to take care of it right away."

I looked up at Dalton and said, "Your Honor, I feel that this lady would make an excellent juror and would be fair to Noi as well as the State of Oklahoma. I feel like she is highly qualified and I feel that she should not be excused for these reasons." I glanced at the woman and saw her mouth twitch as she tried not to smile.

Carson jumped in and quickly said, "The State had no objections whatsoever to excuse her for cause." Clearly, he was anxious to unload her, but it backfired on him.

His attitude sparked her to say, "Now, wait a minute. I can make other arrangements to meet with the Principal." She remained on the jury, and Carson, as you might imagine, was crestfallen.

Maybe she liked being referred to as "highly qualified", I noted.

When we got back to the courtroom, the jury was seated and appeared ready to begin. Several jurors were actually leaning forward, like they could hardly wait to get this show started. I could feel the electricity in the room which seemed to flow through them. I could tell they were excited about being on the jury and equally excited about the trial beginning today. When the Court Bailiff announced, "All rise," we all stood up as Judge Dalton walked into the courtroom.

Carson had his turn first. He had not changed his remarks very much, I noticed, from the first trial. He began by describing the charge against Noi, that of first degree murder. His story was exciting, I'll give him that. He told how Noi was afraid that Bobby would divorce her because their marriage was in shambles. Bobby had almost stopped coming home because things were so bad between the two of them and, in fact, had even begun the process of moving out on the day of his death while Noi was at work at the Monterrey House. Carson emphasized that an intent to kill does not have to take place over any certain length of time. It would be enough that Noi formed the intent to kill him even seconds before she actually killed Bobby.

Carson emphasized that Noi had told Officer Spillman of the Broken Arrow Police Department that she hit Bobby many times with a baseball bat because she wanted to make sure he was dead. Carson also told the jury that Noi had said to the Broken Arrow Police that she killed Bobby because he was going to take her children away. He said Bobby must have struggled more than Noi had planned on since, after all, she'd had to shoot him, fracture his skull at least four times with a bat and then strangle him with her bare hands before she was sure that he was dead. It was not an easy way to die, and I think Carson wanted the jury to feel sorry for the way Bobby must have suffered at the end of his life. He discussed how Noi had certainly gotten the best of this supposed "fight", and if it were an actual fight, it most certainly was not a fair one.

Carson described my tiny Asian client as a shrewd, calculating woman who spoke English well only when it was to her advantage. Carson said, "She had more than one reason to kill Bobby. Her motives will come out in the evidence." He then went on to tell the jury that Noi had dumped her husband's body in his car, still naked, then went back and hid the baseball bat, the gun, the bullets, Bobby's wallet and keys from the police.

Carson shouted, "Ask yourself why she hid and tried to wash the evidence away." I noticed a juror in the back row frantically taking notes. He was scribbling so fast and hard that there were beads of sweat on his forehead and upper lip. Carson went on to explain that when the police came to her home to question her, Noi lied to them over and over to cover up her killing. She was so calm, Carson told them, that she was washing and drying towels when the officers arrived.

Carson summed up by saying he knew they would not like to send a young woman to prison, but that she had come here from another country and had killed an American, a son of Oklahoma. She needed to be punished like any other killer should be punished. He did not want the jury to be distracted by Noi's attractive, subdued appearance and demeanor.

The jurors were spellbound, and it was easy to see why. Carson had fed them graphic details of a brutal and premeditated killing. It was like being in the middle of a supermarket tabloid story with gory details flying at you from every angle until each of your senses had been assaulted. Judge Dalton glanced my way and gave me a triumphant look that seemed to say, *"How in the world are you going to win now??"*

This time, I was ready to give my opening remarks from memory, rather than reading them from note cards like I had in the first trial. I no longer felt sorry for Bobby. I wanted to redirect some of the anger Carson had created toward Noi back toward Bobby. I wanted the jury to know, to really understand, how cruel and brutal Bobby could be. I did not care this time if I offended the Mitchells, all of whom were sitting there glaring at me. I had gotten used to their hostile looks. Nor did I care about Mr. Mitchell's wealth or status in the community, and even though I'm sure Mr. Mitchell didn't want to know it, he was just about to learn what a rotten husband and mean S.O.B. his son actually was in real life. What Mr. Mitchell really didn't want to hear, I'm sure, was that his son might have deserved what he got. And, I knew I was just the guy to let him know it, too.

I walked behind Noi's chair and put both hands on her shoulders to let the jury know I cared about her. I also wanted to reassure her.

I wanted to pretend I was Gerry Spence. I started out quietly and slowly emphasized my words. Just the softer, husky tone, almost a whisper, got the juror's attention much more than Lyon's loud voice. I thought that if a lawyer turned up the volume too loud for too long, then the listeners would tune him out, much like a husband tunes out a harping wife.

I requested that Carson be as courteous to me as I was to him by not interrupting me or breaking my concentration. I watched his features tighten again and felt like I had made another little dent in his armor. If he broke into my opening statement now, it would look like he was being rude.

"Ladies and gentlemen," I said, "this case is about a woman who was terrorized by her husband. He terrorized her on the night of October 5th and the early morning hours of October 6th, 1982. He had left home for a couple of days beginning on Sunday, October 3rd, 1982. He told her he had to go to work. He did not come home at all that Sunday night. Monday, she called his office, but he did not return her calls. He did not come home that Monday night, either."

I then walked over to a spot about ten feet from the jury box. I began to tell Noi's story about what happened the night she killed

Bobby. I reenacted her terror and the fight she and Bobby had. "Bobby brutalized Noi and beat her up many times before," I told them. I wanted to convey to the jury how weak Noi must have been to tolerate this behavior. I also wanted them to understand how weak some women are, unlike the majority of women here in the United States who are strong. Wife-beating is a much more common practice in Thailand where a woman felt like she deserved a beating if she disobeyed her husband.

From the time I took this case, I had visited Noi almost every evening in jail. After I had spent over a month piecing together her story, she finally broke down and told me that Bobby had beat her many, many times throughout their marriage. I knew that Bobby had hit her during their fight, but I needed to know if the beatings were part of a regular pattern of behavior. Noi said she did not want to talk about Bobby hitting her. She was deeply ashamed and began sobbing loudly. I felt terrible for her, but I had to find out more about how he had abused her. She kept crying until I finally gave up that night. She was just too upset to talk about it.

I think Noi had expected me to continue my questioning about Bobby hitting her, because she was much more composed the next night. She was ready to tell me that Bobby hit her often, usually when he drank. He would consume several beers and she would see his face become flushed and his expression turn to rage. He then directed that rage at her. Though not of a large build, Bobby was quite tall and towered over his petite wife as he screamed at her. Noi admitted that she probably deserved to be hit because she could not make Bobby happy and he used to love her. She had already told me that Asian men beat their wives in Thailand. Bobby would curse at her in English and in Thai. His first words he had learned in Thai were curse words and those relating to sexual matters. He had picked up the most descriptive of degrading words in a bar in Bangkok and would hurl those as insults at Noi. He told her over and over what a terrible wife she was, then he would slap her and push her up against a wall, bruising her legs and buttocks. She would cover these areas that showed with make-up when she went to work so no one would see the terrible bruising. But the biggest insult was when he put his feet on her head. It meant she was no better than a dog.

Noi kept repeating that the worst insult was when Bobby would step on her, a degrading maneuver he seemed to do more often when she was pregnant. I could not understand why this had felt so insulting. Noi explained that, in Thailand, there is no greater insult than this. I believed Noi, but for the life of me, could not figure out how I would be able to prove that Bobby had abused her.

In the courtroom, I told the jury how Noi had fought back against Bobby for the first time in their marriage the night Bobby died. I described this fight in great detail; how Noi had struck Bobby with the bat twice and how Bobby grabbed it and slammed Noi with it on both her arms and both thighs. I described how Noi and Bobby had struggled for the gun on the closet shelf and how Bobby yanked the gun while it was in Noi's hand causing it to fire twice.

"They both got their hands around the gun," I recounted, "and pulled and struggled and kicked. They came around to this side of the bed," I continued, pointing to a diagram of the house. "They were in front of the baby bed, and they came on over between the green chair and the television in here." I pointed to the place on the diagram.

"Between the baby bed and the dresser," I explained, "they were struggling and kicking. Noi kneed Bobby in the groin and he dropped the gun. She dove on top of the gun, but he turned her over and jerked on it. She pulled back. That first shot barely missed his leg and left powder burns, or gunpowder stippling, on his right ankle. That bullet went up only thirteen and a half inches from the floor to the dresser drawer. Noi was pulling back. Bobby was on top of her.

"Now, the second bullet, "I told them, "went off when she was lying down. Bobby jerked the gun again and, when he did, the gun went off the second time, and the hammer pinched the web, the fleshy tissue between the thumb and forefinger of his right hand. That bullet went through his chest and continued upward. It

155

actually went seventeen inches from the top of Bobby's head into his chest, and came out his back fifteen inches from the top of his head. The medical examiner will tell you it was two inches upward and outward, and this second bullet came out Bobby's back and ended up in the east wall seven feet and five and a half inches from the floor. That's when Noi drops the gun. Bobby is now on his knees grabbing for it and he gets a hold of it."

I then went on to tell the jury how Noi had hit Bobby with the bat to keep him away from the gun, which was lying in the brown carpet in the bedroom, just a few feet away. I also wanted to impress upon them how Noi grabbed the bat from the wrong end before she hit him with it, which would show two things: (1) that she was panic-stricken and terrified, and (2) that, by using the smaller end of the bat as a weapon, her intention was not lethal. I described to them how Bobby was stalking her out the front door and around to the side of the house all the while holding the gun. Before he makes it inside the garage, he stumbles, falling to his hands and knees and drops the gun. She runs to the gun and throws it as hard as she can, but it hits her neighbor's outside wall and bounces into the neighbor's back yard.

When Bobby finally made it into the garage through a side door, he collapsed. I used a pointer to show the path Bobby took while stalking Noi. My plan was to repeat Noi's story of the fight with each juror every chance possible so it would be as ingrained in their minds as it was in mine.

I tried to explain why Noi covered up evidence and lied to the police. I had to explain it in the context of her culture and her peculiar psychological profile.

"Ladies and Gentlemen," I said, "Noi was born in Thailand on April 19, 2948 which, in Oklahoma, means April 19, 1955. She is twenty-seven years old and the mother of two small children – two little girls she wanted to protect from a violent man. She was faced with this terrifying night, not knowing what to do."

Dalton would not let me go into the details of her background because he said it was irrelevant. I sensed that the Judge felt it might make the jury begin to understand and like Noi. He must have known it would be harder to convict someone who had become a real person to the jurors, especially someone they might like.

Dalton interrupted me, "I'll remind the jurors to understand that the opening statements of counsel are merely statements of what the lawyers feel the evidence will show. The statements are not evidence." He was really saying that the statements were just lawyer talk, and everyone knows about lawyer talk: it cannot be trusted because it is not under oath.

I made a last plea for them to study the evidence, the exhibits, and asked that we then discover the truth *together*. I asked them to return a verdict of "not guilty".

I walked slowly back and forth a comfortable distance from the jury. I tried to focus on each of them periodically throughout my statements so that each would feel I was communicating directly with him or her. I noticed the older man in the back row of the jury box was, once again, furiously writing his notes. I did not know what this meant. Usually, the judges in Oklahoma do not allow this. Finally, I sat down.

Deputy Sheriff Ray Manning waited until Carson and Lewis left for the lunch recess before he slapped me on the back. My whole physiology changed when he grinned and said that he had seen many lawyers and many trials, but that my opening statement had to rank in the best top five he had ever heard. I really appreciated his taking the time to tell me that. I liked that. I also noticed Noi had stopped studying her hands folded on the table and watched me as I talked with the jury. I liked that, too. I guess I was starting to do something right, after all.

CHAPTER 14 – *ALMOST* PICTURE-PERFECT

Perry Mason destroyed the prosecutor's star witness each week on TV with his spectacular cross-examination to such a degree that the witness almost always broke down and confessed to the murder, either gesticulating wildly and angrily or sobbing hysterically. Oddly enough, the confessions would not happen during a jury trial, but at the preliminary hearing stage in front of only the judge. I imagine it was planned that way so the producer would not have to pay for 12 jurors to be fed on the set and saving from paying the high California studio labor union wages. For pure entertainment value, cross-examination in a courtroom ranks right up there with the best. It is to a trial what a fist fight is to a hockey game.

In real life, however, it rarely happens that a lawyer will have a chance to break down the opponents' witness without damaging his own case, so it's risky to base the outcome of your case on that alone. The real purpose of cross-examination is to discover the truth.

My grandfather, Olen Lloyd, born in 1889, told me going to the courthouse and watching a jury trial was more entertaining and enjoyable than going to those fancy air conditioned movie houses, any day. On his death bed, Nancy and I drove to his nursing home (hospice care) to say our good byes. When I told him I was in law school and going to become a lawyer, he spoke his first words in days, "I don't believe it,' he clearly said as tears ran down his hollow cheeks. He held my hands and squeezed them for the longest of times and closed his eyes and fell gently asleep. He passed away that summer during my first semester in law school.

I knew Grandfather Olen would have enjoyed the entertainment of this case so far. On October 3rd, 1983, after taking one solid week to select the jury and give our opening statements, the prosecutors began calling their witnesses to testify against Noi.

The prosecutors wielded the full power and resources of the State of Oklahoma against her. The Oklahoma State Bureau of Investigation, the Sheriff's Office, and the Broken Arrow Police Department were all waiting in the wings to aid them, too. All of these law enforcement agencies are graded by how many convictions they get; no one grades them on how much justice they give. My job would now be to cross-examine each witness, to bring out any possible bias, prejudice or incompetence in order to get closer to the truth. Given how law enforcement agencies tend to close ranks to protect their various agencies' reputations, as well as the reputations of investigating officers, I knew this was going to be a tough row to hoe, as my grandmother used to say.

I wanted the jury to doubt the Broken Arrow Police Department's testimony as well as the officers' quality of investigation. Personally, I saw it as incomplete and shoddy at best; a malpractice of justice at the worst. I wanted the jury to doubt the officers' stories as much as the officers had doubted Noi's. I wanted to paint a picture of a bungling, local police department which was committed to convicting Noi Mitchell whether she was guilty of murder or not. After all, this was one of the few murder cases Broken Arrow had ever handled and Noi was the only suspect. To me, these guys saw it as a slam-dunk, and I believed, had conducted their investigation not to find out the truth of what happened, but rather, in order to secure a conviction of the only suspect they had.

Carson called Officer Tom Powell to the stand first to describe his procedures and to identify the pictures he took for Noi's trial. Powell was the detective assigned to photograph the Mitchell home. He had a round, baby face that looked lovable and sweet. His bright blue eyes seemed to captivate the jury and he had a direct, persuasive smile. He was stocky and muscular and looked, a little, like the Pillsbury Dough-Boy or a huggable little teddy bear.

After Carson was finished, it was my turn to cross-examine. The questions I asked Officer Powell were directed in such a way that he would have to agree with me, which would give me a chance to show how he had contradicted himself. I rubbed it in how he had botched the Mitchell investigation; in fact, I got him to show how the majority of the Broken Arrow Police Force had helped him along.

"Officer," I asked him, "do you feel like it was important to establish and determine the trajectory of the bullet – if you are looking for the truth and justice in this case?" Honestly, he really could not disagree with this noble sentiment; he would be a fool to do so.

"Well, of course," he replied, just as I had expected him to.

"Since you agree that it is so important, did you take panoramic view photographs of the bedroom where the gun went off?"

"No, I didn't," Powell replied.

"Since you agree," I continued, "that it is important to investigate all the facts to determine the trajectory of the bullet, did you determine if a bullet was buried in the wall in that bedroom?"

"I thought it was a scratch in the wall, sir," Powell answered.

I could not believe the officer would call a hole in the wall splattered with blood a mere "scratch," but he did. "As a matter of practice," I pressed him, "do you usually take pictures of mere "scratches" in a wall?" I had a copy of the picture Tom Powell had taken of Officer Donaldson pointing to the mere "scratch" with a pen. I was creeping closer to Powell as I asked him these questions, closing in on him. I knew he hated me from the first trial and decided to use this to my advantage. I positioned myself in front of the jury in such a way that they could see his glares of hatred. The closer I got, the more intense his stares. He was looking less and less like a huggable teddy bear by the moment. I kept inching forward. The jury could see how much hatred he had for me.

Powell stuck with his story, though. "We decided it was only a scratch," he said.

I held up the photograph for him to see.

"When did you decide it was a mere scratch," I asked him, "was that before you took this picture or after?"

"I don't know, sir," he replied. Powell's voice was taking on a high, stressed pitch and sounded tight. It was grating, irritating, almost like a cat when it is cornered and furious.

"Did you think it was important that the wall next to the "scratch" was splattered with blood?" I wasn't about to let him get away with a bunch of nothing answers.

"I don't know," Powell growled.

Clearly, my questions were getting under his skin, and I think the jury was picking up on how little the Broken Arrow Police Department had cooperated with me. "Do you think it's important," I asked him, "to find out all of the evidence to prove a person's guilt or innocence, as the case may be?"

"Yes, sir."

"Did you take samples of the blood spatters on the wall?"

"No, sir."

I put my hand on my chest, like I couldn't believe what I'd just heard and it was causing my heart to stop. "So, you mean to tell me that you did not scrape off a little of the blood with a Q-Tip to take back to the office for a routine lab check?" I asked him.

"No, sir," Powell replied.

"If it was important to determine the trajectory of the bullet, did you think to cut out carpet samples to test for blood so that they might prove the path of the bullet in some way?" I asked him.

Blood on the carpet could help locate exactly where Bobby and Noi had been fighting over the gun. From this point, an expert could trace the path of the bullet after it went through Bobby's body and ended up in the wall.

"No, sir," Officer Powell replied.

Glancing out of the corner of my eye, I could see his facial expression which was one of pure hatred. No more Pillsbury Dough-Boy; no, ma'am. His face was flushed to a dark red and his eyes had turned a deep, cold, icy blue that jumped out in contrast to the crimson of his face. His voice took on more of a smart-alecky tone.

I continued, "Do you think a blood test on the wall and carpet might have been beneficial to determine if it was Bobby's blood and to pinpoint the place of the struggle?"

"I don't know," he replied.

I wanted the jurors to draw their own conclusions as to why Powell didn't know. I wanted to trust them to do what was right, as Gerry Spence had taught me. *Was Officer Powell deliberately trying to cover something up, or was he just plain incompetent?* That's what I wanted the jury to be wondering. "Did you have your blood testing kit with you, sir?" I asked.

"Yes, but we did not think it was important."

"If you did not think it was important," I pressed, "why did you take a picture of the blood spatters?"

"I wanted to do a thorough job, sir," he answered.

By this time, I think his answers were just beginning to sound ridiculous. Apparently, his idea of a "thorough job" did not include using all the tools at his disposal to do so. He was appearing like Barney Fife who had to keep his only bullet in his shirt pocket to keep from wounding himself. Powell was almost pathetic. If his disdain for me hadn't been so blatant, I might have almost felt sorry for him.

"Isn't that what you get paid for by the good people of the State of Oklahoma to do, Officer – a thorough job? – to solve crime by gathering *all* of the evidence?" I wanted to nail Officer Powell now and would not let up or back down.

"Of course, sir," he replied. His words were polite, but his manner was not.

"Did you see any blood spots on the front porch, Officer Powell?" Blood spots would prove that Bobby had followed Noi out to the front porch.

"It was just *possibly* a blood stain," he said. Powell wanted to side-step my question and I understood why. He had said in preliminary hearings and in the first trial that they were blood stains and now he wanted to backtrack. I could not directly use the words "first trial" when I asked him about inconsistent statement because Dalton had ordered me not to. I could, however, make reference to it in some other way to show that he had suddenly changed his mind, and, under oath, too.

"Did you say at an earlier time, under oath, that the stain on the porch was a blood stain?"

"Yes, sir," he admitted this because he knew I had copies of the trial transcript where he had definitely said it was a blood stain.

"What changed your mind about whether it was a blood stain or not since you did not run any tests for blood?" I asked.

"I don't know," he replied curtly. He had stopped calling me "sir."

"Did it look like the same brownish-red color that was set on the door sash, the one the Broken Arrow Police Department removed from the threshold of the door?" I knew that it did.

"Yes," he replied, spewing it like venom at me, yet unaware that he had just wrecked his image with the jury.

"Did you test the sash for blood?" I asked.

"We did not," he said, "because the Oklahoma State Bureau of Investigation did. Why don't you ask them?" he threw it back at me, like a child in a snit on the playground.

"I will do that," I promised. "Well, sir," I went on, "what kind of tests did you run on the blood stains on the front porch, if you didn't test it for blood?"

"Well, sir," he said, mocking me, "we did not have a jackhammer to break the concrete on the porch and take it back to the lab." He was getting very smart with his answers.

"Couldn't you have wiped up the blood with a cotton swab and then test it with your blood testing kit, sir?" I asked him.

"Yes," he admitted.

I decided to change my angle of attack. I had jabbed and jabbed and jabbed at poor Officer Powell until his nose was almost bloody. I didn't want the jurors to think I was heartless; I did, *however*, want them to think I was smart and in possession of more tools of combat – like, *facts*, for example – than just a quick left hook.

There was a mattress in the master bedroom at the Mitchell's home which was spotted with blood stains. The prosecutors had used the theory that Noi shot Bobby while he lay sleeping on the bed. The problem the prosecutors had with this particular theory was that the same blood was on both sides of the mattress.

Officer Maddux had interviewed Noi's six year old daughter, Mia, concerning the blood on the mattress. Mia did not know what it was. She said it looked like cherry Kool-Aid. Mia told Officer Maddux that she had helped her mommy change the sheets and turn the mattress over several months earlier and had noticed those stains on both sides. Noi claimed it was menstrual blood.

Another problem with the ambush theory was that Noi and Bobby had the same blood type, A-Positive. The police could not prove whose blood was on the mattress, but there is a blood test, which is simple and reliable, that identifies menstrual blood. The Broken Arrow Police failed to run this test, even though Noi said it was blood from her periods.

"Officer Powell, you introduced a picture of a cut-out of the mattress from the bed in the master bedroom, did you not?" I asked him.

"Yes, I did," he replied.

"Did you take any pictures of the other side of the mattress?" Powell hesitated. I think he was getting confused, which suited me just fine. I wanted the jury to see him as easily confused and, basically, incompetent and unreliable.

"Did you tell me at an earlier time," I continued, "under oath, that you could not remember the blood stains of different patterns on each side of the mattress?" I wanted the jury to see how Officer Powell had changed his answers.

"Well, now, I remember," he said, "I took pictures of both sides of the mattress." He said this, finally, when I confronted him with two pictures of the mattress showing differently shaped stains in different locations on the mattress.

"Did you see any gunpowder stippling or bullet holes on the mattress to indicate that Bobby had been shot on the mattress?" I wanted the jury to hear it from him that there were no signs of anyone having been shot on that mattress.

"No, sir," he admitted. This testimony blew the prosecutor's theory of an ambush on the bed.

Officer Powell testified about the bullets found in the Marina Apartments Lake by a SCUBA diver for the police department. He said, "Somebody had tried to shoot three of those bullets and they had misfired." This statement was to imply that someone, probably Noi, had tried to shoot Bobby five times. Two bullets fired and three misfired.

Before the start of this third trial, I had the "scratch" on the wall x-rayed with a pipeline x-ray machine like the one used at the Kerr-McGee Nuclear Facility in Crescent, Oklahoma (think of Karen Silkwood). What did it reveal? The x-ray showed a bullet behind the hole. The second bullet was found about 13 inches from the floor in the chest of drawers. So these were the results of the "boom…boom" Noi remembered hearing – just as she testified in the first trial. However, the implication of Officer Powell's testimony was that Noi had pulled the trigger five times trying to kill her husband and then gathered up all the bullets from the gun, even the ones that had misfired. Clearly, this would not be the act of a person claiming an accidental shooting or self-defense. This would be murder. It would be an open and shut case of first degree murder.

Misfiring occurs when the round does not go off after the gun is cocked and the trigger is pulled. The hammer then strikes the firing pin which puts a small indentation into the firing cap (or primer) of the cartridge. Officer Powell testified that morning that he could tell three of the bullets found in the baggie in the lake had been used because there was a little indentation at the end of each of those three cartridges.

I felt my heart sink into my gut. This was serious. Powell could destroy our defense that the gun accidentally went off twice during the struggle between Noi and Bobby. It is just not believable that a shooting could be accidental if the trigger had been pulled that many times. Two times is about as many as I would expect the jury to believe, but five times means someone is dedicated to their efforts and passionate about making sure there's a dead body.

At this point, I really only had two choices and neither was good. (1) I could either figure out a way to undermine Officer Powell's testimony of five trigger pulls or (2) I could steer clear of the whole area and pray that the jury would not be persuaded by those misfired bullets.

I stood there feeling sick when suddenly I had another *Godplop!* It was like a wave of understanding washed over me. Don't ask me how, but I instinctively knew that Powell was trying to mislead the jury with his testimony. I had to believe and put my trust in Noi when she told me that the gun went, "boom…boom". This meant that the trigger or gun was yanked twice and had fired twice. Perhaps the misfired bullets were not the same ones as those recovered from the lake or, perhaps, someone had tested those bullets. These were the only other reasonable possibilities I could think of.

I decided to attack Powell's story. If he was being deliberately misleading, everyone in this courtroom was about to find out. Or else, I would look like a fool for asking a question that I did not know the answer to. It was a huge risk.

"Now, Officer Powell," I asked, "did you initial each and every one of the bullets you recovered from the lake?"

"No," he answered. I wanted to leave room for the possibility that the bullets might not be the same ones recovered from the lake.

"Did you initial any of them?" I was pursuing him and could see him start to sweat.

"No, sir."

"So, you really don't know if those are the same bullets or not, do you?"

"I didn't take the bullets from the package they were in because I wanted to try to obtain fingerprints, if that was possible. That's why I did not take the bullets from the baggie."

"Let's try again," I suggested, feigning compassion, like I was trying to explain something fairly easy to a small, dull boy. "You don't know if these are the same bullets you turned in, do you?" I asked.

"They were the same bullets Officer Adair gave me. If the chain of custody was not broken, then they are the same bullets."

This was not the answer I wanted. I had to show that, somehow, these bullets had been tampered with or tested by someone in the Police Department or by the OSBI – and were not fired by Noi.

I tried another approach. "Officer, as a matter of fact, there are bullets in that bag that have been tested, aren't there?"

"That's correct," he admitted. Now, I was getting somewhere.

"And," I went on, "you don't know what kinds of tests were done on those bullets, do you?"

"No," he replied, "I don't."

"Now, Officer, did you know that Agent Martin Udall, the OSBI's agent and expert on firearms, had tested those three bullets that were marked by being misfired?"

Powell said that he did.

"Could these be the same bullets which you said earlier had misfired, bullets that were tested and returned to the bag?" I wanted to make this perfectly clear to the jury.

"Yes," he said, sullenly.

Even though Officer Powell had not *technically* lied, he gave the jury a half-truth in such a way that he knew his statements would seriously mislead the jury. It made me wonder how many other times half-truths are used to convict an innocent person. Once again, maybe Noi was right in her mistrust of the police.

Since Officer Powell was the officer who took the police pictures of Noi's house, I had to use him to introduce into evidence the blow-ups I had made from these pictures. Powell had used a cheap camera that made very small five inch by five inch pictures. I had them enlarged because I knew the jury would have trouble seeing certain details which I wanted to point out.

Powell had taken about forty-five photographs of the Mitchell residence. He marked on the back side of each with a black felt-tip pen with his initials and the date on which he took them. Before the marker ink had dried, he had stacked the pictures on top of each other; thus, the black marks smudged each photograph except for the lone one on top of the stack.

I asked Officer Powell to identify and authenticate the blow-ups of the pictures that I had made. He smirked and refused to do so. He said he could not say whether they were accurate copies or not and he did so because he knew this would keep me from getting these into evidence. I then asked him about the smudge marks on the blow-ups that matched the smudge marks on the smaller original pictures. He replied that did not prove anything. He said perhaps I, too, had signed the backs of the blow-ups and stacked them before the marker ink had dried, like he had.

I just calmly replied to him, "Yes, I could have done that, if I had been so careless." I then asked him to look at the back of my blow-ups to see if I had, indeed, done what he did. He took my blow-ups, looked at them and shrugged, saying there were no black marks on the back of them that could have smudged the other pictures.

Powell did not want to admit what was quickly becoming obvious, that the entire Broken Arrow Police Department had deliberately made my job as difficult as they possibly could.

Carson had pressed Judge Dalton to order me "not to tell the jury about the way Powell had refused to give me the negatives of his official pictures to make the blow-ups I needed". It cost me $180.^{00} out of my own pocket to have blow-ups made from the pictures without the negatives. Given how this trial had almost wrecked my family financially, that was a big chunk of money to put out when it didn't have to happen that way. Carson should have been embarrassed if the jury found out about his tactic of forcing me to pay extra to make blowup enlargements of the photos. At the first trial, I never did get Powell to authenticate his enlarged pictures.

Just when I felt I had Powell on the run like a hound dog after a raccoon, Judge Dalton called me off. He interrupted my questions to call for the noon recess even though it was only 11:45 am – unusually early for lunch. To me this was clearly to rescue Officer Powell and stop my momentum.

I hollered, "Wait, Judge, I've almost got him treed!"

I heard a few chuckles, but they were quickly drowned out by Dalton slamming his gavel down. He barked back, "Now, *you* wait, Counselor. I called the recess and we are going to have lunch *now!*"

I heard a murmur from the jury, but I didn't know what it meant.

After the jury left, Carson ran to Powell and chewed him out, yelling, "Don't you know what you are doing to this case? Do you want to lose it?" He knew Powell was making the jury dislike the prosecutors by disliking the police. Powell was making Carson look bad. Rex said he could hear Carson's bellow reverberate in the marble hallway outside the courtroom. I don't know if any jurors were still around to hear it, although I hoped so.

Well, I thought with satisfaction, *that was a good morning session and I thoroughly enjoyed the confrontation.*

After lunch, we waited fifteen minutes or so to begin the trial. Officer Powell had still not returned. Just when I thought he was not going to show up, he walked in through the side door and up to the witness chair with an extremely slow and halting gait. He looked like he had been tranquilized.

I started right in by asking him, again, to authenticate my blow-ups of the pictures he had taken and this time, he calmly agreed – *finally!*

Getting the blow-ups into evidence brought me great relief. If I hadn't already felt I was walking a fine line with the Judge, I would have danced around.

One critical point I wanted Powell to substantiate the existence of an oak baby bed in the master bedroom. There were blood spatters on it about twelve to eighteen inches off the floor. This minute concentration of blood would help the jury determine that Noi was on the ground when Bobby jerked the gun as he was crouching over her. This was crucial evidence because my blood splatter expert and my ballistics expert both based their trajectory calculations from the baby bed to the hole in the wall.

I introduced my picture of Noi's bedroom showing the baby bed in the room, but Powell said, "I don't remember the baby bed being in the master bedroom." Every time Officer Powell opened his mouth to speak, he glanced over at the prosecutor first.

He actually looks contrite, I thought. *That must have been one major ass-chewing Carson gave him.* For the briefest moment I felt sorry for Officer Powell.

Then he went too far again and said, "The bedroom has been altered in those photographs."

Any sympathy I might have started to feel for Powell, rushed away. He knew the location of the bed was important to Noi's defense because it would help verify her story about the struggle with Bobby.

"It's amazing to me that an officer trained in investigating crime could not remember that there was a baby bed in the room." I said with narrowed eyes. "It's also shocking that you failed to take critical photos of all the objects in the bedroom."

He just stared at me.

"Do you remember seeing the Bambi baby pictures hanging on the wall next to the baby bed?" I asked.

172

"I don't remember."

I held up the photograph for him to see and asked, "Is there anything else you see in this picture that you do not remember?"

"No," he answered, coldly.

"No further questions, Your Honor."

Carson spotted an opening and pounced. He jumped to his feet and asked Powell, "Would you be surprised, Officer Powell, if you discovered that the baby bed had been placed in the bedroom later?" *What??* I couldn't believe he was doing this. He was trying to convict me along with Noi! *They are accusing me of tampering with the evidence. That's a felony crime in every state in the nation.* If this stunt worked to discredit me, then Noi would get the maximum sentence.

Powell replied to Carson as I would have expected, "Not at all, sir."

Carson kept at it, suggesting, "That baby bed might have been slipped in at any time?

"Yes, sir," Powell dutifully replied while nodding his head up and down.

Then Carson asked, as he waved the baby bed picture in front of the jury, "Would you be surprised to find out that Mr. Lloyd took this picture?"

I quickly stood up and said, "Your Honor, I stipulate that I took that picture." I did this to let the jury know I was proud to document evidence the Broken Arrow Police Department had missed.

Carson then snidely replied, "Thank you," as though he had saved the day.

What a jackass, I thought and at the same time I was scrambling to make sense of his actions. *Did he do this innocently as a mistake or with an evil and deceptive heart?*

CHAPTER 15 – PRIDE GOETH BEFORE A FALL *ALMOST* ALWAYS

The prosecutors called Lieutenant Charlie Reynolds to the stand. As lead investigator, Charlie Reynolds was the officer from the Broken Arrow Police Department who had been in charge of the investigation. Something dark boiled up inside of me when I looked at him. The Scorpio part of me had awakened and I wanted revenge. I wanted to burn and bury Charlie Reynolds just like he had done to me in the first trial.

I thought Lt. Reynolds' weakness might be pride – just a hunch. He was proud of his longtime association with the Broken Arrow Police. He thought it was one of the finest investigative agencies in the State of Oklahoma, and he had told me earlier that Broken Arrow had won an award for the quality of their investigative work.

Lt. Reynolds was an average-looking man with a bit of a pudgy build. I could not read his emotions through his eyes very well because his black, horn-rimmed glasses hid their expression. I began slowly with him. The two of us had not gotten along since Tom Cook and I had gone to Noi's home to do our own investigation without the police department's help. I know he felt I was overstepping my bounds then and stomping all over his toes by doing that, but I did not trust the police department to be honest with me, or even thorough with their investigation of the crime scene.

"How long have you been with the Broken Arrow Police Department?" I asked him.

"Eleven years," he replied, firmly, proud of himself.

175

"In fact, you have never worked for any other police department anywhere else, have you?" I questioned.

"No, sir," he said.

"Did you, at one time, tell me that the Broken Arrow Police Force once won an award for achievement in investigative procedures in Oklahoma?" I was trying to lay a trap.

Proud of this, he was quick to remember. "Yes, sir," he said, "it was 1980. The State of Oklahoma recognized Broken Arrow as being the finest. Also, our department has been nominated again this year for excellence."

"What role did you play in the investigation of Noi Mitchell's case?" I was maneuvering him. I wanted him to take responsibility for the entire investigation. I wanted to pin down *exactly* what he had and had not done.

"I was in charge and I assigned the men to the job. I also followed up by going to the house and supervised my men personally. I took a personal interest in this case," he added.

"Well, as Chief of one of the finest investigative forces in Oklahoma, would you want to gather all the evidence to establish Noi's guilt or innocence, as the case may be? I asked.

"Yes," he answered.

"Then, as supervisor of the investigation, do you think you would be interested in establishing the trajectory of the bullet, if you are looking for truth and justice?"

"Yes," he answered again.

"Do you think it would help establish the trajectory to see if the hole in the wall had a bullet embedded in it?"

176

"Yes," he replied, "if it were a bullet hole." He was not going to give me a thing.

"And, how would you go about determining that?" I was trying to see what normal procedures would be used to discover if it was a bullet hole. Actually, months earlier, I had discovered it *was* a bullet hole by having an x-ray company come out to the house and x-ray the wall. Sure enough, the x-rays showed that the bullet was there, and it had a slight dent on the end of it. Even the staples and nails in the wall showed up on the x-rays.

"Well," he replied, "I thought that the scrape in the wall was a scratch." Then, he added, "It could have been anything."

And, he was right, of course, it *could* have been anything, even a staple or a nail, but in this case, it was a bullet, one that a good investigator would have found *if* he had wanted to find it.

It was notable to me that the subject of our conversation was *holes*, because this guy was digging one for himself, deeper and deeper. I almost didn't have to say anything. It was an interesting coincidence, too, I thought, that both Reynolds and Powell used the term "scratch" to describe the hole in the wall, almost as if they'd been practicing their testimonies, getting their stories straight, you might say.

"In your quest to discover all the evidence, who made the decision that it was a mere scratch so that there was no need to perform any other tests?" I asked. The hardest part was trying to keep the sarcasm out of my voice.

"I did," he admitted.

"Did the OSBI or Creek County Sheriff's Department or anyone else make any suggestions about what to test in this case?" I pursued.

"Absolutely not," he answered defensively.

"Then, it was your decision alone to determine it was a scratch, not a bullet hole?"

"It was mine alone," he replied.

"And, you made that decision after you saw the blood splattered all over the wall?"

"Yes," he replied and his voice had turned cold and hard.

His eyes had lost their veiled expression and were now glaring at me. He looked like he might lunge for my throat. I was thinking I had better not get stopped for speeding through Broken Arrow any time soon.

"Do you think it might have been beneficial for the finest investigative police force in Oklahoma to determine exactly where Bobby bled on the carpet in the bedroom to determine the trajectory of the bullet?" I asked him.

"I do not know, sir," His face looked determined and hard, like it had been chiseled from granite. He was becoming more and more tense and was slapping his clinched fist against the palm of his other hand. I'm betting he was wishing that open palm was my face.

"What about the mattress?" I asked. "What happened to it? I really wanted to know.

"It was taken to a landfill," he said. "We had finished our investigation by then," he added, like that would make it okay. I couldn't believe what I was hearing.

"You mean you gave the order to bury it?" I asked.

"Yes, sir," he replied.

I wondered why the Broken Arrow Police Department hadn't cut out the blood stains from both sides of the mattress to introduce as evidence. *Hadn't they, in fact, now destroyed the evidence?* "Did you see the pictures of both sides of the mattress?" I pressed.

"They looked like pictures of the same side, to me."

I went on to question him in detail about what else the Broken Arrow Police Department had done to determine the trajectory of the bullet besides bury the mattress. I asked him if he had ordered his men to test for blood on the front porch.

"No," he replied, as the rhythm of his hands slapping together quickened.

"Did you test for blood in the garage?"

"No."

"Did you test for menstrual blood on the mattress?"

"No."

"Did you test for blood on the wall surrounding the hole?"

"Yes."

"In fact," I said, "you waited six months to have it analyzed, didn't you?"

"Yes."

"Do you think more extensive testing for blood would have made the investigation more complete, Lieutenant?" I asked.

"I do not know." By now, his hands were knocking together almost violently.

I asked him, "Now, Lieutenant, did you see Noi before she was transferred to the Tulsa jail?"

"Yes, sir," he replied, "I helped my men when they brought her in."

"Now, Officer, did you observe any bruises on Noi, bruises which might prove that she was in a struggle?" I asked.

"No, sir," he said. "She looked fine to me, just a little tired, that's all."

There were bruises on Noi that the Broken Arrow Police Department had failed to see. Bruises meant she had been in a fight and, perhaps, was beaten up. Bruises would not fit the prosecutor's theory that Noi had killed Bobby while he was helpless to defend himself.

I remembered back when Noi was first charged for the murder of Bobby Mack Mitchell, III. The Broken Arrow Police had already transferred Noi to the care of the Tulsa County Jail. I needed to get pictures of any bruises Noi suffered in her fight with Bobby. Tom Cook and I asked the Sheriff to allow us to take pictures of her. The Sheriff sent a deputy officer with us to meet her.

I explained to Noi, "We need to take pictures of your bruises so we can show the jury what Bobby did."

The three of us went into a drunk tank, a small cement room about eight feet square. Noi stood on the side opposite from the "hole" in the floor, which is used as a toilet. Noi knew she had to take off her clothes (the orange color now indicated she was a medium-risk prisoner); but she hesitated. Her modesty touched us and we became very silent out of respect for her and to acknowledge that we knew how difficult this must be for her.

Slowly, as if stripping gracefully to music, but with her facial expression impassive, she raised the orange prison garb over her head. It was bulky and fit her loosely but, surprisingly, she was quite shapely as she stood there wearing only a bra and panties. She looked like a girl-woman as her long black hair was brushed back into pigtails bouncing off her shoulders.

Then, without saying a word, she pulled the bra straps down and unsnapped the hooks. She was beautiful. I felt embarrassed and awkward, almost as much as Noi did. I remember a wave of heat going up my neck that reddened my ears. I usually blush brightly when I get embarrassed or frustrated. Noi felt a sense of humiliation from having been beaten and shame from having us see her naked, I'm sure. She stood several feet from us with her eyes downcast. I noticed everything about her... no make-up. Her nipples were brown not pink. *I am a professional*, I reminded myself... *but so much of me is "mere man", with all the weaknesses that go with being one.*

Sometimes, the difference between success and failure hinges on how observant you are. I was very observant. I noticed all of the bruises, the scratches, and the smooth skin which showed no signs of stretch marks from her two pregnancies. Even though more than a week had lapsed since her fight with Bobby, Noi still had baseball-sized bruises on each upper bicep and high up on each thigh as well as on her hips but, unfortunately they had turned yellow and the flash only made them fade out more. Her dark skin also did not show bruises as well as a lighter skin tone would, but, still, they were easy to spot. *The Broken Arrow Police officers, apparently, were not as observant as I was in detecting signs of physical abuse*, I thought. *It's almost as if they didn't want to see it. Imagine that.*

I remembered all of this and had to force my brain to make its way back to the courtroom because I was not *quite* through with Lieutenant Reynolds.

"Did you see the baby bed in the bedroom when you came out to supervise?" I asked.

"No, sir," he replied, "I do not believe it was there."

"Did you make any molds of the tire tracks on the oil and gas lease where the Creek County Sheriff's Department found Bobby's body?" I asked him.

"No, sir." He was giving the same answer to all of my questions and it wasn't boding well for him. He knew it, too.

"Did you take pictures of Bobby's hands to see if they showed scratch marks where Noi said she had clawed him?"

"No," he grumbled.

"Did you take pictures of Bobby's hand to show the pinched web he got when he pulled on the gun?" I asked. I held up my own hand and pinched the web between my thumb and forefinger so there was no mistaking what we were talking about. I made sure the jury saw me do it.

"No, sir," he growled.

"Did you run any tests or take pictures for gunpowder stippling on Bobby's shins, ankles or hands which might have remained with him from the fight over the gun?"

"The OSBI probably ran those, sir," he responded, looking away from me. I could hear his hands beating rapidly. I noticed the note-taking juror was no longer writing. His pencil was slapping against his notebook in time with Reynolds' beating hands, so those hand sounds were distracting to more people than just me. *Should I just go ahead and ask him to please stop? Why doesn't Dalton make him quit it?*

Finally, I looked right at Lieutenant Reynolds and said, "Will you give the jury this much? Do you think the investigation your office ran was as complete as it should have been?"

He swallowed hard. "No, sir," he reluctantly admitted. His face was like stone. This prideful man so bursting with enthusiasm for his investigative team had just been laid low; had been forced to admit that their work on what was one of the most noteworthy cases their department had ever handled was, in fact, not much better than shoddy. Actually, "shoddy" would have been a compliment.

It was time to prepare for the next day's trial.

CHAPTER 16 – *ALMOST* THE BEST DETECTIVE

Prosecutor Lewis called Detective David Anderson to the stand – what a look on this guy! He looked like the arch-villain in some silent movie with a pencil-thin mustache curling slightly at the ends. He talked with his hands a lot using aggressive gestures; and he was tall, muscular and large enough to be intimidating. I'd heard he held a black belt in karate.

Anderson was the detective who questioned Noi and took the recorded confession. He had also searched the Mitchell home and found a bullet in the dresser thirteen inches off the floor. He found lead and a copper jacket fragment lying intact in the partition between the drawers in the dresser.

Anderson testified he met Noi on Thursday, October 7th, 1982, around 11:30 am. He described how he had gone to Creek County to view Bobby's body, and that the license tag number on Bobby's Pontiac led him to Noi's address in Broken Arrow. He introduced himself to Noi and told her there had been an unidentified body found in Creek County. He asked her if Bobby Mitchell was her husband and she replied that he was. He asked Noi when she had last seen Bobby.

Anderson said, "Noi coolly replied, 'He work all time.'"

Detective Anderson asked, again, "When was the last time you saw Bobby?"

He said, "This time she replied, 'He not say anything. He say he need practice. But, some day, some night he tell me all time, he say he need practice.'"

Golf clubs were found in Bobby's abandoned Pontiac, so Detective Anderson interpreted Noi's answer to mean he was going to the driving range to practice golf.

Anderson testified that Noi told him she put the children to bed then went to bed herself. When she got up the next morning, Bobby had already left for work. Anderson asked her how she felt about Bobby leaving for work without saying anything to her.

The detective testified that Noi answered, "Not much because he do that before."

Anderson said he asked Noi if there might be something wrong since she had not seen Bobby for the past two days and she repeated that Bobby worked all the time. Anderson then asked if she could let him borrow a picture of Bobby for the Medical Examiner to use in order to determine if it was her husband's body that had been found. He said Noi then left the room and returned with a family picture album. The detective testified, "Noi asked, 'Okay?' and she seemed anxious."

Anderson continued, "She asked me, 'What can I do, what can I do?' She asked me to leave so she could call Bobby's father. I suggested she wait to find out whose body was in the morgue before she raised the alarm and she nodded that she would. I told her I would be back to give her the news one way or the other," Anderson told the jury.

He testified that the medical examiner, Dr. Masood, made a positive identification of the body of Bobby Mack Mitchell, III. Since there had been so little blood in the car, Anderson said that he knew Bobby had died before his body was placed there.

Detective Anderson testified that Lt. Charlie Reynolds called him and said it was possible the crime could have been committed in Broken Arrow. Lt. Reynolds then ordered him to return to the Mitchell home.

Anderson said, "The first time I returned to the house, Noi was not there and her car was gone. The next time I went there," he said; "when I rang the doorbell, there was no answer, but I noticed there were reddish-brown stains on the front porch. When I looked around, I saw black trash bags out by the curb, which had not been there before."

Anderson continued by testifying that Officer Maddux, Officer Powell, and he opened the trash bags and found egg cartons, diapers, tin cans and several bloody cloths and paper towels. "We decided we would remove the bags and put them in the trunk of the police car because they might be evidence," the detective explained.

When they walked back to the front porch, they could hear the clothes dryer running. Anderson said he thought it was very unusual that Noi was washing and drying clothes and leaving the house to run errands in her car while she waited to find out if her husband was still alive.

Anderson testified that, while he was standing in the driveway of the Mitchell home waiting for Noi to return, a neighbor walked over and asked him what was going on. When he filled her in on what he knew, she said she had noticed a tall man standing in the garage the night of Bobby's death. The man got into Bobby's car and drove away and she assumed it was Bobby. Anderson said he returned to the Mitchell home at around 5 pm and that, this time, he found Noi at home.

Anderson told her that he needed to talk with her and told Noi her husband was dead. Anderson said she did not appear to be upset or surprised at the time, only confused, as if she was waiting for someone to tell her what to do next. He then asked if she would mind coming down to the police station for an interview. She said that she would go with him, but wondered what to do with her children. Who would take care of them while she was gone? So, Officer Maddux stayed behind to baby-sit with the two little girls.

Anderson said they drove the ten-minute distance in complete silence. He stated that he had not handcuffed her and that she was not crying.

At the station, Anderson seated Noi in a training room by herself for several hours. He said he checked in on Noi from time to time and she was sitting in the chair, grimacing. She was not actually crying, but she was twisting her hair into knots, first with her right hand, then with her left, over and over. He said he had no trouble conversing with Noi but, in order to prevent any future problems regarding Noi's understanding of her constitutional rights, they wanted to get an interpreter.

The problem was they could not find someone who understood or spoke Thai well. They settled for Kao Vue, a Laotian refugee. Kao Vue arrived at the station around 7 pm. Anderson said that Noi and Kao Vue appeared to understand each other and even laughed at the same time. Anderson then moved Noi and Kao Vue into the interview room with a DO NOT DISTURB sign posted on the front door.

After referring to his notes, Anderson testified that he read Noi a consent form allowing the Police to search her home. Kao Vue then translated the *"Consent to Search"* form. After Noi signed the form, Anderson read her another form that informed her of her Miranda rights. Kao Vue translated again. Noi then signed the *"Miranda Rights Waiver"* form in two places and verbally agreed that she understood her rights and was willing to answer questions and to make a statement.

"She said, 'You ask, I answer'," Anderson told the jury.

Anderson then reviewed for the jury what he remembered Noi saying in her long confession.

"She repeated that Bobby had left Tuesday night to play golf. I asked her if it didn't sound a little strange to her that Bobby was going to hit golf balls alone at ten o'clock at night."

He related how Noi explained, in broken English, that Bobby told her the driving range never closed, year-round.

Detective Anderson asked her what Bobby was wearing when he left Tuesday night. He testified that Noi said Bobby was wearing light blue shorts and a t-shirt.

Anderson testified that Noi told him that she had talked to Bobby's secretary and left a message asking him to pick up the children Wednesday after school. Noi said she went ahead and picked them up herself because she was ill and returned home from work early.

Anderson said he asked her if she had made any attempts to locate Bobby Wednesday night when he did not come home. Noi said she had called Bobby's Dad and cousin to find out if they had seen him.

Anderson then testified that he asked Noi if she had set out any trash that day and she said she had. Anderson told her that they had found bloody cloths and paper towels in the trash and asked if anyone in her home had suffered an injury in the last few days. Noi was unclear about what an injury was. Anderson told her it was like a cut.

Anderson told the jury how Noi began laughing uncontrollably and said the blood was from her period. He asked her if she and her husband had an argument or fight in the house and she replied that they had not. He said she could not stop laughing, which he found disconcerting. Anderson testified, "Noi said, 'I don't care what he does.' I then asked her how she accounted for the blood in the trash bags and on the front porch and she said she didn't know."

Anderson asked Noi if her husband's car was in the driveway Tuesday night and she replied that it was not. "I told her that we had witnesses who saw a white male raise her garage door," he said, "and pull that silver car into the garage Tuesday night at 12:30. And she did not answer.

"I asked her what her response was to that. Were these people lying – did they make it up? All she could say was 'No', but when I asked her if the silver car was there that night, again, she said 'No.'

"I told her we had witnesses and valid information that she and her husband got into an argument Tuesday night. She said that she did not lie. I told her that her argument woke up Mia and asked her if her daughter lied. She replied that her daughter was not a liar.

"I asked her about the fresh scratches and bruises on her hands and she told me that she cut herself at work.

"I went back over all of the evidence against her, statements from witnesses, her inconsistent statements and confronted her with it all. I pleaded with her to tell me all she knew about her husband's death and told her she had the opportunity right now to explain. I then said that the door would close behind me and she would be on the inside and would reach a point of no return and could not come back at a later date and tell me what she knew.

"She began to cry and asked me to tell her the answers. I knew she was lying and concluded the interview at 10 pm that Thursday night. I asked a woman Officer, Earlene Spillman, to do a pat-down search and to book Noi for the murder of her husband. Just as I was getting ready to go off duty, Spillman said Noi wanted to tell me everything.

"When I got back to the interview room, I plugged in my tape recorder and asked Noi to sit back down and face me. I said, 'Noi, tell me the truth.'

"She responded, 'I have to. He wanted to do something to me.' I asked her, 'Why did you have to?' She said, 'He couldn't take my kids.'

"I asked her who helped her. She said that nobody helped her. 'He try to do a lot of things to me and then I kill.'

"I asked her when she did it and she said, 'Tuesday night.'

"I asked her who the neighbor had seen at the house on Tuesday night. She told me that he was one of her friends and that his name was George. I asked her what George did to help her and she said he just helped her load the body into the car.

"I asked her if she and Bobby had been fighting for quite a while and if he had tried to hurt her before. She said, 'Yes.' I asked her if she had gotten tired of all the fights and all the times he had tried to hurt her and she answered, 'I know.'

"She admitted that they had a fight with a gun Tuesday night and that 'we both have gun in same hand.'

"I asked her what she did after she shot her husband and she said that Bobby had thrown the gun away. She told me that she took Bobby in the house and told him to see the doctor.

"She told me they fought over the gun in the bedroom and said, 'When he run out, I go run with him, too.'

"She said she took him back into the house after he was shot and then they went into the garage and he died there. I asked her what she beat Bobby with and she told me the baseball. I asked her if she meant the thing you hit the baseball with or the baseball. I had to illustrate that the bat was the long thing used to hit a baseball." He confirmed, "The OSBI agents found the bat cleaned up and hidden in the attic."

Detective Anderson continued to relate Noi's confession to the jury, "I asked her what had happened to her husband's billfold and the keys to Bobby's car. She said she cut up the contents of the billfold and threw them into a trash can at the apartment complex where George lived. She flung the keys out by Bobby's car where she had parked it with his body in it.

"I asked her who had helped her move the body. She said that she went to her friend George and asked him for a favor. She told him that someone had died and she needed help because she didn't know what to do. He decided," Detective Anderson stated, "she should leave Bobby's body near Kiefer, Oklahoma. The next day, Noi brought George Rivera the gun and a baggie of bullets. George and his Puerto Rican friend, Wilfredo Torres, threw them in a lake at the Marina Apartments where George lived." Anderson told the jury that Officer Adair recovered the gun and bullets from that lake by the Marina Apartments.

Anderson said, "Noi concluded her confession by saying, 'I not understand why this happen between me and Bobby.' "

I noticed Anderson had a smug expression on his face as he glanced at the jury with this parting shot. I saw the note-taker shake out his hand and nod slightly at Anderson.

It was now my turn to cross-examine Detective David Anderson. He thought he was the coolest detective on the police force, I'm sure. I recognized that it would be very difficult to get Anderson to lose his composure, but I welcomed the challenge. And, so, I began.

"Do you, as an officer trained to uphold the law," I asked, "search for all the facts so that you do not charge an innocent person – is that right?"

"Absolutely," he assured me.

"In fact, Officer Anderson, you spent over three hours with Noi trying to discover the truth, isn't that correct?" I pressed.

"That is approximately right, yes, sir," he answered.

"You have told all the ladies and gentlemen of the jury all of the lies she told you. Did you ever ask her why she was telling them?"

"No, sir," he answered.

"What, exactly, did you say to her?" I asked.

Anderson replied, "Well, she volunteered that 'Maybe I tell all lies.' "

"Now, Officer," I continued, "in your training as a servant of the people, don't you think it is important to determine what the trajectory of the bullet was?" I started in on my familiar pattern of questioning and heard a couple of people in the courtroom groan, as if to say, *Oh, brother, not this again.* Well, they could be as bored with it as they wanted to. I was not there to entertain them, but to defend my client against a murder charge.

"Yes, sir," Anderson replied.

"Did you ask Noi where she was when the gun went off?"

"No, sir," Anderson replied, then exhaled, like he was also bored with it all.

"Did you ask her how many times the gun fired, Officer?

"No, sir."

I then went on to explain that Noi would never volunteer information, that she would only answer questions. "You knew that," I said, "she even told you that." Then I asked Anderson if he had asked her questions that would explain what had happened.

"No, I had not."

I asked Anderson if he asked Noi how the bat got into the fight or if Bobby had hit her with the bat.

No, he had not asked Noi that.

I asked Anderson if he had asked Noi to reenact what happened.

No, he had not.

I asked him if he remembered that Noi admitted they had been fighting.

He testified, "She had said, 'We fighting.' "

I asked Anderson if he had asked Noi about the pinched web on Bobby's hand.

"No, I had not."

I summed up by asking Anderson if he had asked Noi everything that would be necessary for a complete investigation.

Very sarcastically, he said he thought so.

I showed Anderson a blow-up of the picture of the mattress in Noi and Bobby's bedroom. "Do you know what happened to the actual mattress?" I asked.

"Well, you know the answers to these questions before you even ask them!" he exploded and began to rise out of the witness chair. He quickly regained his composure, though, when he saw Carson stare him down.

"Well," I calmly said, "the jury doesn't know them, do they?"

"No, sir," he replied. He looked subdued, but then grudgingly admitted, "Yes, I buried it in a landfill, forty feet under the ground." He smirked then continued. "We already had pictures of it, so we did not need it." Just like the other officers, he was trying to justify the destruction of evidence.

"Who decided to bury this evidence?" I asked.

"Lieutenant Reynolds gave me the order," he replied.

"You did test for blood on both sides of the mattress, didn't you?" I asked him. I was not going to let him off the hook so easily.

"I do not think so," he replied.

"If the Police Department had not tested both sides of the mattress or taken pictures of both sides of the mattress, why did you think we did not need the mattress anymore?" I pursued.

"I do not know," he said, giving me his standard answer, "I did not give the order."

"Officer Anderson, what did *you* do to prove the trajectory of the bullet that killed Bobby Mitchell – besides burying the mattress in a landfill, I mean." Someone in the courtroom giggled behind their hand. Anderson's face began to turn a dark red.

"I don't know, sir."

I asked him if he had seen bruises on Noi and he replied that he, perhaps, saw a few scratches on her right hand and that he remembered she was wearing a long-sleeved shirt, so he really could not tell.

"Do you remember where the baby bed was located when you went to Noi's home to investigate the death?"

"Yes, it was in the middle bedroom and not in the master bedroom," he answered. It seemed like he'd been coached to reply to a question I had not really asked of him.

"Did you know that Agent Oswald with the OSBI told me that the baby bed was in the master bedroom?" I asked.

"No, sir," he said, losing some of his smugness.

I was finished with David Anderson.

CHAPTER 17 – HONESTY IS (*ALMOST*) THE BEST POLICY

Prosecutor Lewis announced his next witness was OSBI Agent, Kenneth Oswald, who was boyish-looking with light brown hair and blue eyes. Agent Oswald had worked with the OSBI for over two years when he got called by the Creek County Sheriff's Office to investigate an apparent homicide.

He went out to Bobby's car to view the body. Arriving at the lease property off Highway 75 in nearby Creek County at about 9:30 am on October 7th, 1982, he and his partner, Robert Driscoll, removed everything from the car. Driscoll packaged the contents into bags and labeled them while Oswald listed the contents of each bag on inventory sheets. Oswald ran down the license registration and read the name printed on a blank, personal check he'd found folded in the glove compartment. This identification led to an address in Broken Arrow, Oklahoma.

Oswald interviewed Mack Mitchell, Jr., who was the father of the deceased, in order to determine the last time that Mr. Mitchell had seen his son. Mr. Mitchell told Oswald that he and his son were not especially close and he would not be aware if Bobby disappeared for several days. "I could tell," Oswald said, "just from the level of his grief and anger, that Mr. Mitchell did indeed love his son very much, but I surmised that there must have been a rift between the two of them at some point – most likely over Bobby's marriage to an Asian woman from Thailand. Still, that was just a guess on my part."

Agent Oswald said Theresa McComb was more helpful. "She divulged that Bobby and Noi's marriage had dissolved to a point where they were considering divorce. She confessed Bobby had spent Sunday and Monday nights with her before he disappeared." Oswald continued to testify, "The last time she said she saw Bobby, he said he was moving out and only going back home one last time to collect his clothes. From the interviews and physical evidence, I determined that Bobby died within the jurisdiction of the Broken Arrow Police Department and notified them of the apparent homicide.

"Several hours later, David Anderson told me that Noi had signed a consent form to search her home for evidence so I could go to the Mitchell house." Agent Oswald explained that he, Powell and Officer Reynolds drove out together, combining forces to comb the area around and inside the house.

"From a walk-down of the entire house, we narrowed our search for clues to the master bedroom," Oswald detailed for the jury. "We pulled back the covers and sheets on the bed in the master bedroom and discovered blood stains on the mattress. Flipping the mattress over, we found blood stains on the other side, too. We also found a piece of lead near the chair in the nap of the carpet."

Prosecutor Lewis nodded encouragement so Oswald continued.

"We discovered a blood stain on the metal door plate at the bottom of the inside garage door and we found blood on the front porch. Anderson called me at the Mitchell home and told me that Noi had confessed to beating Bobby with a bat. We looked for that and later found it while searching the attic."

After the prosecution was finished with him, I began to question Oswald about what he learned concerning the relationship between Theresa McComb and Bobby Mitchell.

"Did she indicate to you whether they had a personal, close relationship?" I asked.

"They dated at one time," he said.

"How recently?" I asked.

"They dated several months before Bobby married Noi and they began the relationship again in the recent past," Oswald answered.

"Officer Oswald, is it your opinion that they were having a sexual relationship?"

"Yes, I guess so," he replied.

"Now, when you handled the investigation of the car, did you vacuum the car to get hair samples or gather blood scrapings?"

"No."

Oswald said that Driscoll was the person to determine what they should remove from the car as evidence.

"What did you do with the golf clubs in the back of the car?" I asked.

"We just brought them into the station," he said, "they were too large for our bags," he answered.

"Did you see any blood in the car?"

"There were no large pools of blood, but there was a smear near the roof on the passenger's side."

"Did you run any tests on it?"

"No."

"Did you dust the car for fingerprints?"

"I don't know," he answered.

"Who has jurisdiction of this investigation, the OSBI or the Broken Arrow Police Department?" I asked.

"We both do," he said. "We decided who could do what best. It didn't matter which agency conducted the investigation."

I looked right at him. "Now, this," I said, "is a very important question…" and I waited for Carson' inevitable objection.

Carson scrambled to his feet and shouted, "I object, Your Honor, to Jimmy Lloyd editorializing as to what is important."

"Sustained," bellowed Judge Dalton.

"Do you remember a baby bed in the Mitchell house?" I asked.

"Yes, sir, I do," he replied. "It was in the master bedroom. I remember the blood spatters on it."

I felt so relieved, almost like hearing the best news of my life. I'm sure I let out a sigh. "Thank you for your honesty," I said.

Every Broken Arrow Police Officer involved in the case either denied the existence of the baby bed or could not recall having seen it in the master bedroom. So, the question suddenly became: *Who is the jury going to believe – Agent Oswald from the OSBI or the Broken Arrow Police Department or the prosecutor who suggested I staged the evidence by placing the baby bed in the master bedroom before taking the photo?*

Had I discredited the police enough to help the jury question the animosity directed toward Noi?

Had I spotlighted their incompetence enough that the jury would believe Agent Oswald rather than the Broken Arrow Police and the prosecution? My mind was buzzing with these thoughts as we moved on.

CHAPTER 18 – *ALMOST* A WITNESS

Prosecutor Carson called as his next witness Earlene Spillman, a woman police officer who was calm and self-confident. She was just the opposite of Noi, it seemed to me, who was so scared and insecure she seemed about to crumble at any moment. Spillman was around 5'3" with shiny, wavy brown hair. Although she was not directly involved in the investigation, still, she made several startling and damaging disclosures to the jury. These made my heart sink down into my socks whenever I heard them.

Spillman had worked for the Broken Arrow Police Department for nearly three years when David Anderson asked her to do a pat-down search of Noi. She described this as a normal procedure to find any hidden weapons.

She, like the other Broken Arrow Police Officers had done, said she had no problems understanding and speaking to Noi. Spillman also said Noi responded like she understood everything perfectly. She said Noi pulled down her jeans and pointed to the bruises on her legs which, since they were still rather fresh, were about the size of silver dollars, and also pointed out the scratches on her hands. Spillman said these injuries appeared to be minor and did not seem to be causing Noi any discomfort.

Spillman testified that she waited for Noi while the defendant was in the interview room telling Detective Anderson "everything". When Noi was finished, Spillman and Anderson went with Noi to the Marina Apartments where her accomplice, George Rivera, lived.

First, Anderson and Spillman drove by the restaurant where Noi worked. They wanted to discuss certain details of the investigation with the OSBI. When they got to the Marina Apartments, Noi pointed out George's apartment.

Spillman said she only had one question to ask Noi, which was why she had hit her husband with a baseball bat. Spillman testified that Noi said, "To make sure he was dead."

My cross-examination of Officer Spillman was short, but not very sweet. I asked her, "Do you recall whether or not Noi indicated to you that she hit him with the bat right after the gun went off?"

"Noi said she hit him afterwards," Spillman replied.

"You did write these statements into a formal report?" I pressed, expecting to hear what I had mostly heard from the Broken Arrow Police Department when it came to something important they had failed to either document or do. Again, I was right.

"No, I did not," she said, crossly.

CHAPTER 19 – AN EDUCATED GUESS (IS STILL ONLY *ALMOST* FACTUAL)

The gun and ballistics expert for the OSBI, Agent Martin Udall, took the witness stand the next day. He was a very fair-skinned man with jet black hair. His thick, dark eyebrows dominated his face in an almost cartoonish way, making each of his expressions that much more dramatic and intense.

He identified the weapon which had killed Bobby as a .38 caliber RG pistol, a very cheap gun, which has a special guard lever. This lever is supposed to spring up between the hammer and the firing pin if the cocked hammer is bumped. This is to prevent accidental firings.

After the agent explained how the gun worked, the Judge asked me if I had any objections to the gun being submitted into evidence. I said I wanted to look at it and to hold it first. As I held the gun, I cocked the hammer and barely pushed it. The hammer slammed down as if it would fire had it been loaded. It was almost shocking how forceful and loud it was. I did this several times and the gun clicked loudly each time.

Finally, Carson, getting peeved, rose and said, "I object to him squeezing the trigger and firing the gun, Your Honor."

I responded, "Your Honor, look at this. I barely *touch* the hammer and it accidentally goes off." I cocked the hammer, held my finger up and gently, like a butterfly landing on a lily, lightly touched the tip of my finger on the hammer. It *SLAMMED* down, loud and hard. I proved my point. This happened as I was standing in front of the jury. Their eyes widened. (Melvin Belli taught me this technique).

Judge Dalton became a little agitated and called a recess.

When we reconvened, the Judge asked Agent Udall. "Would the gun fire if it had live ammunition in it and the cocked hammer was pushed into the firing pin?"

Udall responded. "The shield is "supposed" to rise up if the hammer is not activated by the trigger."

I handed the gun back to Carson who placed it on the table with the Prosecutors' other evidence.

Udall also examined the bullets which were marked as State's Evidence and identified them as the same bullets removed from Marina Lake. He testified that he ran tests on only three of those bullets found in the bag and they had misfired, presumably because they were very old or water-logged from having been submerged in the lake.

He testified that there were two different types of gunpowder grains found burned into the decedent's skin. When he examined some of the grains from the skin on the victim's leg and compared them to those found on his chest, Udall said he noticed that some of the grains were coarse and some were fine. He concluded that two different types of bullets had been fired.

Udall said that he would have expected to find burns on the decedent's hands if he'd had them around the gun when it fired. "When a gun fires," he explained, "the gunpowder explosion creates gases that shoot out from the barrel of the gun and escape from around the cylinder. These gases would cause burns on the skin. There was no evidence of burns on the deceased's hands," he said.

The prosecutors tried to introduce a picture of a gun fired in the dark which graphically showed the explosion of fire shooting from the barrel and cylinder of a gun. I objected because the gun in the picture was not the gun which shot Bobby, nor was it even the same caliber or model of weapon. This time, Judge Dalton sided with me and kept the picture from being shown to the jury.

Agent Udall also testified that the first bullet, which lodged in the dresser, had been fired at a downward angle. In his opinion, the fact that the second bullet ended up seven feet, five and one-half inches from the floor did not prove that the gun was fired at an upward angle. He said that, once a bullet travels through a body, ballistic science is unreliable to prove the actual path of a bullet once it has exited a body. He then gave an example of a strange experience he had read about where a bullet actually entered the neck area and exited the leg. He testified that bullets can ricochet inside a human body. He suggested that the bullet which went into the decedent's chest at a slightly upward angle zoomed outwards and possibly hit the decedent's fifth and sixth ribs causing it to then ricochet upwards.

Carson then turned Agent Udall over to me for cross-examination. I approached the witness chair in the front of the courtroom.

"Mr. Udall," I began, "how long have you been with the OSBI?"

"About eight and a half years," he replied.

"In that length of time, have you ever heard of Lucien Haag?"

"Oh, yes," he said, "everyone in the field of ballistics has heard of Lucien Haag. In fact, I took a course from Mr. Haag and have read many of the articles he has published."

"Would you respect the quality, reliability and the results of his ballistics testing?"

"Yes. He is *THE* expert in the field," Agent Udall responded.

"What about the fact that this gun is so cheap," I began, "have you known of any cases of lawsuits where someone was shot when the gun misfired because the safety device did not work?"

"Yes, I know of several times when people have been accidentally killed," he responded.

"Could that have happened in this case?" I asked.

"Anything is possible," he replied.

"With respect to the burns you thought would have been present on Bobby's hands from the escaping gas around the cylinder, did you actually run any tests on this gun or is your testimony a generalization on all firearms?"

"I didn't run any of those tests on this gun," Agent Udall admitted.

"Then you don't know if any of those gases escaped from the cylinder of this particular gun, do you?" I questioned.

"Well, the cylinder was loose and gases would escape," he answered, a little flustered.

"Without actual tests, though, the best that you can say is that you are making a guess, isn't that right?" I asked.

"Yes," he persisted, in a very business-like voice, "but it is an educated guess, sir."

CHAPTER 20 – *ALMOST* HIS BROTHER'S KEEPER

Prosecutor Lewis then announced Bobby's cousin, Rob Schaeffer, would take the stand. Schaeffer slowly and hesitantly walked toward the front of the courtroom, like he really didn't even want to be there. He was probably in his mid-thirties, with a slender build, blonde hair, and had begun to sprout a dark brown beard.

When Lewis asked Schaeffer to describe the last time he saw his cousin Bobby alive, Schaeffer's large, blue eyes began to brim with tears. He testified that he and Bobby got along better than most brothers. "Bobby," he said, "was my golfing buddy and his best friend."

He testified that Bobby had come over to his house quite early on Tuesday morning and said that he could not bear to live with Noi any longer. Bobby asked his cousin if he would take a day off work and help him move out. After Schaeffer called work to get the day off, he and Bobby drove in separate cars to the Mitchell residence where they spent nearly four hours carefully separating and loading Bobby's belongings into the cars.

Schaeffer said that Bobby walked back into the house and stood there looking at everything he was leaving behind. The phone rang and Bobby went into the kitchen to answer it. Rob attested he heard Bobby promise to pick Mia up from school that afternoon.

Schaeffer said Bobby came out of the kitchen and told him that he was sorry, but, after talking to Noi, he decided that he would stay there and tell Noi face-to-face that he was leaving her. Schaeffer said he tried to talk Bobby out of staying, but Bobby said he had to see her one more time to tell her he was leaving, that it felt like the right thing to do. Schaeffer said he unloaded his car and left Bobby standing on the front porch.

Lewis asked Schaeffer if he had ever seen Bobby act aggressively towards anyone. Schaeffer replied that Bobby was a true diplomat and, to his knowledge, always settled any differences without any kind of aggressive acts or harsh language. Rob said, "Sometimes we had a problem, but Bobby was able to smooth things over." Schaeffer looked up at the jury as he recalled his memories of his cousin. Tears rolled down his cheeks as he rubbed his eyes. I was touched by his heartbreak and, in glancing around the room, I noticed that everyone in there seemed to be deeply moved.

Lewis then asked Schaeffer about his own relationship with Noi. Schaeffer replied that he and Noi never really got along because he found it so difficult to talk to her. It was not because of her having to wrestle so much with the English language; it was because they had nothing in common and she seemed so secretive.

Rob testified, "I was surprised when Bobby brought her back to the States with him because Bobby had always had so much success with women, in general. Marrying a woman he couldn't even talk to didn't make sense to me."

Schaeffer said, "I regretted seeing Bobby so unhappy with his life and his marriage during the last four or five months before his death." Schaeffer summed up his testimony by saying, "When something hurt Bobby, it hurt me, too."

Lewis had nothing more to add.

In my cross-examination of Schaeffer, I asked him, "If you and Bobby are such close friends, how many times were you invited to their home for dinner?"

"She never invited me. I never could understand why not."

"Well, then," I countered, "how often did you see Bobby?"

"At least twice a week," he said, "we would meet out on the golf course or maybe go somewhere for lunch."

"How do you feel about Bobby's marriage to an Asian woman?" I asked.

"I felt fine about it," he replied, "as long as Bobby was happy. I felt badly when Bobby felt like a failure because his marriage was falling apart."

I walked back to my chair feeling less than positive about my cross-examination. I glanced over at Nancy who was sitting next to two Thai women. The look on her face told me that Schaeffer had just struck a major blow. Sympathy for Bobby was at an all-time high in the courtroom.

The next character witness to testify was Bobby's friend and co-employee, Philip Odom. He testified how gentle Bobby was and about his reputation for non-violence. He was on and off the witness stand in under ten minutes. He didn't raise the sympathy like Schaeffer had; therefore, he didn't hurt us.

Odem walked to the back of the courtroom and as he headed to the door, a large man patted him on the back and hugged him. That man is a local lawyer, Mark Lindberg, who worked with Odem and came to give him moral support and pray for him. He became the Adult Sunday School teacher for Nancy and me. It's a small world. Indeed!

Jim Lloyd and Jody Seay

CHAPTER 21 – A LIFE & DEATH *ALMOST* EXAMINED

Each of the prosecutors was responsible for prepping their own particular witnesses to testify. Eddie Lewis continued his parade of experts, beginning the third week of the third trial, with the formidable Dr. Omar J. Masood, a man who looked like he meant business. There were frown lines stamped in his forehead and around his mouth, as you would expect to see on the face of man who witnessed death on a daily basis and still, always, had to keep wondering what happened and why.

Dr. Omar Masood had represented the Medical Examiner's office since 1979 and had performed thousands of autopsies. He had gone to school in Bombay, India, although he was a native of Pakistan. He had practiced as a pathologist in the United States for at least fifteen years and was fluent in English.

At 1:15 pm on October 7th, 1982 Dr. Masood identified the body lying on the table in the examining room as that of Bobby Mack Mitchell, III. Dr. Masood performed an external examination of the body and made several tests from internal specimens. He determined that the cause of Bobby's death was multiple blunt traumas to the head, a gunshot wound to the chest, and strangulation. He also concluded that the manner of death was homicide.

Prosecutor Lewis asked him if he would please tell the jury what wounds he found on the body.

Dr. Masood replied, "There were many lacerations, with three deep ones. One was on the left side of the midline, three and three-fourths inches from the top of the head. Another was behind the right ear. The third was under the chin." He went on to say that there was extensive hemorrhaging due to the fractures at the base of the skull.

"Did all of the lacerations hemorrhage?" Lewis asked.

"Yes, sir," Masood replied.

"Was the victim alive or dead when he suffered these lacerations?" Lewis asked.

"Alive, because the blood stops circulating at death and there would be no more hemorrhaging," Masood answered.

"What kind of instrument would have made these lacerations?" Lewis asked.

"A blunt one, like a rod or a bar," Masood said.

"Could the instrument have been a bat?" Lewis asked.

"Most definitely," Masood agreed.

Dr. Masood also described the multiple abrasions around Bobby's neck and the fracture of the thyroid cartilage. He said the abrasions and wounds in the neck showed manual strangulation. He testified that, since there were markings from what looked like "fingers working on the neck", the victim must have been strangled by someone's hands.

He also mentioned he found abrasions and excoriations on the hands and ecchymosis of the right orbit. He said he found the victim's fifth and sixth ribs had been severely traumatized. He testified there were several wounds on the body which the victim sustained after death.

Masood had measured the entry wound in the victim's chest as seventeen inches from the top of the head and testified that the point of entry was surrounded by an area of dense gunpowder

stippling about six inches in diameter. He traced the wound tract –
the path of the bullet – from the chest through the right lung and
out through the right chest wall. The bullet traveled front to back,
outward and upward. Dr. Masood testified that the exit wound was
two inches higher than the entry wound. He found 2,000 cubic
centimeters of blood stagnated in the body's right lung.

Dr. Masood testified that he found gunpowder stippling in the
chest area and on the side of the right leg, below the knee cap.
Masood had pulled the victim's knee toward the chest and traced
the pattern of stippling from the chest to the leg, which, he
concluded, occurred at the same time the bullet shot. He testified
that, from the pattern of the stippling, it was not possible for the
victim to have had both feet on the ground at the exact time the
gun fired. He cleverly suggested the path of the bullet and the
stippling was consistent with the victim being in a sitting or lying
position.

Lewis wanted to make sure the jury understood the importance of
Dr. Masood's testimony. "Then, are you suggesting that the victim
was lying down or sitting down at the time the gun went off?"
Lewis asked.

Dr. Masood looked at the jury and agreed with Lewis, "Yes, sir."
His large, dark brown eyes and stern gaze riveted the jury's
attention.

Lewis was not finished, though. "Were the decedent's arms raised
up in front of his body when the gun fired?" he asked.

"Dr. Masood replied, "I don't know, sir. They may have been. The
absence of stippling, gunpowder or soot on the area suggests that
they were not in the firing range."

Shit. Whether it was true or not – and, I knew it *not* to be – the jury
could now picture a scene where Noi surprised Bobby with a gun
pointed toward his chest as he lay on his back.

Lewis then asked, "Well, what kind of soot did you find on the victim's body?"

"None," Dr. Masood answered, "not even on the right lower leg that had been burned by gunpowder."

"What does the absence of soot mean to you, Dr. Masood?" Lewis inquired.

"Soot present on the body around the entry wound indicates the firing range is less than six inches," Dr. Masood explained. An absence of soot meant that the gun fired at Bobby from more than six inches away, which discredited Noi's story that the gun accidentally discharged when Bobby pulled on it.

Lewis asked, "Was there any soot on the hands of the body?"

On its face, this was a straightforward question; but this single question, in my mind, is the most telling question asked during the entire third trial. It's important because of *who asked the question* and in terms of *the expected answer.* A short time later, the hidden value of this question and testimony would become exposed. But for now, Prosecutor Lewis asked, "Was there any soot on the hands of the body?"

Dr. Masood replied, "No, there was no soot on the decedent's body."

"Did you determine the range from the muzzle of the gun to the entry wound of the body? Lewis asked.

"Less than seven feet," Masood replied.

Lewis then summed up, "Well, what was the cause of death?" Everyone in the courtroom, including the juror who had been scribbling his notes so fast and furiously, looked up, listened, and held their breath. It seemed to me that half the people in the courtroom were now leaning forward in their seats.

Dr. Masood answered, "The gunshot wound, strangulation, and the blows to the head, individually and in combination, killed the victim." Lewis sat down triumphantly. No one moved. Dr. Masood's testimony blew Noi's story to pieces. I could feel prickly goose-bumps rise, one by one, on my arms, even though the courtroom was stuffy and warm. The Prosecutors thought they had Noi convicted.

Dalton called a fifteen minute recess.

During the break, Dr. Masood approached me and asked if I would draw up an estate plan for his family. I needed the business; maybe Dr. Masood knew that, too. Maybe he felt sorry for me because he knew his testimony would shatter my whole defense strategy, but I didn't really think of that until later. At that moment, despite the fact that I needed the money, I was concerned about whether the promised fees would give the appearance that I would go easy on him during my cross-examination. Fortunately, I did not have time to give him an answer because the bailiff announced that the Judge was ready for my cross-examination to begin.

Despite Dr. Masood's extensive knowledge and experience testifying in court, he looked very nervous to me when I stood close to him as I began my cross-examination.

"About your theory that Bobby may have been choked, Doctor, did you find any petechia around his neck?" I asked.

"No," Dr. Masood admitted.

"What is petechia?" I asked him.

"It is a small amount of bleeding in the eyelids and windpipe caused by lack of oxygen," Masood explained.

"Would petechia appear only above the point of strangulation or pressure?" I asked.

"Yes, sir," he answered. "Any instrument or pressure on the blood vessels of the neck cause a backward engorgement within the veins, capillaries would break and there would be petechia."

"As a result of what?" I asked.

"Compression of the neck," he answered.

"Is there always petechia when there is strangulation?" I asked.

He refused to draw the conclusion that one did not occur without the other. I asked him to read from the most widely accepted medical textbook of the day which stated that there is always petechia when there is strangulation. Stubbornly, he refused to agree with the medical textbook.

"Isn't it possible for a sudden blow to crack the thyroid cartilage instead of strangulation?" I asked.

"Yes," he answered.

"Were the decedent's vocal cords damaged? I asked.

"No, sir," he answered.

"Was the trachea or windpipe damaged?"

"No, sir," he answered, again.

"What about the supposed path of the bullet? Did you know that Officer David Anderson discovered a bullet fragment in the chest of drawers and there was another one in the east wall, so there were two bullets fired from the gun?" I asked.

"No, sir," he responded, "I did not know that."

"Does this affect your guess about Bobby's position when the gun fired?"

"Yes, sir. The knee could have been burned by one of the shots and the chest by the other. I am not a ballistics expert," Dr. Masood said. He had seemed so certain, when questioned by Lewis, about the path of the bullet entering Bobby's chest. I now had the good doctor in a delicate position, but he was too much of a professional to strike back at me. He was nervous, sure, but did not appear to be upset.

"I want to discuss what you indicated earlier about not finding any soot on Bobby's hands," I began. "When you got the body, was it wrapped in a plastic bag?"

"No, sir," he replied, "the officers brought it in on a stretcher, covered by a blue blanket."

"What had been done to the body before you saw it?" I asked.

"The procedure is to wash it and refrigerate it until I can perform my tests," he replied.

Ah ha! You see, less than a week before the third trial began I was handed another *Godplop!* in the form of a hunch as I reviewed the preliminary information. Now, preliminary information is also known as the criminal complaint. I was studying the list of the State's endorsed witnesses when one name just jumped out at me… Deputy Sheriff Bob Westover… but he was not called to testify by Assistant D.A. Eddie Lewis. And that struck me as odd, very odd. As I said, *Godplop!*

Because of my unease, I drove out to Creek County, to Sapulpa, where Deputy Sheriff Westover was assigned, but he was not there. Unexpectedly, I found him in Bristow sitting behind the Sheriff's dispatcher's desk. Together we drove back to Sapulpa looking for his photos. We found them at the bottom of the twelfth and last evidence locker at the Sapulpa jail.

This was just three days before the beginning of the third trial. That's when I discovered that Creek County Deputy Sheriff Bob Westover had taken pictures of Bobby's hands, which clearly showed evidence of gunpowder and soot. The powder on Bobby's hands would substantiate Noi's testimony that Bobby had pulled on the gun. Before that time, I never could prove that there had been gunpowder on Bobby's hands *at all* when he died.

Creek County Chief Investigator Deputy Sheriff Bob Westover specifically placed the victim's hands in baggies and taped them shut to keep the soot from getting lost. That was standard – and proper – police procedure.

But I did not have this information before cross-examining Dr. Masood in the previous trials. Right here, in this discovery, was proof of both soot and another *Godplop!* I was so grateful and hoped blessings and great evidence would continue to find their way to me; still, living this way and trying to win a court case this way was unnerving.

Now, back to where we left off during my third trial cross-examination of the Oklahoma State Medical Examiner, Dr. Omar Masood.

"Dr. Masood, did you examine the blue blanket for soot?" I asked.

"Well, I did not test for it, but I always look over everything on the table with the body."

"Can soot rub off?" I asked.

"Yes," he replied, "easily."

"Did you run any microscopic tests to determine if there had been any soot on the decedent's hands at the time of death?"

"No."

"Then, you would really not know if there was soot on Bobby's hands or not?"

"No," he replied.

"Do you know in what order the victim suffered his injuries?"

"No, I have no way to determine that," he answered.

"Did the gunshot kill him immediately?"

"No," he answered.

"Could Bobby have remained conscious if he was shot first?" I asked.

"Yes, for a certain length of time."

"Would it be possible for the decedent to have run around inside the house after he was shot?"

"Yes, sir."

"Would it be possible for the decedent to have run around the outside of the house after he was shot?"

"That is correct, sir."

"Did all the lacerations cause hemorrhaging?" I asked.

"Yes," he answered.

Dr. Masood then explained that this meant all the lacerations were inflicted while Bobby was still alive. I asked him for more details about the post-mortem wounds. He told me that the wounds he referred to as post-mortem were superficial and could have been caused by dragging the body across a rough surface.

"Did you say earlier that the decedent had ecchymosis of the right orbit?" I asked him.

"Yes, sir," he replied.

"Just what does that mean to most of us?" I asked.

"It is commonly referred to as a black eye," he responded.

"Now, the excoriation, or abrasions, of the hands that you referred to, could they have been caused by fingers scratching him during a fight?" I asked.

Masood said that they could.

"Now, Dr. Masood, didn't Bobby bleed to death?"

"Yes, he did," Masood responded.

"By the way, did you take any photos of the hands BEFORE you washed them?" I inquired.

"No, but his hands were pristine clean, both before and after I washed them. I only took photos of his hands after washing them. There was no gun powder or soot on them."

Strangely enough, Dr. Masood never mentioned taking the baggies taped to the wrists off or testing them for gun powder or soot, and I had not yet discovered this fact until just *three days* before the third trial began. See how stressful a *Godplop!* can be? I'm still amazed my hair didn't all fall out before the end of the third trial.

I think it was significant that the Prosecutors gave the jurors three ways in which Bobby died so that they would have a choice. This would force Noi to defend all three methods of killing her husband.

Dr. Masood hurriedly left the witness stand and the courtroom after his testimony without once looking back at me. I never did do any estate planning for the doctor. I would have; I certainly needed the business, but he never called me.

CHAPTER 22 – THE *ALMOST* SUCCESSFUL MARCH OF THE WHORES

The next day was actually fun. I have always referred to the introduction of these next witnesses as the "March of the Whores," not because of their sexual activities – I didn't care about that – but because I felt they had prostituted themselves to the State of Oklahoma to get Noi convicted.

First, the State introduced Jenny Sanders, a dark-haired woman who was a little overweight and looked every bit her age of thirty-nine. Her face was weather-beaten from too much sun and there were deep crow's feet around her eyes. It didn't help that she wore quite a bit of pancake make-up, which seemed to accentuate the lines and wrinkles, creating deep and severe-looking crevasses in her face. It all served to give her a hard, tense look.

Carson began questioning her. "Miss Sanders, are you acquainted with Bobby Mitchell, III?"

"Yes," she replied, "I've known him since 1963. I was married to him."

"How long were you married to him?"

"I was married to him on two occasions. The first occasion was for a little over two years and the second occasion was approximately six years."

"How long did you know him before you married him?"

"Two years," she answered.

"Are you familiar with his tendency for violence?"

"He had none," she replied.

"Why do you say that?" Carson asked.

"Because he was very passive – virtually, a timid man," she replied.

"Did you and Bobby have any fights?" Carson asked.

"You bet," she replied.

"Was there any person who would start the fight?"

"Me, usually," she answered.

I nearly dropped my pen. I could see she was playing the heavy and building Bobby up as a mouse, not a man, just the opposite of his relationship with Noi.

"Can you think of any specific instances?" Carson asked.

"Yes, sir, I can think of three instances when we got into a physical situation."

"What were those, please?"

"The first would have been at a Christmas party early in our first marriage. We were both drinking; everyone at the party was, which was in our home, and we – well, one of the guests and I had been kind of going back and forth all evening."

"Is that arguing – in what sense?"

I jotted down in my notebook, "arguing – in what sense?" *Could it be that Bobby was jealous?*

Jenny then told the jury that Bobby had overheard what she said to the man and had misunderstood it. "He reached over and popped toward me to say hush. After I stomped out of the room, Bobby followed me and apologized."

I wrote down "popped toward me?" I bet he slapped the hell out of her like he had Noi. She was trying to make it sound like he swiped the air and had missed her.

She went on, "It really made him feel bad. That was all there was to it."

Carson continued his questioning, "Concerning his drinking, what kind of a drinker was he?"

"Only socially," she replied, "and, usually, very moderately." Again, she was trying to make him out to be an angel, one that didn't booze it up at home, only when partying.

Carson then asked her, "Would he ever get violent when he drank?"

"Never," she said.

"What about his work habits?"

"He worked long hours. He would work even when he didn't feel well. He was very dedicated to his job."

"Any particular reason why he would work such long hours? Did he enjoy it?" The patter between Carson and Jenny Sanders seemed, to me, to be well-rehearsed, painting Bobby as this hard-working, dedicated employee. Bobby's long working hours were supposed to be real working time and not used for whoring around town, which is what we knew to be true of him when he was married to Noi.

"What about the other two times when you got into a fight?" Carson asked.

"One of them was an occasion right after we had remarried and I had been nagging at him all morning. He reached over and grabbed me and told me to hush, that he was tired of hearing it."

"How did he grab you?"

"By both arms. As I remember, he yanked me up out of the chair and it flashed in my mind he might hit me. And, I dared him, 'Go ahead and hit me.' He left the room after that."

I'm betting he grabbed her by both arms as he had repeatedly done to Noi when he would grab her and shake her and throw her up against a wall.

"What about the third occasion?" Carson asked.

"The third occasion," Jenny Sanders replied, "was, again, when we were first married. We had an argument and I was going to leave the house. I said, 'I've had it and I'm not going to put up with it.' He reached to stop me and I whirled around and came back in the house and he, again, took both my arms like he was trying to get something through to me. He was trying to calm me down and talk to me and I was hysterical and just panicked and I hauled off and slapped him and his eyes got wide. He took a couple of steps back, turned around and went into the bedroom.

"I was shocked that I had ever struck him," she continued, "and, of course, went right behind him. He was so upset he got a nose bleed. He just couldn't take a lot of stress. He would go out of his way to avoid an argument."

Somehow, I felt that her testimony was helping my case more than hurting it at this point. Still, I knew I couldn't become complacent. Things can turn quickly in a courtroom.

"Would Bobby argue with you much?" Carson asked her.

"No. In fact, I said to him, on occasion, 'I wish you would fight back. I don't know how to talk to you because you won't argue back with me.' "

"Did he have a general way for you to resolve problems?" Carson asked.

"He'd get up and walk away."

Jenny went on to testify that Bobby was a loving man and children responded to his love. She also testified that Bobby had a great need for a child.

"We tried for seven years to start a family and I was not able to and had to have a hysterectomy. Knowing how much he wanted a family of his own and that he was not willing to adopt or... I left him because I just couldn't cope with it."

"Did you and Mr. Mitchell remain friends after your second divorce?" Carson then asked.

"Yes, we have."

"Had you ever seen or talked with each other after that?"

"Yes, we have. We had lunch on several occasions. I live out of the state now, he was there on business and once we had dinner when he was there. We talked on the phone every month or two, you know, just to say what's going on, how's your love life, and how's the job going."

"Was there any indication to you from the conversations after the divorce that he was changing?"

"No."

"Did you and he ever discuss Noi Mitchell?"

"Yes, we did."

"Did he tell you how he met her?"

"Yes, he did."

"How was that, please?" Carson asked her.

At this point, I stood and objected because what Bobby said to her would be considered as hearsay. The rules of evidence are designed to keep out evidence that distracts a jury rather than helping it to discover the truth. A trial is supposed to be a truth-finding process. The hearsay objection specifically keeps a witness from testifying to what someone else said to him out of court. This forces the State to bring in the person who actually made the statement. Opposing counsel can then cross-examine that witness. The jury members can then see for themselves what the witness is like and decide how valuable this testimony is by evaluating the biases, prejudices and credibility of the witness.

This hearsay objection is deeply ingrained in our Anglo-American judicial system. It originated in England in the sixteenth century due to public outrage when Sir Walter Raleigh was convicted for treason and, ultimately, beheaded. In that trial, the only evidence against Sir Walter Raleigh was a signed statement from a convicted traitor who was still jailed in the Tower of London. In a beautifully impassioned plea, Sir Walter Raleigh asked the court to bring this traitor before the court from his prison cell, which was only a hundred yards away, so that he could confront this man face to face with his accusations. The man was never brought to court. After Raleigh was beheaded, Parliament changed the law to eliminate this type of sham. A person accused has the right to look his accuser in the eye and face him.

Judge Dalton decided to ignore the hearsay rule. He must have been curious to hear what she had to say. Carson continued his line of questioning.

"How was that, please?" Carson asked her again

"Bobby told me a friend had arranged for Bobby and Noi to meet. She said Noi was working as a prostitute and Bobby's friend had hired her to provide sexual entertainment when he was there."

"When were you told this?" Carson asked.

"When Bobby called me from London," she replied. "I'm not sure of the exact date. It would have been, probably, sometime in early 1977. I'm guessing. Bobby had been to Indonesia and had met her on the way. He had finished his job there and had gone back to London where he had, like, six weeks, I believe, of vacation time coming. And he called me and said he needed advice. He had met this girl and had been totally captivated by her child and by her. He wanted to try and make arrangements for them to come to the United States. I said, 'Well, what are your alternatives? How did you meet her?'... these types of questions. He explained how he met her and told me..."

I interrupted at that point to make a continuing objection to the hearsay statements. I was furious at the Prosecutor for stooping to these tactics and upset with Dalton for allowing them to continue.

"Overruled," said Dalton. His ears perked up and he leaned forward in his chair, like he was anxious to hear the more titillating parts of this testimony.

"Continue," Carson coaxed Jenny Sanders.

"He was trying to decide about bringing her home and I suggested that he tour Europe and use his vacation, then see how he felt. We talked at length about it.

I suggested to him that I didn't understand how he thought he could introduce her to his family and asked if he would just try to keep it a secret? He couldn't decide exactly what to do. Could he bring the child without Noi? He felt he could not, that Noi would not release the child to him because she wanted to come, as well." She kept talking. "I asked him, 'Is there no arrangement that you can make?' He said there was none."

"Okay," Carson said. "Now, when he came out to California, I think you said, on business once?"

"Yes."

"You had dinner with him?"

"Yes."

"Did you have some conversation about how things were going with him then?"

"Yes. He told me that he was a little disillusioned."

"Was Noi here in the States?"

"Yes. They were married by that time."

"Was there anything untoward about your meeting him there for dinner?"

I jotted down "untoward?" *Did that mean an unlawful assignation or illegal sexual affair?* I had never heard the term "untoward" used like that before.

"That was just normal for you all, right?" Carson asked.

"Yes."

I guess she was saying it was normal for him, as a married man, to take her out to eat without expecting sexual favors in return.

"What kind of conversation did you have about her then?" Carson wanted to know.

By this time, I was becoming upset and adamantly objected. The Judge finally agreed with me. He must have realized he had allowed Carson to go too far.

"Did he give you any indication of a violent temper?" Carson asked.

"Bobby told me they fought quite a bit and one day, when they were fighting, Noi grabbed a knife and threatened him, and then, attacked him with it. I don't remember if he said she threw it at him or came at him with it. My reaction was to wonder why in the world was he still there. He told me there was a child he had to take care of."

"Thank you," Carson ended the examination.

I looked at my jury. Her testimony was definitely making an impression, but, for the life of me, I couldn't be sure of exactly what it was.

Now, it was my turn to attempt to expose her bias and to attack her credibility. Sometimes, you can't make opposing counsel stop using unfair tactics in court, but you can, sure as heck, make him wish he'd never started it.

"Is it Miss or Mrs.?" I cautiously began.

"Mrs."

"I assume that Bobby loved prostitutes so much that you were one when he married you, is that right?" There was a concerted gasp throughout the courtroom. It was hard for me not to smile. Lewis put his head in his hands. Dalton's bushy eyebrows shot way up. Noi's friends giggled quietly among themselves and gave each other looks, which promised they'd be laughing over this one many times to come. The Mitchells were stunned. I know Carson thought I was acting like a mad dog. His mouth opened so wide he looked like a gaping carp. He leapt to his feet and threw his pen down on the table. "Oh, Good Lord, Judge, I'm going to object to that!!"

Dalton recovered and said, "Sustained."

"Were you a prostitute when he married you?" I asked Jenny Sanders.

"No, sir," she replied in mock disgust. Her rough voice became even rougher, it seemed. She looked like she was about to blow a cork or throw a temper tantrum. I don't blame her for that. I had started off by insulting her, but I needed to let her and the prosecutors know I wasn't going to let their damaging descriptions of Noi go unchallenged. Besides, I wanted to even the score.

To be sure, it was both immature of me and borderline unprofessional to ask this type of question. I regret having done so and apologize to Mrs. Sanders and ask for her forgiveness. It is not my style to act this way and I am so sorry for any pain I caused you. The same goes for the next question.

Here's the problem a trial lawyer faces. He hears something damaging to his client in court and has to make a spur of the moment decision: How to respond when the other side makes a vicious attack and gets it into evidence when you believe it to be untrue in the first place and not relevant in the second place and highly inflammatory in every place? The appellate courts have a system when the scales of justice get tipped too far over; especially when it's due to a lawyer's misconduct. They allow the wronged lawyer to use self-help to cure – to even – the score. Even if it means the trial takes on the ambience of a dirty bare knuckles brawl, a lawyer can use words to equalize the playing field.

"Were you a prostitute who'd had venereal disease when you had your hysterectomy?"

Carson jumped to his feet and objected in a loud and angry voice and declared, "I've had enough!"

Dalton, of course, sustained his objection. However, he recognized he had allowed the prosecutors to commit an error in the first place and I had gotten more than even. But, enough was enough. He now had to solve the very problem he helped create, by doing the only fair thing he could. He admonished the jury not to consider the testimony about Noi's having been a prostitute and told them that this was hearsay. He admitted, "I should never have allowed it in the first place."

Judge Dalton then asked the jury, "Do you understand? Will you tell me at this time you'll not concern yourselves with any of this prostitution business at all in this case?" All of the jurors nodded their heads.

Satisfied with this response, Dalton looked at me and said, "Very well. You may continue."

The problem with telling a jury something like this is that the information is already in their heads; it can't be eliminated just because someone tells them to forget all about it. That's like telling someone, "Don't think about pink elephants. Now, think about elephants. What color are they?" Well, they are pink, of course.

I responded to the court's instructions, "In that regard, I'm afraid, independently of the court's admonishment – and I appreciate and can trust the jury – but, independently, for the preservation of the record, we move for a mistrial. We're afraid that the court's admonishment would not properly cure such a blatant error."

The Judge overruled my motion for a mistrial and, again, admonished the jurors not to consider the issue of prostitution. I was then allowed to continue my questioning of Jenny.

"Since your arrival here from out of state, have you stayed over at Mr. Mitchell's residence?"

"No, I have not," she replied, indignantly, as she leaned back.

"Who are you staying with?" I asked.

"My mother."

"You're aware, are you not, that Mr. Mitchell, Bobby's father, is a multi-millionaire?"

"No, sir, I am not."

Carson objected. "That has nothing to do with anything," he whined.

The Judge sustained the objection.

I continued, "When you said Bobby slapped you, how many people were in front of you when he slapped you?" Earlier, she had said that he "popped toward her" and I interpreted that to mean that he had slapped her. Her instant answer proved my hunch was right.

"One that I can remember," she then added, "maybe two."

"At a party?" I wanted to show that he would slap women around, even in public, which would mean that maybe Bobby wasn't the sweet and shy guy she'd been trying to make him out to be.

"Yeah," she said, but she was becoming more abrupt and I noticed beads of perspiration dotting her upper lip, just resting there, like little raindrops atop that thick and goopy layer of pancake make-up on her face.

"Do you remember his face turning red just before he slapped you?" Noi said he always would get red in the face just before he slapped her around.

"No," she replied.

"When was your last divorce from him?"

"1974."

"And, when was your first marriage to him?"

"1965."

"And, the first marriage ending in a divorce was when?"

"1978."

"Your first marriage ended what year?"

"I meant 1968. Excuse me."

"All right. Now, during the time you were married to Bobby, did you observe him smoking marijuana?"

Carson quickly objected and the judge overruled his objection. Jenny answered, "No, sir."

"Did you observe him shooting cocaine?"

"No, sir."

"Alcoholic is the only thing you observed him doing?" This was an intentional twist on the word *alcohol*, which I wanted to plant in the minds of the jurors, that Bobby was an alcoholic, a raging and violent alcoholic.

"Yes, sir."

"Do you recall what year it was when he grabbed you by both arms and yanked you around?"

"It was probably 1965, the first year we were married."

"Did you feel you deserved that?"

"Yeah."

"When was your last association with Bobby Mitchell?"

"The last time I talked with him was probably four or five months before he was killed."

"When was the last time you saw him?" I asked.

"Sometime in, I think it was, December of 1980."

"And, he came to you?"

"He went to California; he was in California."

"And, where do you live now?"

"California."

"I have no other questions," I said.

Judge Dalton allowed the prosecution to call the next witness, Jackie White. She was quite pretty: petite, yet buxom, red-headed with a fair complexion and turned-up nose and big, blue eyes. She dressed conservatively and looked every bit like a sweet, wholesome school teacher, right down to the low-heeled brown pumps she wore. Lewis began the questioning.

"When were you contacted to testify in this case?" he asked.

"Last night," she replied.

"Did you know Bobby Mack Mitchell, III?"

"Since I was a senior in high school."

"Now, ma'am, at that time when you were a senior in high school, what was your relationship to Bobby?"

"Friend."

"Did, at any point after that, your relationship become closer to him?"

"Yes."

"At what point of time was that, please, ma'am?"

"1975, at the beginning of 1975."

"Can you briefly describe the relationship?"

"We started dating in December of 1974, and continued dating until July of 1975, and then we started living together."

"How long, please, ma'am, did you live with him?"

"Two years."

"Did Bobby ever have any occasion to use physical violence upon you?"

"Huh-uh," she replied, shaking her head *no*.

"Please describe Bobby."

Jackie White replied, "Well, he was a hard worker. I remember that about him - always concerned with how well he was doing his job. So, I guess I would say he was a very conscientious person, especially when it came to his work."

"Did he ever mention his time in Thailand?"

"Well, when he got back from overseas, he told me he was going to bring her..." she nodded to Noi; "... over here and, the best I can remember, he called me the night before she got in."

I stood up and said, "We object because Counsel has been admonished here." I didn't want them to go back into slandering Noi again by talking about prostitution. She was never a prostitute.

"I'll sustain the objection," Judge Dalton properly ruled.

"Please, ma'am," Lewis continued, "did you ever have an occasion to interact with Bobby after Noi came to this country?"

"No."

"Thank you. Now, ma'am, do you have an opinion as to Bobby's violent tendencies, or lack thereof?"

"Well, he didn't have any that I knew of."

"That's all; thank you," Lewis concluded.

Now, it was my turn to cross-examine her and I began.

"How many times have *you* been married?" I asked this question a little sarcastically; I know, but there was a reason for it. I wanted to show the jury that hardly anyone is a true expert on relationships; that people are all different and respond differently to each other, and that response is often based on their own background, personalities and proclivities.

I did not hear her answer; it didn't matter; I just pressed on.

"Did you consider yourself as being common-law married to Bobby?"

"No way!" she said emphatically.

"Do you have any children by Bobby?"

"No."

"Now, ma'am, would you please tell the ladies and gentlemen of the jury about your educational background."

"Objection; it is irrelevant and immaterial what her educational background is," Lewis complained.

"Overruled."

"My education?" she asked.

"Yes, ma'am."

"I graduated from high school, have gone to keypunch school, and I'm currently attending Tulsa Junior College."

"What is your occupation or vocation?"

"I work for an independent oil company. I do the payroll, operate the computer, and I help with accounting."

"Ma'am, do you consider yourself to be a rather strong-willed person?"

"At times."

"And assertive?"

"Not especially, no."

"I mean, you wouldn't let anybody walk over you, would you?" When Noi was pregnant, Bobby – literally – walked and stomped on her in his attempt to degrade her. Sometimes he would put his feet on her head to really insult her.

"No way."

"And, you would tell them, in fact, that 'Nobody is going to walk over me!' "

"Yeah."

"Do you know about the meek and timid personality traits of Noi Mitchell?"

"I don't even know her."

"Have you ever met her before today?"

"No."

"Now, ma'am, do you understand some people aren't as strong as you?" Do you understand that? Some women are not assertive and strong."

"Objection as being irrelevant," Lewis said.

"Overruled," Dalton replied.

She just looked at me, wide-eyed.

"You may answer," I said.

"Yes," she replied.

"Would you characterize your relationship with Bobby, during your two years of association or living arrangement, as a good, harmonious relationship?"

"Yes."

"You weren't married to anyone else at the time during that arrangement, were you?"

"No."

"So, you were free to marry him if you had chosen to do so?"

"Yes."

"And, he was legally free to marry you?"

"Yes," she continued in her quiet, patient voice.

"Thank you very much," I said. "Your Honor, I have no further questions." I theorized: *If Bobby was such a sweet and nice gentleman, then, why didn't she marry him? And, if he was the kind of guy who, as his cousin had implied, wanted to do the right thing, why hadn't Bobby married her?* I decided to trust the jurors and let them draw their own conclusions about Jackie White's "harmonious relationship" with Bobby.

"You may step down," Judge Dalton said to Ms. White. "Thank you."

Lewis announced, "Your Honor, at this time, the State will call Theresa McComb to the stand."

Theresa, a tall blonde, made a striking picture with her extremely shapely figure wrapped in a tight-fitting red dress. On closer scrutiny, however, I noticed she looked a little like an aging showgirl, like she'd been "rode hard and put up wet," as ranchers in Oklahoma would say.

"Ma'am," Lewis began, "did you know a man named Bobby Mack Mitchell, III?"

236

"Yes, I did," Theresa replied.

"How long did you know this person?"

"Since 1976."

"Please, ma'am, at that time, what was your relationship with him?"

"I worked with him."

"Did your relationship ever change?" I assumed what Lewis really wanted to ask her was when she started having sex with Bobby. Lewis was always so polite.

"Yes, it did."

"Could you describe that change, please, ma'am?"

"In 1977, we became very close friends." She made it seem so natural that close friends always have sex with each other.

"And, did you have occasion to date Bobby at that time?"

"Yes, I did."

"Thank you very much, ma'am. Now, ma'am, did you ever have occasion to meet a woman known to you now as Noi Kanchana Mitchell?"

"Yes, sir."

"Is that person present in the courtroom at this time?"

"Yes, sir," Theresa said, narrowing her eyes at Noi. Her eyeballs disappeared, actually, as she rendered them into tiny slits to show her disdain for the defendant.

"Judge," I offered, "we stipulate that Noi Kanchana Mitchell is present and that the witness can identify Noi."

"Very well," Dalton said.

"Ma'am," Lewis asked, "did you ever have occasion to interact with Noi?"

"Could you rephrase that?" the confused witness asked.

"Did you ever have occasion to interact, to associate, with Noi Mitchell?"

"Yes, I did."

"Were you present at a Christmas party that Noi and Bobby attended?"

"Yes, I was."

"Who were you there with, please ma'am?"

"My fiancé."

"What is his name?"

"Leo."

"Ma'am, could you describe the set of circumstances which occurred there in reference to the winner of a prize?"

"Yes," Theresa said, "there were papers stuck under the chairs, and you were to pull them out, and whoever's number matched the centerpiece won it. Bobby won the centerpiece."

"What, if anything, at that point in time, occurred?"

"At that point in time, the party wasn't over, but, at the end of the party, they were to take the centerpiece home."

"Did someone, in fact, go over and pick up that centerpiece?"

"No. Bobby turned around to get the centerpiece to give to Noi and she just went into a rage right there."

"Could you describe that, please, ma'am?"

"I could not understand what she was saying because she spoke in Thai. She went into a rage, and then Bobby pushed the centerpiece towards me."

"Did he ever actually give you that centerpiece?"

"No, sir."

"What, if anything, did you do when he pushed the centerpiece towards you?"

"I backed away."

"What, if anything, occurred next?"

"After that, Noi went into the restroom. My fiancé and Bobby and two other couples went into the foyer to get their coats and I sat on a chair, waiting. Noi came out of the restroom and started hollering and yelling at me."

"What was she saying, at that point in time, if you remember?"

"I cannot tell you because she was just raging."

"Ma'am," Lewis asked, "had you done anything whatsoever to provoke this ranting and raving on the part of Noi?"

"No, sir," Theresa cooed, as if to say, *Heaven forbid.*

"Had Bobby done anything whatsoever to provoke this rage?"

"No, sir."

"Ma'am, what, if anything, did you say or do when Mrs. Mitchell started hollering at you?"

"I said, 'We're not going to stand out here,' and I took her by the arm and led her into the restroom.

"Now, ma'am, what, if anything, did Bobby do when Noi started hollering at him at the table earlier when he pushed the centerpiece towards you?"

"He looked very embarrassed."

"Did he say anything to Noi whatsoever?"

"He said, 'Shoo!' "

"Did he raise his arm?"

"No."

"What occurred after you took Noi into the bathroom?"

"I told her Bobby had brought her over from Thailand because he loved her very, very much and that I was engaged to marry my fiancé. The basis of our whole conversation was how much Bobby loved her and that he had brought her over here because he loved her and that he did not love me, he loved her." Theresa seemed pleased and proud of her pep talk with Noi. She sat up a little taller and puffed out her chest. She also swayed very slightly in the witness chair as she spoke, back and forth, as if she were hypnotizing the jury with the movement of her body, like a cobra. It was a little spooky. *Did she mean to be doing that? I don't know.*

"Thank you very much," Lewis said. "Now, ma'am, do you recall when Noi initially came to the United States?"

"In 1978."

"Did you have occasion, please, ma'am, to spend any time with her when she initially came to the States?"

"Yes. I met her one day that week and then I spent a week with her the following week."

"And, where was Bobby when you spent the week with Noi?"

"In Houston."

"Thank you very much," Lewis said. "Now, ma'am, during that period of time, did you have occasion, during the period you spent a week with her, to have a conversation with Noi?"

Bobby asked Theresa to teach Noi how to cook the American dishes he liked, while he was in Houston. Noi was eager to learn and wanted to cook things that would make Bobby happy.

"Yes, I did," Theresa replied. "I visited her every day."

"Now, ma'am, how long, in terms of years, did you interact with Noi, if you can estimate for us, please?"

"1978 at the Christmas party was the last time I saw her."

"How far do you live in Broken Arrow from the Mitchell household?"

"I live on one intersection corner and they live on the other intersection corner."

"So, you live directly across the intersection, diagonally?"

"Uh-huh." She nodded *yes*.

"Now, ma'am, can you see the Mitchell household from your front yard?"

"No, sir."

"Can you see the Mitchell household from your house?"

"No, sir."

"If you walk out into your yard, can you see the Mitchell household?" It was obvious to me that Lewis was unfamiliar with the area. Theresa actually lived one short half-block up, only two houses down and around the corner from Noi's house. Theresa's home faced a different direction from Noi and Bobby's; theirs faced south and hers faced west.

"No, sir," she replied.

Since I knew her home location, too, I knew this was untrue. Standing at any point on her lot you can see the Mitchell home. *Why is she lying about a physical fact? And why would Lewis even ask?*

"Are you within earshot of the Mitchell household?"

"No, sir."

"Now, ma'am, did you ever have occasion to hear unusual noises at the Mitchell household?"

Dalton spoke up then. "I'll sustain the objection, the continuing objection, to hearsay, I assume," he said, trying to keep out any more appealable errors. Maybe he was trying to help me out when I should be objecting. Either way, I appreciated him doing that.

"Yes, Your Honor," I said.

"It will be sustained," he said.

Lewis then jumped back in. "Ma'am," he asked, "do you know what Noi's reputation for peacefulness is in the community?"

"No," Theresa replied, "I don't."

"Was Bobby ever physically violent towards you, please, ma'am?"

"No, sir."

"Ma'am, can you tell me what you opinion is as to Bobby's reputation for peacefulness?"

"He wouldn't hurt a fly."

Wait a minute! I thought. *Isn't that a line directly out of the movie, Psycho, 1960?*

She added, "He was very calm, very sweet." When she said 'sweet', it seemed syrupy-thick and unnatural, somehow.

"Thank you very much, ma'am," Lewis said. "I pass the witness now."

It was my turn to cross-examine this witness. I slowly stood and walked to a spot about eight feet in front of her, very close to the jury, because I wanted them to concentrate on me and not on Theresa. I began.

"How many times have *you* been married?" I asked this in a bored-sounding voice, like, *here we go again*.

"Three," she answered.

"And, when was the first time?"

"1961."

"And, who were you married to then?"

"Jeff Neal."

"And, when did this marriage end?"

"1966."

"And, when was your second marriage?"

"I believe it was 1967."

"And, who was that to?"

"Jay Millman."

"When did that marriage end in divorce?"

"I'm not sure," Theresa said, "I cannot give you the year, the date."

"All right," I replied. "When was your third marriage?"

"1979."

"That was Leo McComb?"

"Yes."

"And, when did he divorce you?" Notice how I pointed out who divorced whom? I was hoping the jury noticed that, too.

"1981."

"And, he divorced you because of your affair with Bobby?"

"No, sir."

"He never found out about it?" I asked this with raised eyebrows. A male juror in the first row now looked at Theresa in disgust.

"I divorced *him*," she said, emphatically. I noticed that Theresa's story was changing a little and that she was evading my question.

"And, what was the time span you were married to Leo McComb but were having an affair with Bobby?"

"I was not having an affair with Bobby when I was married to Leo," she replied. She looked huffy, indignant, like she'd been insulted to the deepest degree.

"When was your divorce to Leo McComb?"

"May, 1981."

"When did your affair begin with Bobby?"

"Two or three months before he was *murdered.*" She tried to harpoon me by telling the jury that Bobby had been murdered. *Cheap shot.*

"You were there," I asked, "on the night of the fight between Noi and Bobby, were you?" I wanted the jury to understand that the only way she could say Bobby was unlawfully killed – *murdered* – was if she had actually seen it herself.

"I don't understand the question."

"You weren't present on the night they had the fight, were you?" I wanted the jury to see she was really showing her bias against Noi by saying "murdered" and had no basis of knowledge for her statement.

"No."

"Hmm," I waited a beat to let it land and then changed direction. "Did you ask at the Christmas party if Noi hated you?"

"No, sir."

"You don't recall asking her that?"

"I did not ask her that."

"Did you ask her if she didn't like you?"

"No, sir," she replied.

"You knew she was upset with you, didn't you?"

You could hear a pin drop in the courtroom even though the gallery was busting at the seams and there was standing room only with people packed in like a Tokyo subway train.

"I knew she was upset with something."

"You say Bobby was very sweet to you?" I began to hammer away at her, and I wasn't going to let up, either. *Jab.*

"Yes."

"Do you think it was very sweet of him to have an affair with you while he was still married to Noi?" My questions flew at her like left jabs, over and over again... *jab... jab...*

"Bobby was very sweet to Noi," she protested. "He gave her everything she ever wanted."

"Was that being sweet to her?" *Jab.*

"To give her what she wanted?" She asked. "Yes."

"*Did she want him to have an affair with you?*" BOOM! *Knock-out punch.*

"Objection, Your Honor!" Lewis sputtered. "This witness can't respond..." What he was really saying was, *'Call him off, Judge. He's like a mad dog!'*

Judge Dalton, however, wisely said, "Overruled."

Theresa McComb just sat there with her mouth gaping open like she'd just been doused with cold water. I looked at her and after a long awkward pause, said, "You don't have to answer. That's all the questions I have." She hunched her shoulders and slumped down a few inches.

The courtroom was buzzing, like there was an electric current running through the room. I was pretty buzzed, too. The term "emotional high" doesn't come anywhere close to the feeling I had. *Wow.*

Judge Dalton called it a day after the three women had testified. I could hear laughter ringing down the hallway. People had gathered in small groups and were talking excitedly, many using large hand gestures. The hallways in the courthouse are usually sterile, quiet and restricted, like a hospital corridor. Dick Hynd, my friend who was looking after Noi's children and who had gotten me started on all this, walked up to me and shook my hand. He said, "It's great fun to join the ranks of trial lawyers, isn't it, Jim?"

Rex and several other people congratulated me on my "courtroom flair." I was pumped up and feeling good, no doubt about it.

Ray Manning, the Deputy Sheriff who escorted Noi back to the Tulsa County Jail, was especially friendly to me that evening. I think Ray usually pulled for the underdog in these court fights, especially if it was an underdog he liked.

When Rex and I got home from court that day, we were slapping our sides and almost falling over from laughing so hard. Buddy ran up to me from his spot at the garage door and said, "What's so funny, Daddy?"

"Well, son," I said, "the prosecutors sent their best guys to get Noi, but we attacked them and got them instead."

"Oh, I get it, Daddy. It's kind of like checkers, isn't it? They made a sacrifice play and sacrificed some of their best guys when they tried to get her." My son is almost spooky smart sometimes, like his Mom. Buddy understood advanced checkers strategies since we studied the various moves from books and he was just a tiny boy, only barely older than a toddler. I've always been astonished at how beautifully his brain works.

"Yeah," I told him, "that's kind of what happened, son." I hoped this was how the jury saw it, too. Buddy walked over and picked up his kite from the living room floor, the one I had promised to help him put together, but never got around to it. He looked at me sweetly and said, "Daddy, tomorrow twist them in the wind."

"OK," I replied, "I will do my best son."

I hoped the prosecution had not had as much fun as I had. At least, maybe the jury had been entertained and would be in a receptive mood when I began presenting my case the next day.

Weeks later, when the case was over, I would talk with the jurors about how the "March of the Whores" affected their decision. This was an important way to gain insight. To win a case, a lawyer really needs to perceive his case through the jurors' eyes. Gerry Spence taught me to always ask someone I trust, "W.G.O.?" This means, "What's going on in the courtroom?"

I could not wait to ask the jurors about the particular testimony where Jenny claimed that Bobby had said Noi was a prostitute. I wanted to know how that testimony had affected their decision, and in what way, if it had any impact. After the trial, one woman, a doctor's wife, asked me to come by and visit. She told me that this testimony had made no difference whatsoever. On the contrary, she and all the other jurors had *always* thought Noi was a prostitute. Most of them were aware of the sex trade industry in Thailand and they were sympathetic to a young woman there needing to do what she had to in order to get by.

I was blown away by this information – it was the last thing I had expected! The assumption the jury had made never crossed my mind. I am now thankful I was not aware of their feelings toward Noi during the trial.

CHAPTER 23 – *ALMOST* HUMAN

I began to present my witnesses for Noi's defense and, oddly enough, my first witness was Noi, herself.

The courtroom was packed, but still, it was hushed. There was a current of anticipation in the room, a poised tension like everyone in the courtroom had taken a big breath and were about to explode into action. This was a pivotal moment. We all sensed it.

I remember asking the prospective jurors during jury selection for a show of hands to vote on whether or not they felt Noi should testify in her own defense.

"Folks," I told them, "I feel like I am between a rock and a hard place. I need to know something. If my client exercises her Fifth Amendment right and doesn't testify, I'm afraid you'll feel that she's guilty. If she does testify, I'm afraid that you'll think she's lying just to save her own hide. How many of you – deep down inside – would want to hear Noi's side of what happened without her hiding behind the Fifth Amendment?"

They looked at each other, with uncertainty, and, then, one by one, hesitantly, raised their hands. It was unanimous vote. They all wanted to hear Noi's side of the story. I had tried to explain to Noi that she was not required to take the stand and testify and that the Fifth Amendment to the United States Constitution protected an accused from testifying. A criminal defendant cannot be forced by the State to take the stand. It's how our judicial system is set up. Noi would be waiving her Fifth Amendment rights when she took the stand. Never mind that she didn't understand what waiving her Fifth Amendment rights actually meant; she only knew that she would have to talk to the jury.

I had reminded the jury that it was the prosecutor's burden to prove Noi was guilty beyond a reasonable doubt. The law does not require the accused to put on a defense at all. However, in reality, I knew that most people consider a person to be guilty as charged. After all, most people trust the Police to be honest and competent. *Why else would the police charge a person with a crime, if they weren't guilty?* That's how most people think.

I acted as if Noi's decision to take the stand was the jury's idea. I had put the responsibility on their shoulders and it greatly sparked their interest. Three weeks earlier, when the jury had voted for Noi to testify, I had made a pact with them that she would tell her story. So, this was the big moment. The question in my head was: *the jury is ready, but am I?*

Noi was sitting at the table in front of the jury on the south side of the room behind the prosecutor's table. She always looked down at her hands in front of her. I could see that her fingernails were bitten down to the quick. She was wearing Nancy's navy blue suit and a pink, Oxford cloth shirt. Matching navy blue pumps completed her outfit. I wanted to give the jury the impression that Noi was a conservative and sharp dresser, just as they were.

Before the very first trial, I rummaged through Noi's closet to see which outfits she would wear to court. All she had were bright red and mustard-yellow silk-type dresses with large slits up the side or back. These would never do! These clothes were not appropriate for a murder trial in Oklahoma, not in any courtroom in America that I could think of. I did not feel that an accused killer should ever wear red and I knew a slitted dress in court would send absolutely the wrong message. It was clear that she needed different clothes and I was afraid I would have to spend more money to buy a suitable middle class-type wardrobe for her.

Nancy decided to lend Noi some of her clothes to wear to court. By sheer luck, Noi wore the same size as Nancy, even though Noi was a little smaller in the waist and hips. Lending Noi her clothes was a big deal to Nancy. Even though my wife was not at all happy I had taken this case, spent so much time on it, and spent most of our money helping Noi in such a personal way, this was an important contribution to helping me defend Noi in this murder case. I'm sure if I talked from now to the end of time, I could never make Nancy understand how grateful I was for that kind gesture.

Nancy was a Certified Public Accountant at that time and proud of her career. She dressed very professionally in tailored business suits of demure colors and styles. They were perfect for a court appearance. I took Noi a fresh change of clothes to her jail cell each morning of every trial. I remember the very first time I brought her Nancy's clothes. Noi asked, "Where my clothes?"

I said, "They aren't right for the courtroom. Nancy is letting you use hers."

Two days later, Noi used the telephone at the jail to call Nancy. Noi was crying and saying she did not like Nancy's clothes, that they were ugly. Her new "friends" at the jail were saying they would never wear anything that drab-looking to court. Of course, Nancy flared up like a firecracker, as you might imagine, turned around and thrust the phone at me, like a sword. I don't doubt that, if the phone had been a knife in Nancy's hand at that moment, she would have plunged it straight into my chest, splaying me open like a ripe melon, that's how pissed she was at me, at Noi, at this whole mess I'd dragged us all into.

I don't think my wife was ever able to forgive Noi for refusing what Nancy considered to be a very personal and generous gift. I got on the phone and lost my temper with Noi for the first time. I told her she had to wear suitable clothes for the jury and it didn't matter that Bobby had liked her clothes. Noi probably did not understand what I was saying, but she did understand my anger. She just sobbed and whimpered into the phone like a child and did not respond.

Noi came to court that next morning with her shoulders slumped forward, looking so awkward and uncomfortable in the borrowed clothes. Still, I was very relieved to see her wearing them. I hoped they would make a big difference in how the jury perceived her and, eventually – hopefully – in how she perceived herself.

By this time of the third trial, several of her jail and Thai friends had complimented her on her new look. It seemed she liked the impression she was making and began liking herself better, too. She even sat up straighter.

In fact, I thought it was funny when Noi gave one of Nancy's favorite navy skirts to a jail buddy of hers because the friend said she liked it and asked for it. Nancy wasn't too pleased about that one, even when I tried to explain Noi's pathetic need to be liked by everyone. In everybody else's world, the real world, including Nancy's, you don't give away something you have borrowed from someone else no matter how huge your need to be liked may be. It's just not done – everybody knows that. Except Noi, of course.

October is a crisp month in Oklahoma, usually. The hazy heat and humidity of summer, especially in Tulsa, which makes it feel as if you are breathing through a sponge, have lifted and the sky looks brighter. The air smells cleaner. It smells like hope, to me. Summers in Oklahoma can be relentless, starting way too soon and dragging on through most of September. Just when you're sure you can't take any more of the heat and humidity, almost suddenly, in flies October like the flashy cousin who cruises in once a year to visit, with its clear skies and bright colors of leaves beginning to turn. It always makes me feel hopeful. On this October morning when Noi was to testify, however, the morning dawned hot and hazy, too hot for this time of year. October had thrown me a curve. The early hours were quite still and humid; there was a sensation that a storm was building.

Noi looked serene, like an angel. She was especially pretty in Nancy's navy blue and pink and looked like she couldn't harm a fly. A co-employee of Noi's once told me that, whenever Noi was asked to kill a fly or bug at the restaurant where the two of them worked, she would always refuse to do so. She would say, "It's only a baby, don't hurt him." *How could she have done all those terrible things to*

252

Bobby?" That's the question I kept asking myself. That's the question I had to answer in the jury's minds.

Noi kept her hair long and parted down the middle. It hung down her back like a dark waterfall. Since she had not been outside in the sunlight for over a year, her skin was bleached out and almost white, which was enough to give her an exotic look when contrasted with her dark eyes and coal-black hair. When she was not looking straight downward, her eyes darted around all over the room. This worried me. I was afraid this scared-rabbit look would make the jury distrust her. I wanted the jury to see her like I did, as someone kind and timid who operated out of fear and concern for the safety and well-being of her children as well as herself.

Noi and I both sensed that her testimony would be the final act in this drama. There was a keen sense of finality. Like a bell once rung that can never be unrung, I knew the case would hinge on whether the jury liked Noi enough to believe her.

When Noi settled into her wooden chair on the witness stand, I asked a series of questions designed to allow the jury to get to know her as a human being with feelings and responses like theirs. I wanted them to form a common bond.

"Noi?" I asked in a quiet, almost intimate voice.

"Yes, sir," she responded.

"You understand you have to tell the jury what happened that terrible night."

"Yes, sir."

"You understand the jury is here to help us find the truth together."

"Yes, sir."

"You understand that nobody in this room will hurt you for telling us the truth. You understand that?"

"Yes, sir."

"How do you feel about being here?"

"I am scared."

"What are you afraid of, Noi?"

Carson vaulted to his feet. He towered over me by about eight inches. He liked being on his feet, stretching out his body, as if to show me he was the stronger man. The Thai support group that showed up every day called him "Skunk" because of the peculiar ball-shaped white patch on the back of his head of dark-brown hair. This was his trademark. A lawyer friend of mine heard that classmates of Carson' in elementary school had called him "bird shit" because of that white spot on his head. *Admittedly, it was hard to not think of bird shit whenever I saw it... or, skunk... both of those names made me feel better when I felt he was trying to intimidate me.*

Carson said, "Objection, Your Honor." I expected that one and Judge Dalton sustained the objection. Noi would not be allowed to answer my question. My stubbornness, however, forced me on. "You understand," I said, "that nobody, including Mr. Carson, is going to hurt you?"

"Objection, Your Honor," Carson said, again.

"Sustained," replied Judge Dalton.

Carson and Dalton both thought I was trying to appeal to the jury's sympathy and I'm sure they were right about that. I'd go after that any chance I got.

"Noi," I continued, "do you understand that nobody in this courtroom, including Mr. Carson and the jury, nobody in this courtroom wants to hurt you? You can trust us. Do you understand trust?"

"Yes, sir."

It was important that the jury understand her fears, but it was more important that they understand that she and I trusted *them*, because in the process of seeing us give them our trust, they would give us theirs.

I next asked Noi about her childhood. I wanted the jurors to see her as a little girl living on a farm in Thailand with her parents, her two brothers and three sisters, a regular family. I tried to draw out some common experiences that she might have with members of the jury even though she is of a different race and culture. I wanted them to see Noi growing up and falling in love with Bobby.

For this part of my story, once again, I am asking that you indulge me here; humor me just a little more. I have never written a book before, but my friend, Jody Seay, an award-winning author and the woman helping me put this tale together, has assured me that having to read a hundred or so pages of dialogue with someone speaking broken, barely understandable English is a quick way to get a book thrown across the room and never picked up again. Thus, I am summarizing this part of the trial – Noi's testimony, her personal narrative – which was sometimes achingly hard to decipher. I will, of course, insert into this narrative the places where I had a specific question, or, where there was an objection or other things pertinent to this case. Once the prosecutors begin their cross-examination in this story, I will revert back to the dialogue, distracting and disjointed as it may be. I am hoping you trust me by now because I am trusting *you*, as we embark upon this journey of discovery together. This is Noi's story.

Noi and her siblings helped their father farm rice, care for hogs and chickens, and care for the banana trees. They went to a public school about three miles away, when they could. Noi was a friendly, well-liked slender little girl with jet-black hair. Her school grades, however, were low, so there was little chance she would attend high school. When her older sisters got married and left home, the rice and banana farm was too difficult to care for, so her father traded it for a fruit farm at the base of some mountains in northern Thailand.

One year, the rains in the mountains were saturating. The soil was washed away in the valley and floods finally came crashing down onto their farm. The rampaging water swept the pigs and chickens away; Noi saw the animals floating, desperately swimming, trying to stay alive, and then be dragged under by the current. She later had vivid nightmares of the animals screaming as they drowned. After the devastation of the flood, her father's health weakened and he died several months later of some tropical disease.

Noi's mother could not afford to pay the tuition required for public school. Since Noi had the lowest grades and was the oldest child living at home, she was sent to work for a Japanese conglomerate as a clothing inspector.

"How many years of schooling did you have?" I asked her.

"It eight year," she said.

"Through the eighth grade?"

"I don't finish last year."

"What kind of training did you have after you finished your eighth year?"

"Well, go to what you call, make dress, cut dress, tailor."

"About how old were you at this time?"

"Between fourteen, fifteen."

"Why did you quit school in your eighth year?"

"Well, mom didn't have…so poor, we all family poor, and mom can't everything, go school everyone. Sister come out school and help in farm, and little one go to school. Nobody want to get out from school, and I had low grade in the family. I told my family I get out school."

Noi was brought up accustomed to making sacrifices. Giving up her education meant that she would not be able to progress either financially or socially. Thai people are very family-oriented. I wanted the jury to try to understand Noi's nature a little better. The jury could also reason that Noi did not have the education which would give her the freedom to walk out on Bobby. In situations of domestic abuse, the question is often asked, *"Well, why didn't she just leave him, if he was so mean?"* And, this is the answer, not just to Noi's personal situation, but to so many others. They are stuck, mostly due to factors beyond their control.

Noi's uncle wanted her to learn a trade, so she went to work in a textile mill. As was the custom in Thailand, she was expected to send any money that she could back to her family. She lived in a large dormitory next to the factory to save money so that she could send most of her paycheck back to her destitute family. In the textile mill, she crated bolts and lifted stacks of material. She was a hard worker and became lean and strong.

Noi lived by the textile mill for about three years. She became tired of living in the girls' dormitory and felt she was not making enough money; plus, she had no future where she was. After her nineteenth birthday, she moved to Bangkok, like so many of the people did, to find a better-paying job. She found one in an automobile supply store, and, much to her surprise, realized she had an almost photographic memory when it came to categorizing parts and organizing the nuts, bolts and supplies in the parts house.

After she worked for about a year, Noi married the man chosen for her. Both families had arranged this marriage when the children were about two years old. Noi had grown up with this Thai boy. His father had given her father some farm animals to seal the deal. Noi married him because her family told her to. This was part of the Asian sense of family duty. After she gave birth to Mia, her first daughter, Noi knew there was something seriously wrong with her marriage. She felt her husband was more of a brother to her than a husband because she had known him too well as a child.

Noi was also honest enough with herself to realize that he had never wanted to marry her and did not love her, either. Both had married because their families thought it was best, and both felt a sense of relief when he moved out, even though she was left with a newborn infant.

Her older sister babysat Mia when Noi returned to work in the automotive parts store. Noi cared for her sister's baby every evening. Noi slept with Mia each night, as this was the custom in Thailand; children sleep with their parents. The Thai way of life is very child-oriented, even more so than the American way.

I had Noi discuss her bittersweet relationship with Bobby. When Mia was about a year old, Noi's best girlfriend asked if she wanted to double-date with an American in Indonesia. Bobby worked on a field audit for an oil and gas company. This was 1977, the peak of offshore drilling along the Indonesian coast. Bobby had a fifteen-day stay in Bangkok. They asked Noi to be his tour guide, even though she could only speak two words in English: *yes* and *no*. An interpreter chaperoned these early dates.

Bobby took Noi out to some of the best and most expensive clubs in Thailand and bought her a beautiful silk dress. Noi fell in love with a man she thought was wealthy, warm, loving and who could be a good father to Mia. Bobby was six feet and three inches tall, and fair-skinned. Thais like height in a man and many of the women were very attracted to him.

Noi was also drawn to Bobby's worldliness and apparent maturity. He was thirteen years her senior. She still missed her father terribly and Bobby reminded her of him. Bobby seemed attracted to Noi, perhaps it was her beauty and Asian mystique. His ex-wife had been mouthy and demanding, according to Bobby, whereas Noi made no demands on him. Bobby had a normal fear of venereal disease, which was common in Thailand, therefore, theirs was an exclusive relationship.

When Bobby left Thailand, he promised Noi he would return to see her. He kept his promise and four months later proposed marriage.

Bobby paid Noi's mother $1,000 as a gift and Noi left Thailand and flew to San Francisco where she and Bobby were married. At first, they seemed happy together. Too soon, however, Noi realized Bobby wanted her because he enjoyed the power he could wield over her. In a twisted way, what he really wanted was a doormat, someone who would not challenge him in any way and not be too upset when he walked all over her. This is what Bobby expected an Asian woman to be, especially to an American man, as sick as that was.

In getting Noi to describe all of this, I wanted the jury to see Noi as a disillusioned woman who was trying to make a better life for herself and for Mia. I also wanted them to see a marriage which had no hope and I wanted them to hate Bobby. I wanted them to hate him *a lot*. Knowing what I had learned about him from Noi, I sure did. I saw him as an abusive and power-hungry man, a bully who only put his own needs and wants first in a relationship.

Soon after she married Bobby, Noi began to see another side of her husband he had kept hidden from the world. Most people who knew him considered him to be a successful, hard-working accountant who was somewhat of an introvert, a gentle man, in other people's eyes. They didn't know he tried to prove his masculinity by completely dominating Noi. He would do this by isolating her so that she had to turn to him for all of her emotional needs. Bobby reminded her constantly that she was now in "his" country and, if she wanted to know anything, she must ask him and no one else. He demanded that she stay at home with the baby while he worked. He wanted her to stay inside and wait for him to come home, even though he would not let her know when to expect him. He wanted to exclusively control what she learned about American ways, and cut her off completely from the Thai community in Tulsa. He refused to eat Thai food, something he seemed to enjoy while they were dating in Bangkok. Bobby also refused to let Noi speak Thai around him because the sing-song quality of the language irritated him. He did not want her to learn how to drive, even further isolating her.

Bobby would occasionally slap Noi around, or grab her by the shoulders and shake her, if he thought she had disobeyed him. One psychological tool he used was to threaten to beat her with a leather belt he kept wrapped in a coil on the top shelf of the bedroom closet. He had beaten her savagely with it enough times that just the threat of it kept her fearful and in line.

The complete isolation depressed Noi to the point that she felt like she was losing her sanity. She became so miserable that she finally struck out on her own. She learned to drive a car and took a job as a waitress a few miles from home at the Monterrey House restaurant. By dealing with the public, her English steadily improved. Her marriage, however, deteriorated even further as she became more independent. As Bobby and Noi drifted apart, she relied more and more on her colleagues from work to give her the emotional support she craved. Bobby began spending more and more time with his former girlfriend, Theresa. He began working longer hours. Noi said Bobby no longer told her that he loved her, even though that shouldn't have been too hard to figure out, if you ask me.

When Noi became pregnant in March of 1981, she was excited and prayed that this child would save their marriage. When she shared this good news with Bobby, he became furious. Since he had never fathered a child before, he thought that this child could not possibly be his. He hit and slapped Noi that night and accused Noi of having an affair with a Puerto Rican man, George Rivera, who was friendly with her at work.

It was a long, miserable pregnancy. After the second baby daughter was born, Bobby and his dad ordered that the Tulsa hospital run a blood test on the baby to determine the child's paternity. The test results showed that there was a ninety-nine percent chance that Bobby was, indeed, the baby's father. Bobby's dad, Mack. Mitchell, still denied his granddaughter. He had a deep and abiding hatred for anyone who was Asian. Mr. Mitchell was a product of his generation – he and his friends had fought the Japanese in World

War II and thought all Asians looked alike, had the same accent, and thought alike.

Any love Bobby and Noi might have felt when they were first married was completely gone after Maggie was born. Bobby began a pattern of beating Noi. He would warn her never to tell anyone about her bruises because it was a family problem, and she obeyed him as a dutiful wife would in Thailand. She testified that when she saw Bobby's face turn red, she became terrified because that was the sign he was going to beat her. After the beatings, she would run into Mia's room and cry with her daughter for comfort. "Why this have to happen to me?" she would cry to Mia. To me, this action demonstrated how weak Noi was, psychologically. Noi would go to Mia for strength and Mia was only six years old. When Bobby died, Mia was, in a sense, stronger than her own mother.

Noi fooled herself for a while and kept trying to think her marriage was going to work out. She was happy when a doctor verified that she was pregnant in March, 1982. She felt that her prayers had been answered. She'd had a dream the week prior that she was holding a newborn son. She had always wanted a boy. However, Bobby didn't want to be a daddy again. He tried to reason with her and told her it was too soon to have another baby. He told her that she must get rid of the baby. She pulled back in horror and said, "No, I can't. Besides, it might be a boy baby."

According to Noi, Bobby flew into a rage. Noi cried all night, but, still, Bobby insisted that she get an abortion. He drove her to an abortion clinic in Tulsa and marched her into the office to make sure the deed was done. This broke her heart; she was devastated. During this part of Noi's testimony, I saw a middle-aged male juror in the back row wipe his eyes.

Now, I wanted Noi to describe the events leading up to the terrible night Bobby had died. "Noi," I asked, softly, "what happened on October 3rd, 1982?"

"Bobby," Noi told the court, "not come home on Sunday." He said that he had to work late. Nor did he come home on Monday, either.

Noi said she called Bobby at his office and he left her on hold without talking to her. He did not return her calls, so she did not talk to him on either Monday or Tuesday of that week.

Noi recreated the night's events – the night her husband died – in her unique Thai way. The jury was getting used to her high-pitched voice which trailed off at the end of every sentence, even though, at first, it was very distracting and often irritating.

"I get home 9 o'clock, maybe," she said. Noi refused to speak to Bobby at all when she got home from the Monterrey House. He had already eaten at the China Palace in Broken Arrow not far from their home. Noi fixed supper for herself and the children and they ate in silence. Noi quietly put the little girls to bed and looked at Bobby, who was in their king-sized bed reading a magazine. She slid in next to him and raised her voice. "Where have you been?!?" she shouted at him. Bobby snarled that it was none of her business.

"I can do what I want to do and go where I want to go without answering to you!" he shouted back at her. They both got out of the bed and stood up.

Noi was so angry and so hurt that she did something she had never dared do before, even though he had beaten her badly many times previously. She turned toward him and slapped him as hard as she could. It was the very first time she had ever struck him. She was so terrified when she realized what she had done that she began to back up. Bobby grabbed her and slammed her against the wall so hard she crumbled to the floor. Scrambling up off the floor, she ran down the hallway. She was going to cry with Mia. Her young daughter, however, was already asleep and Noi did not want to wake her on a school night, so she did not lie down with her.

Noi was still shaking with anger and fear when she spotted her baseball bat lying on Mia's bedroom floor. It had her name etched on the handle and adhesive tape wrapped around the handle for a better grip. She had used the bat earlier to play softball for the Monterrey House team. She took the bat and ran back to her bedroom. She saw Bobby standing there at the mirror examining his face and looking at the cheek where she had slapped him.

Noi swung the bat against Bobby's head as hard as she could. I don't doubt, in her anger and terror, she really wanted to knock his head off. And truthfully, I couldn't blame her for that. She hit him only once, but she was strong and the blow was enough to gash his scalp. Of course, head wounds bleed more than most other wounds, so blood had splattered everywhere, including on the mirror attached to the bedroom dresser. Bobby turned toward her, wrenched the bat away from her and pounded her hard – once on each bicep and once on each thigh – with her bat, keeping up his pattern of hurting her in places that were not obvious. She screamed out in agony, which woke the baby up. Noi kept Maggie in the bedroom with them in a baby bed up against the north wall. With the baby crying, Noi ran to the kitchen to heat up a bottle of formula for the baby.

Noi hurried right back to the bedroom where Maggie was still in the baby bed, screaming at the top of her lungs. She picked Maggie up and carried her to the bed to feed her. Looking up, Noi saw Bobby standing in front of the mirror with blood dripping down his face. He turned around to face her, and then hurled the bat at Noi and the baby. The bat narrowly missed the screaming baby and ricocheted off of Noi's left hip.

Quickly, Noi laid Maggie down on the floor. All she could think of at that moment was how much Bobby must hate them all and that the bat could have killed Maggie. Noi threw herself at Bobby, beating his chest with clenched fists. He slapped her and threw her onto the carpet. She jumped up and Bobby pushed her toward the bedroom door – *literally*, shoving her out of the room. Noi lay crying in a heap in the hallway, trying to decide what to do when she saw Bobby run to the bedroom closet. He reached up to the top shelf where he kept that coiled leather belt and a .38 caliber pistol.

Noi tells the jury that she was terrified of the belt. "Oh, my God, he beat me," she said. All she could think about was stopping him and she runs back into the bedroom, grabbing his arm as he reaches up toward the shelf. Her long fingernails leave deep scratch marks on his right hand and wrist. She could not stop him from getting the gun, but she holds onto it, too. They both have their hands on the gun and pull back and forth. It was a close match. Noi is a very strong woman and, even though Bobby has a height advantage of almost a foot, he only outweighs her by thirty-four pounds. Of course, Bobby isn't fearing for his own life or the lives of his children, as women are prone to do, something which, most likely, added to Noi's strength at that time.

Noi knees Bobby in the groin and he drops the gun. She then dives on top of the gun and cradles the weapon to her chest. Having been a wrestler in high school, Bobby uses a pinning half-nelson move to turn Noi over onto her back. He rolls her over on the floor in a space between the baby bed and the dresser so that she lays flat on her back. Noi still hangs onto the gun, with the muzzle pointing right at Bobby. Her middle finger gets caught in the trigger guard. When Bobby jerks on the gun to get it away from Noi, it goes off. Noi feels herself jerked off the floor either from the concussion of the bullet firing or her own startle reflex. It whizzes past Bobby's ankle and lodges in the dresser, about thirteen inches off the floor. Bobby jerks on the gun again, this time so hard it yanks Noi up into a sitting position and the gun fires. This bullet goes through Bobby's chest, out his back, and slams into the east bedroom wall sideways, precisely seven feet, five and a half inches from the floor.

Noi panics, she does not realize that Bobby is shot. She pulls away from him and drops the gun. She sees Bobby on his hands and knees, reaching for it. A cold fear grips her. She knows he will kill her if he gets his hands on the gun. She is temporarily frozen and looks about the room, which is dimly lit only by a small reading lamp and she sees Bobby groping for the gun.

He's getting very close to it and she knows she has to stop him. She grabs the bat by the large end, which is closest to her, and hits

Bobby on the head. She hits him very hard five or six times. He doesn't let go of the gun. Noi said, "Bobby still have gun, so I run."

She just wants to get away. She flees down the hall and out the front door, runs to her parked car in the driveway when she realizes two things: she does not have the keys to her car and she is only in her underwear. She then runs to the side of the house and waits. She is so terrified her senses are heightened and she can hear Bobby… coming… he's stalking her. He comes out the front door and she hears him wheezing and gurgling as his lungs fill with blood. The only way back into the house is through the side garage door, so she pushes it in. She forgets, however, about the heavy tool box blocking the door and the new carpet Bobby had installed which is curling up in front of it. Noi stands there in front of that door and freezes.

Bobby is now behind her. She knows he will kill her and the little girls, too. Just as she stands there, waiting for her own death, Bobby drops onto the grass face down. She hears his labored breathing turn into a death rattle, like a big coffee percolator at its peak of operation. Noi runs to Bobby, grabs the gun and throws it over the fence and into the neighbor's yard. It hits the neighbor's outside bedroom wall and bounces into the neighbor's back yard. She then heaves the side garage door open, opens the kitchen/garage door, locks it, and runs back into the house and locks the wide-open front door. She runs into the master bedroom, locks the door and waits for Bobby to come crashing through it and into the room. She waits, terrified.

"What did you do, then, Noi?" I asked, quietly.

She said that she was dizzy, sick to her stomach. Then, she spots the baby. Maggie was still and covered with blood. Noi said. "I screamed, 'Oh, God, oh, God.' I grab her with arms and shake her, blood all the time." The baby looked like she had been massacred in a blood bath.

Anytime Noi or any other witness mentioned Noi's two children, Lewis just stares at her while Carson grimaces – his face becomes hard and his mouth turns white around the edges. They were concerned, I'm sure, that the jury would let Noi go to care for those two tiny children who had already lost their father.

Noi testified that she's weeping for her dying baby and carries nine month-old Maggie to the bathroom to wash the baby off and see where she's been hurt. "There no bullet holes," Noi exclaimed after a thorough check. That's when Noi realizes Maggie must have crawled through the blood and then fallen asleep. Noi said Maggie stretched her little chubby arms up toward her mother and began to cry. "She not like fuss". The baby was upset by the night's many disturbances. Next, Noi put on a t-shirt and jeans and fed the little girl, cradling her in her arms.

She was afraid Bobby was still coming after her and, indeed, as it turns out, as the evidence came to show, she was actually right about that.

"If he come in back door, I going out front door," she said.

As Noi described her fears, I felt chills coursing up and down my spine as I envisioned her terror and her silent vigil. I noticed that, even as she told me about this night of horror, her eyes darted back and forth all over the room. She was transported back to that wretched, blood-soaked night as she testified in this courtroom.

I asked her if she went to sleep that night and she said she had not. She spent those long, dreadful hours watching and waiting, needlessly, as it turned out, all night long. The Medical Examiner for the State of Oklahoma determined Bobby's death to be, probably, between fifteen minutes to three hours after he fell in the garage, trying to enter the house, so he *was*, we think, still trying to get to Noi. For what, there is no way to know. To say good-bye? Doubtful. To exact revenge? Most likely. I left that for the jury to decide. Bobby Mitchell bled to death in the garage of their home, face down, still naked.

Noi continued her story. When the sun comes up, she finds the courage to creep into Mia's room to look out the window for

Bobby. He's not there. She looks in the living room and, finally, tiptoes into the garage. When she sees Bobby lying there, she races to him, crying, and hugs him. She said, as she shakes him, "Bobby, Bobby, why this happen to me?"

Noi is now almost hysterical again as she recounts this part of the story. I had to practice asking her questions many times because, in the first trial when she was nervous, her voice trailed off and she would look away. If I got impatient listening to her high-pitched voice dropping off, I knew the jury would, too. Noi was really trying this time to keep her voice loud enough at the end of each sentence to be heard by everyone in the courtroom. By now, though, she had reverted to her old habits and I could see all the jurors leaning forward, straining to hear her better. I remind her to speak up. Just that simple statement broke her state of mind so she could pull herself together.

Noi continues with her narrative, her testimony, of what happened next. She tells us, "Bobby will not talk to me." Then, she feels his skin and it is very, very cold. She just stares at him. Then, she gets up and closes the side garage door.

Noi climbs up into the attic to get some boxes, which she then stacks around Bobby's body so Mia will not see him. Then, she said, she goes about her regular morning routine, as though to block out the terrible things that happened. She does several loads of laundry and begins to clean the house. She finds the bat still lying on the bedroom floor, the tape around the handle covered in Bobby's blood. She unwraps the bloody tape from the handle and tosses it in the trash can. She washes the bat with soap and water to remove the remaining blood stains on the handle, then climbs back up into the attic and hides the bat behind several storage boxes.

Noi said, "Think time to get Mia up and blood all over the floor in my room, and I don't know what to do." She goes back to see Bobby in the garage and sits next to his body. She is completely confused. She gets a sheet and covers him, then she sits back down next to Bobby again. She then stacks more boxes around Bobby's body again to make sure neither Mia nor Maggie can see him.

She heats water and puts hot-soaked towels on her sore, bruised body, alternating them with cold towels to help ease the pain. She then begins her regular morning routine of getting Mia up to go to school, fixing her breakfast and packing her lunch. Noi takes Mia to school, just like always, never saying a word to her about Bobby. Noi then goes next door to ask her neighbor for permission to go into his yard to get a toy Mia had thrown over the fence. Of course, the "toy" is the gun Noi had grabbed after Bobby fell down between the houses.

"Then what did you do, Noi?" I asked.

Noi said she went to work, since she was scheduled for about three hours during the lunch shift at the Mexican restaurant. She said she felt dizzy, too weak and sick to her stomach to stay for her full shift, so she drove back home, went into the garage, and sat next to Bobby. Noi began quietly sobbing into the courtroom microphone.

Never before had she been so completely on her own. A man had always been there to tell her what to do – a father, husband or supervisor. Women in her culture do not make decisions. She remembered, suddenly, that she did have a friend who might be able to help her, George Rivera, a Puerto Rican man who had worked with her at the Monterrey House. He was twenty-one years old and a student at the Spartan School of Aeronautics. He lived down the street from Noi's babysitter.

The first time she drove to his house, George was out. Unfortunately for George, he was there later when she returned about 10 pm that night.

"He keep asking me what bother me, and I tell him people die in my house and I don't know what to do," Noi told us. She said George did not ask who it was and she did not volunteer any information.

My brother Rex heard one of the Mitchell clan whisper to an elderly woman that Noi must have really been mixed up if she asked a Puerto Rican for help. Several people overheard the man; I noticed a titter in the courtroom and saw several smiles.

Noi said that George did not say anything for a long while, walked into the kitchen and, when he returned, said, "Well, okay, I help." George had worked in Creek County, so he knew the area around Kiefer, Oklahoma well, which is why he decided to dump the body there. Noi did not tell George it was the body of her husband. Noi said George helped her because, "he know I don't have nobody here." Then, she added, "And, he don't know who killed him." I winced a little with this comment, even though it was almost funny in a pathetic way.

That night, Noi testified, she took Maggie and Mia over to the babysitter's house. Noi picked up George and drove him to her home. He helped her load Bobby's naked body into the hatchback of Bobby's Pontiac Sunbird. George Rivera was superstitious and refused to drive in a car with a body in it, so, Noi drove Bobby's car with the body in the back seat and followed George, who drove Noi's 1974 Chevrolet Caprice.

George drove straight to an oil lease near Kiefer, Oklahoma, and they parked the cars side by side deep in a grove of blackjack oak trees, the thick, dark green leaves of which don't fall in October, as most leaves tend to do. This seemed like a good place to stash Bobby's car with his body inside it. Noi got out and left the body in the car.

She got into the car with George and they did a slow U-turn through the grove of trees, making their way back out to the road. Then, the unlikely criminal duo drove home in Noi's car, with the very nervous George behind the wheel. He was so badly shaken that he went the wrong way on a one-way street. The Police stopped them and issued a warning ticket. Still, George was so nervous, Noi drove the rest of the way to his apartment, dropped him off, and then went on to the sitter's house. The babysitter asked her if anything was wrong. Noi replied, "No, it's Bobby. You'll see." Then, she took Maggie and Mia home. It was 1:30 am.

When they got home, Noi put the girls to bed, then did more laundry. She washed the sopping towels she had used to wipe up the blood from her fight with Bobby. She then tried to clean up the blood from the bedroom so the children would not be inquisitive. It was then that she thought of the gun. Noi drove back to George's apartment the next day, bringing George and two of his friends the gun along with a sack of bullets as a present. She said she did not even know the names of these friends. Noi was still in a state of shock, so she was acting in a way many people would find bizarre and incomprehensible.

"Noi, why did you take the tape off the bat?" I asked her.

"It so bloody," she responded.

"And, why was it so bloody, Noi?" I asked.

"I used that end to hit Bobby about the back," she answered.

"Then, you hit him with the wrong end of the bat, didn't you?" I asked. I wanted the jury to understand that she had picked up the bat without thinking.

"Yes, I do," she answered, "it closest to me when I pick up."

"Noi, why did you give George the gun?" I asked.

"I was scared Officer Anderson going to see the gun," she responded.

"You just handed it to him?" I asked.

"I hand it to friends," she replied.

Noi described how the Broken Arrow Police Officers came out to her home and talked with her. She said they took her into the police station, asked her many more questions and booked her for first degree murder of her husband.

By this time, I felt like the jury and I were almost in a trance, as if we'd been hypnotized. It was so still in the courtroom, as if all the air had been sucked from the space. I had concluded my questioning. It was Carson's turn now.

Carson began strutting back and forth in front of the jury as if he was trying to make them think he had control of this case.

"After the first interview with David Anderson, you went in and had another interview, correct?" Carson asked.

"Yes, sir," Noi replied.

"And, you told the officer you were going to tell him the truth when you had the first interview, right?" Carson asked.

"Yes, sir," she answered.

"In fact, later, didn't you tell David Anderson that you told him all lies before?" Carson asked.

"Yes," Noi admitted.

"You were crying and sobbing like you did on the stand today, right? Do you remember how you did that?" Carson asked.

"Yes, sir," Noi whispered, her eyes wide.

"And you were telling us the truth today in court, weren't you?" Carson asked.

"Yes, sir," Noi responded.

"And you were telling David Anderson the truth, weren't you?" Carson asked.

"Yes, sir," Noi replied.

"Noi, the stories are different. Which story is a lie and which is the truth?" Carson persisted.

"Same story," Noi answered.

"You remember that you told David Anderson that Bobby threw the gun over the fence, and today, in court, under oath, you said you threw the gun over the fence?" Carson said.

"Well, I scared," Noi replied.

"Answer the question," Carson persisted. "Did you tell David Anderson lies out there?"

"That's when I scared. Everybody ask me all the question and I thought I might do something wrong," she replied.

"Did you tell him the truth?" Carson pressed.

"Yes, sir," Noi answered.

"Noi, when was the first time you mentioned to anyone about two shots?" Carson asked.

"I tell my lawyer," Noi replied, pointing in my direction.

"When?" Carson asked.

"When he come and see me," she replied.

"After they found the second bullet and your attorney told you about it, then you changed your story to say, 'boom ... boom' didn't you?" Carson asked. By this time, he was standing next to Noi as she sat on the witness stand.

"No, I tell him first," Noi responded.

"Noi, you said Bobby fell in the grass, isn't that right?" Carson asked.

"He sort of lying down on the ground," Noi replied.

"He didn't go all the way down on the ground, then?" Carson asked.

"Yes, he did," she said.

"Look at these pictures of the body, Noi. Do you see any particles of grass in his hair there, Noi? Do you see any particles of grass in his leg hairs, or do you see any in his leg hairs, or do you see any in his chest hairs, Noi? Where is the grass he would have gotten from laying down on the ground, Noi?" Carson persisted.

"I don't know, sir," Noi replied. "He don't lay down on the ground, he just fall down. He not laying down."

"It was a grassy area, wasn't it, Noi?" Carson asked.

"Yes, sir," she responded.

"Then why isn't there any grass on the body?" Carson asked.

"I don't know," Noi said.

"Noi, remember telling the Police Officer when you were booked into jail your physical description, five two; weight, one hundred ten pounds?" Carson asked.

"I don't know how many I am tall or how weight," she replied

"Who ran to the closet first, Noi?"

"Bobby," Noi answered.

"Bobby ran to the closet first?" Carson asked.

"Yeah, I go behind him," Noi replied.

"He got into the closet first, didn't he?" Carson continued.

"Yes, sir," Noi responded.

"How tall is the shelf, Noi?"

"Well, I don't know how tall. Over my head little bit," Noi answered.

"How far over your head? Five or six inches?" Carson asked.

"I don't know, sir," Noi replied.

"Put your hand over your head. How much over your head is that?" Carson persisted.

"Well, I don't know," Noi answered.

"Well, put it there, would you?" Carson insisted. "How high do you think it is?"

Noi placed her hand over her head.

"About there," Carson went on. "Would you say that's about five, five and a half inches over your head, right? And the gun is back on the shelf, right?"

"Yes, sir," Noi replied.

"You had to go through Bobby to try to get to that gun, didn't you?" Carson asked.

"I saw hand grab and I know gun is there. I know the gun in top shelf," Noi said.

"You *knew* the gun was there?" Carson asked, incredulously, with a wide-eyed look.

"Yes, sir," Noi replied.

"You had known it was there when you started the fight, right?" Carson asked.

"Yes, sir," she admitted.

"He stood in front of you to reach up and get the gun?" Carson asked.

"Yes, sir," Noi answered.

"How could you reach up on a man six feet three inches high when you are five feet two and reaching on the closet shelf?" Carson asked.

"Just like in the part of the side here," Noi responded, demonstrating her actions.

"How could you reach up and scratch his arm, Noi? It's impossible," Carson said.

"No, sir," Noi replied, adamantly.

"Oh, it isn't? You weigh one hundred and ten pounds. How could you sit there and fight with a guy who is six three and one hundred and forty-five pounds?" Carson asked.

"I don't know, sir," Noi replied. "When I'm scared... I don't know... just grabbed. He grabbed and I just grab, and I don't know."

"You weren't standing on a chair in there, were you?" Carson questioned, trying to make her look foolish.

"No, sir," Noi replied.

"Noi, after you took the body out, you said you cleaned up. Did you ever clean up the dresser?" Carson asked.

"Yes, sir," Noi answered.

"You hit him with the bat while he was standing at the dresser – did you tell me that?"

"Yes, sir," Noi replied.

"There would have been blood spatters, wouldn't there?" Carson asked.

"I don't know, sir," Noi answered. "I don't look."

"Then, if your story is right," Carson went on, "we ought to be able to see that and verify it." Carson seemed proud of his conclusion. "Noi, how many different stories have you told in everything you did? A bunch, isn't it?" Carson asked.

"No. I told one to Broken Arrow Police. I told already everything," Noi insisted.

"Noi, was Bobby trying to harm you when you went after him?" Carson asked. Without waiting for an answer, Carson continued. "Bobby never tried to harm you!" Carson took a stab at Noi with this statement.

"Well, he do when he start argument over in the bed, and he slap me in the head," Noi said.

"He slapped you on your head?" Carson asked.

"Uh-huh," Noi replied affirmatively.

"Did you have any injuries from where he slapped you in the head?" Carson asked.

"I know I hurt. When I find out in the morning I find all over me, I was sore," Noi said.

"You had a bruise on your left arm; a little bruise on your upper left thigh; and a very old, very faded bruise over your right knee – is that right?" Carson asked.

"I don't know, sir," Noi responded.

"Did you have any broken bones?" Carson asked.

"No, sir," Noi answered.

"Did you have a bloody nose?"

"No, sir," Noi replied.

"Busted out teeth?"

"No, sir," Noi said.

"Did you have a fractured skull?"

Noi shook her head *no*.

"Let me ask you, Noi. What did Bobby do to you so bad you had to shoot him with a gun?" Carson asked.

"I don't shoot him with the gun," Noi replied.

"Tell me the injuries you received. He got a gunshot wound to the chest. He was beaten about the head with a baseball bat, and he was choked. What did you get, Noi? You got three bruises," Carson said.

"I jump and I jump away," Noi responded, weakly.

"Did you receive any other injuries?" Carson persisted.

"No, sir. When he go hit, I just jump, I just jump," Noi replied.

"You ambushed, you brutalized, you beat him with the bat and you choked him. When was it you choked him?" Carson went on.

"I never put my hands on his neck," Noi said, adamantly.

"You did put your hands on his neck," Carson insisted.

"I never did," Noi dug in. "I just hit."

"How did you choke him?"

"I don't know, sir. I don't even know." Noi replied.

"Why doesn't any of the story you're telling us check out, Noi?"

"I never put my hand on his neck," Noi said.

"Noi, you told a lot of different stories and lied to a lot of people, haven't you, Noi?"

"No, sir," Noi replied.

"Noi, you're talking to me here without the use of an interpreter, aren't you?"

"Yes, sir," Noi answered.

"You haven't requested one, have you, for this trial?"

"I don't request," Noi admitted.

The prosecutors wanted the jury to know Noi had a motive to kill Bobby. Carson insinuated that, if Noi did not kill Bobby for having a mistress, she may have killed him for money. *Would Noi be a rich widow if Bobby died?* It was in the prosecutors' best interest if the jury thought so. Carson sneaked in, "How many life insurance policies did Bobby have?"

Noi answered that she did not know.

"Oh, you don't know?" Carson answered her, in mock surprise.

"I don't know, sir. I never see anything."

"He had about a half a million dollars in insurance and you're the beneficiary and you didn't know that?"

"I don't know, sir. I never saw him or anything." Noi was forever getting her pronouns mixed up.

My ears burned. All the jury would remember from these questions was that Bobby had half a million dollars. Half a million dollars sticks in your mind, especially in 1983, when half a million dollars was a big chunk of money. I had to do something so I objected, saying, "We don't object if Mr. Carson will bring in the policies. He can bring them in, *if they exist.*"

"You know about the claims that have been made for the proceeds on your behalf?" Carson kept charging like a wild bull.

"Be what now?" Noi was thoroughly confused and I was upset at this cheap shot.

"And, Noi, it is also a fact, and you know, if you are proven to be his murderer, you don't get the insurance money?"

"Ask me what now, sir?" If Noi was pretending that she had trouble with the English language and American ways, she was doing a good job of it right now.

Noi looked at Judge Dalton and asked, "What the answer now?"

I almost started to chuckle, because the prosecutors had been trying to imply that Noi was faking her language problems and this line of questioning surely demonstrated just the opposite. If it had worked, it would have been a sound strategy, because faking a language problem would have made Noi seem shrewd and cold-blooded. Instead, they just proved she was a confused and frightened foreigner. She looked really confused and pathetic when she turned to the biggest authority in the room, Judge Dalton, and asked him, "What the answer now?"

Judge Dalton looked at Noi and said, "If you know, you may answer the question. *The court* does not answer the question."

Carson then moved in for the kill. "If Bobby's death is shown to be an accident," he said to Noi, "you get half a million dollars?"

This half a million dollars in insurance policies was pure fiction. I had seen what little assets and insurance Bobby had. A lawyer takes an oath of office and this type of questioning was against that code of ethics. We are only allowed to ask questions which have a basis in truth. The official probate file kept by the District Court Clerk made no mention of a half-million dollar insurance policy. Insurance policies would only be inventoried by the Administrator or the Personal Representative if the beneficiary were listed as the "Estate" instead of an individual.

> (NOTE: I found a $100,000.00 policy with her as the primary beneficiary with a double indemnity clause for accidental death which makes it a $200,000.00 policy. This is the policy that is cited in Chapter Two which made it in the law books now taught in American law schools. I never did find the other $300,000.00 in insurance proceeds that Carson was so certain existed. Maybe Bobby's father was the beneficiary and never told me.)

Because I knew this information was wrong, I objected. I would have said more, but I was too shocked and angry by Carson' blatant disregard for rules of procedure and what I considered to be a serious breach of decency.

Noi blurted out, "I don't know anything. He no tell me."

The funny part about these mysterious policies was that the prosecutors never did introduce a single one – not one! To this day I believe the jury saw past these unfair tactics.

The prosecutors then produced another motive Noi may have had to kill Bobby. They wanted the jury to think she killed him because she was not an American and would be deported if Bobby divorced her.

Carson wanted to trap Noi with a convoluted question. "Isn't it a fact, if you're divorced, Noi, you can be deported back to your homeland?"

Noi thought she knew the answer to this question and replied, "I go back my home."

"You would be sent back home and would not have beautiful America?" Carson mocked. He wanted the jury to think a foreigner might kill to stay in this wonderful country.

"I go back my home," Noi persisted.

Carson still was not through with her. "What happens if you're a widow, Noi?" Carson asked.

"If I what?"

"What happens to you if your husband dies? Do you get to stay in this country?" His voice sounded like he was getting exasperated with her.

Noi replied, "I go back home." She didn't sound too upset by this prospect.

Carson jumped up and down. "No!" he said, "you're allowed by law to stay in this country if you're a widow, as opposed to divorced..." The implication was clear. She would have to kill to stay in this country, according to Carson.

"Objection, Your Honor," I said.

"Sustained." Dalton knew that this argument had gone too far. He did not want to be reversed on appeal.

Carson, however, kept right on going, as if he had never heard Judge Dalton tell him to stop. "You know that, Noi," he hollered at her, shaking a finger right in her face.

Judge Dalton finally halted this attack by calling a lunch break. I skipped lunch and ran over to U.S. Congressman Jim Jones' office to grab a copy of the United States Code which governed this area of immigration laws. Luckily for me, one of his staff members was still there and skipped her lunch hour to help me research. I came back armed for battle. I had the law on my side, something I am always grateful for. The law always comes through for me when I need it to.

When the trial reconvened, Judge Dalton let me start first. I introduced the law which clearly shows the United States could not deport Noi even if Bobby divorced her because she had been legally married to an American citizen. I could not help but wonder, *Who gave Carson his information on the law or is he just making things up to suit his end goal.* This *was* the final round. *It looks like the prosecutors are going after a knock-out punch. Is Carson experimenting with his own brand of trial tactics?* In my mind, with his theatrics, soft underbelly groping, and his bullying techniques, he vacillated between being a jackal and a thug. I easily saw him both ways.

I glanced to the galley and saw my private investigator, Tom Cook, give me a wink of approval and that helped me center myself. *Ok,* I thought to myself, *I settled our false immigration issue, now Noi needs to get back on the stand and Carson will probably be back on the attack.*

He was. Carson began with, "Noi, I want you – with the court's permission – I want you to stand down here just a second."

Judge Dalton said, "Very well."

Noi stepped down from the witness stand and stood next to Carson. He picked up the gun and waved it in front of her face. She instantly arched her eyebrows and shrank back in horror.

"The gun's not loaded," Carson said, as if admonishing her for being so silly. "I want you to hold it for a second. Hold the gun!" he shouted.

Noi reeled back even more as he reached for her hand.

"Put the gun in your hand. Hold the gun," Carson insisted.

I said, "Your Honor, I object."

Judge Dalton stepped in, saying, "She evidently does not want to hold the gun. You can return to your seat, Noi."

Noi just stood there, reeling back, with her hands covering her eyes.

Dalton said, "Noi, you can return to the witness stand here."

That little demonstration was the strongest "testimony" I have ever seen. Not only that, but the Judge had referred to her as "Noi," too, a clear indication to me that he was now seeing her as a real person rather than an unhappy and difficult defendant accused of murder.

As soon as she sat back down in the witness stand chair, she blurted out in a wooden tone, "I promise to myself I never touch gun anymore in my life."

CHAPTER 24 – JUDGE NOT, LEST YE BE *ALMOST* JUDGED

By the beginning of the fourth week of the trial, I was still uncertain of the outcome. This uncertainty gnawed at me like a hungry hyena, wrecking my appetite, shortening my temper, and keeping me awake at night. I watched the spectators and monitored their reactions. By now, I knew most of the regulars in the courtroom; except I did not know one man who showed up on Monday of the trial's third week and had been in the courtroom every day since.

Maybe this "mystery man" belonged to the insurance company or he was Mr. Mitchell's secret weapon. Thoughts like this hammered away in my brain constantly. On Tuesday, I had a chance to "visit" with him in the hallway.

"Are you with the Mitchells?" I asked him.

"Oh, no," he said, "I don't know them."

"Then, you're a friend of Noi's?" I assumed.

"No. I don't know her, either," he said with a smile.

The bailiff came out at that moment and walked over to where we were standing. "Judge Dalton is waiting for you," she announced.

"Thank you," I told the bailiff and on the way back in I walked by my brother Rex and whispered, "Find out all you can about this 'mystery man'."

Finally, on Wednesday, Rex was able to talk with Mr. 'Mysterious Man'. Later that night, as we drove home, Rex was grinning with delight.

"What's so amusing?" I asked.

"Well, you know the mystery guy you wanted to know about?"

"Yes, what did you find out?"

"He came to the courthouse on Monday during his lunch break to pay his taxes. While he was there, he poked his head into a few courtrooms just to see what was going on. When he got to Noi's courtroom – *your* courtroom – he was so captivated, he stayed the rest of the day. The next day, he called in to work and took a day of vacation. When he found out that the trial would probably be over in a few days, he took the rest of the week off.

He said his wife thinks he's lost his mind. She couldn't understand why he would spend the rest of this year's vacation on a murder trial, especially when he didn't even know anybody involved! He said he had a hard time trying to explain it to her, and I bet he did. Poor guy. I bet she cannot relate to the fact that he is hooked."

"That's wonderful, Rex," I said. "Do you know what this means?" I could hardly contain my glee.

"You tell me," he replied.

"It means we're keeping the jurors entertained. It means that, if a stranger can care about Noi, then, perhaps, the jury will care about her, too. This is great – I don't believe it! It's too good to be true! WOO-HOO!" I yelled, whapping my hand on the dashboard. What a fantastic sign. *Why, if we could generate this type of empathy and interest in the "mystery man," well, no telling what good things might happen.*

When we got home, Rex and I danced a jig together in the kitchen. We hollered and screamed and laughed. Nancy thought we had gone completely crazy, and she was right. We were crazy with joy.

286

"What happened? What's going on?" Nancy wanted to know.

We had the best of times telling and then re-telling the story of our "mystery man." You would have thought we'd already won the case by the way we were acting.

Nancy had trouble sharing our excitement about the interest we were generating in the courtroom. She was constantly worried about the money and time being sunk into the defense of this case, which was something I had grown to expect from her. I needed her to understand my joy in realizing that some of the things I'd learned from Gerry Spence were paying off – finally! Nancy, however, just felt that there was nothing yet concrete enough over which to celebrate.

To me, though, the "mystery man" was a good omen. He made me realize that, for the first time in my career, I had the power to control everything that went on in the courtroom. It was up to me; not the Judge, the prosecutors or the witnesses. I began to see that the jurors looked at me warmly when I spoke to them. I recalled one woman in particular who had been cold and distant at first. She now leaned forward and sometimes even smiled when I looked her way. Yet, she crossed her arms and looked away whenever Carson spoke. I had a new-found love for the jury and felt at ease with myself. I measured the result of everything I did by observing the jury's reactions. I was, in a sense, watching and gauging the juror's reactions. As if they were a thermometer, I was constantly checking the jury members for a temperature rating on Noi's defense.

Of course, in the world of law, nothing is ever completely smooth-sailing, and, even though so many things were working well in terms of my relationship with the jury, my relationship with Judge Dalton felt mostly tenuous, at best. I had been aware for some time that Dalton had been letting the jury know in very subtle ways that he thought they should convict Noi. When I would question a witness or make a comment, he would sit way back in his black chair, surrounded by his black robe, his eyes almost half-mast, looking like a tired, bored crow, as if to get away from what I was saying. If I continued to speak, he became instantly and obviously disconnected and detached. Sometimes, I thought he looked as if he was ready to fall asleep. This behavior was beginning to make me a little crazy, in truth.

In contrast, whenever the prosecutors presented evidence, he would shake himself to attention in his chair and appear that he was looking on with approval. I knew these actions on his part could easily bias the jury's verdict.

I developed a strategy. When I addressed Judge Dalton during a bench conference, I whispered very softly. He was then forced to lean forward in his chair to hear what I had to say. This would indicate to the jury – I hoped – that Judge Dalton had become more interested which, in turn, caused the jury to become more interested.

My strategy worked until the day Dalton threatened me with contempt of court. He and I had a head-on collision that day. Dalton had ordered me not to bring Noi's children to the courtroom. Carson and Lewis had convinced him that the presence of the children would make the jury sympathetic toward Noi. He told me if the children somehow found their way into his courtroom, he would hold me in contempt of court.

During the trial, my Thai interpreter, Kosin Ponpayuhakiri, was unable to get a babysitter to watch his children while he was in court. I told him it would be all right for him to bring his kids with him. When Carson and Lewis saw Kosin's two little girls sitting in the courtroom, they ran to Dalton and asked for a recess in the Judge's chambers. Dalton was furious with me, thinking I had purposely disregarded his order to me. After I explained that these girls were not Noi's children, Dalton and the prosecutors attempted to contain themselves, realizing, of course, that there was nothing they could do. Even though these little girls did not belong to Noi, the fact that they were small and Asian would remind the jury of Noi's two little ones. It was as effective as if Noi's two tiny girls had actually been sitting there themselves! It was, indeed, another *Godplop!*

Dalton then threatened me, "If those are Noi's children, I am going to have you thrown in jail for contempt of court," he promised.

I asked that a record be made. Dalton then asked the court reporter to come into his chambers.

I said, "With all due respect, Your Honor, I cannot effectively represent my client because you have intimidated and threatened me. I am afraid that I am being ineffective counsel because I am afraid of you and the threats you have made. My client's right to effective assistance of counsel, as provided for in the Sixth Amendment of the United States Constitution, is being violated. I move for a mistrial."

Dalton looked genuinely surprised at my motion and asked Lewis and Carson if either of them had anything to say.

Carson said, "Judge, I don't know what to say."

Lewis piped in, "Judge, I don't think you are intimidating him."

Dalton said, "The motion for mistrial is denied."

After that, however, I was not again threatened with contempt of court and the Judge seemed to be much more respectful. A big plus was that he did not shout at me in the courtroom ever again, so my strategy worked. He also began to rule more in my favor, I noticed.

In baseball, an umpire who blows a call, making a blatantly bad one, will often turn right around and make calls favoring the other team just to even things out or to keep from being considered biased. *Was I now learning the Oklahoma court rules correctly? Or, had I just better-established my position with the Judge?* Time would tell.

CHAPTER 25 – ROUNDING THIRD, *ALMOST* HOME

A fresh, new wind was now blowing into my sails. With the appearance of the "Mystery Man" and Judge Dalton's major attitude change toward me, I sensed the tide of the trial as changing in our favor. This feeling made me happier than I could ever say, like something deep inside me was gigging all the time. Still, I knew better than to let down my guard and coast. Like I said before, things in a courtroom can change quickly and not always in the direction you want.

My next witness, Lucien Haag, was dynamite, if you'll pardon the pun. He is one of the nation's foremost ballistics experts. I hate using that metaphor to describe him given what he does for a living, but really, what he has to say is accurate, well-respected, and often blows an opposing testimony right out of the water. The United States Congress actually requested that Lucien Haag reinvestigate the assassinations of President John F. Kennedy and Dr. Martin Luther King, Jr., that's how good he is at what he does. There is an old expression, "He carries the weight," which means that someone is worth what he charges because he is the one who has the knowledge, who shoulders the burden and who gets the job done. Lucien Haag carried the weight, for sure.

Haag walked to the witness chair like he was in charge of the court. Judge Dalton even looked at him in awe. Haag had an all-American clean-cut look, an appearance which could have been lifted from a Norman Rockwell painting, with his sandy hair, freckled skin, rugged body and wholesome smile.

Carson and Lewis both wanted me to skip the usual questions about why an expert is an expert. These questions are designed to let the jury know just how good your expert is. The prosecutors were aware that Lucien Haag had given their own ballistics expert, Martin Udall, his training, so, in terms of credentials, the stack-up would not come out in their favor. I wanted the jury to know Lucien Haag would win this battle. After all, that is why he can command a large fee and deserve it. He carried the weight.

"We will stipulate that Lucien Haag is a ballistics expert," Carson said.

"I'll accept your stipulation that Haag is an expert if you'll agree he's the best ballistics expert in the country," I countered.

Carson shook his head. "We can't do that," he said.

I was then allowed to qualify my expert.

Lucien Haag commanded respect and it was clear he got it. The jury became even more alert when he told them he was asked by the U.S. Congress to reinvestigate President Kennedy's assassination. Haag could have been a great trial lawyer. When he testified, his eyes conveyed a message to the jury that he spoke the truth and his intensity captivated them. They all looked, listened and believed. He could have worn a torn shirt and dirty overalls and it would not have diminished him as a witness at all. He was perfect.

Mr. Haag had gone to the Mitchell home the day before to take measurements and get the information he needed for the trial. Rex and I saw him measure angles using strings and a compass. Remember, this was 1983; a long time before laser measuring devices had come into existence and much more sophisticated equipment had been developed to do this job. Haag measured the distance from the bullet hole in the east wall of the master bedroom to that area of blood-soaked carpet where Noi said she and Bobby fought. He made dozens of calculations. Haag also measured the hole in the dresser about thirteen inches off the floor. From these measurements and strings drawn taut around the room, he determined the angles of trajectory of the bullets.

Lucien Haag began by explaining to the jury how he determines a bullet's trajectory. It turned out to be a fascinating lesson for the jury and for me. The jury relaxed and I did, too. Haag testified that his calculations showed the gun was level when the first shot was fired. This supported Noi's story about Bobby's having jerked her into a semi-sitting position when the first shot went off. His testimony contradicted that of the prosecutor's expert witness, Martin Udall. Agent Udall had said the gun had to be pointing downward at a twenty-degree angle when it went off, striking the dresser thirteen and a half inches off the floor.

Lucien Haag gave his expert opinion that the second bullet, which ultimately killed Bobby Mitchell, had traveled *upwards* from the floor to the hole in the wall at an angle of thirty degrees. The significance of the trajectory of the bullet is that it proved the gun was pointed upward when it fired. This confirmed Noi's story that she was underneath Bobby when the gun went off. It also proved the approximate location of the struggle when the gun discharged. I really needed Mr. Haag's testimony to prove the physical evidence was consistent with Noi's testimony, and it had. Lucien Haag had just verified Noi's story.

Mr. Haag also helped me in another important way. He testified that the wound on the web of the decedent's right hand was caused by the hammer of the gun striking it. Haag was certain about this. Bobby, when he pulled on the gun fighting with Noi, caused the hammer to strike the web of his own hand.

As an expert, Lucien Haag was shocked and appalled to discover that someone in the Oklahoma State Medical Examiner's Office had completely washed Bobby's body before Dr. Masood performed the autopsy. He said this was destroying evidence, and I had to agree with him – it was.

It made me wonder: *Had someone told Dr. Masood to destroy the photos made of Bobby's hands before they were washed? Had he been urged by someone to leave those photos back at the lab? What happened to the baggies taped to Bobby's hands? Had someone convinced the good doctor to commit perjury on the witness stand – commit perjury twice in two jury trials?* Things just seem too fishy to me so I worried at it over and over. *This was terrible procedural work. In terms of actually getting to the truth of what happened – this is the core of their jobs – the behavior of the prosecutors and several of their witnesses seemed borderline unethical – at best.* As I mentioned before, leveling a charge such as this at other attorneys is huge and not something tossed around lightly, especially when it's something I could not entirely prove to be true. Nor did I want to prove it. I just wanted everyone involved to behave professionally. *I'm not as experienced at trial law as they are,* I reminded myself. *Both prosecutors in this case are good trial attorneys. They are smart, powerful men with sterling reputations. As much as I don't like them for how hard they fight me, how they humiliate me in the courtroom and even make my job more difficult, I still admire them for their legal minds, their tenacity, their trial expertise and their tremendous drive to succeed. I can't believe they would risk their reputations to pull underhanded tricks;* and I realized I really meant that. *So what was going on? As facts were being revealed and things progressed, it began looking more and more, to me, that my hunches were spot-on. Call me paranoid,* I mused, *but things looked pretty flaky to me.*

Lucien Haag testified that there were two different types of gunpowder fired from two cartridges. There were two kinds of stippling marks on the decedent's chest and shin. He defined stippling marks as little black dots, tattooed on the body where gunpowder was burned into the skin. He also educated the jury on the type of gun which killed Bobby, saying it was a .38 caliber RG pistol, a weapon gun experts consider to be a very cheap, dangerous and poorly-designed weapon. It is so dangerous because the hammer strikes even when barely touched so the gun can easily misfire.

I had to secure a court order to get custody of the gun and the bullets before the prosecutors would let us have them for Lucien Haag's tests, which still angered me. Another thing they did to keep me from finding out the truth and keeping me hamstrung. I realized, on some level, they felt they were just doing their jobs, but their intent seemed to be to create more hoop-jumping for me and to distract me from properly defending this case.

The prosecutors wanted Lucien Haag out of the witness chair as soon as possible, so Carson did not ask too many questions. Their objective was to discredit Haag's trajectory calculations. Their own expert, Agent Martin Udall, had claimed the second bullet could have ricocheted up at high velocity, backwards against a rib, and been knocked off course. If that were true, it would be impossible to prove which way the gun was fired.

Mr. Haag was ready for them, though; he had considered this possibility, he explained, which is why he had studied the X-rays of Bobby's body which showed the bullet's path was a through-and-through flesh wound. The bullet had actually gone right between the fifth and sixth ribs. It did not hit any bones. The fact that the decedent's ribs had been traumatized did not necessarily mean that the bullet had hit and ricocheted off of them. In fact, Haag determined that it was highly unlikely; the rib damage was not bullet-type of damage.

I felt a warm glow of satisfaction from knowing I had made the right decision in hiring Lucien Haag to help me with this. I'd had to borrow the money to cover his expenses and fees from my parents, but Haag was worth every cent. He carried the weight, for sure.

I could not help but smile recalling the first trial when Dalton chewed me out as I tried to explain to the jury what a poorly-made gun the RG pistol is. As Lucien Haag was leaving the stand on this day of the third trial, I carefully picked up the gun and barely touched the cocked hammer. It *slammed* down and clicked loudly, which proved my point one more time. This little impromptu demonstration had great impact on both the jury and on Judge Dalton. I felt incredibly high, almost euphoric, like I was racing with a tailwind.

I was on a roll now. It was time for my blood spatter expert, Keith Inman, and I called him to the stand. He did not have the air of authority that Lucien Haag had, but his credentials were nearly as impressive.

He looked like he was from the Golden State of California with his short, neatly-trimmed brown beard and gold, wire-framed glasses. Inman's full name had five names in it; one was his wife's maiden name. I thought, *maybe this is a California custom. It was something definitely not heard of in my very conservative Oklahoma. He looks a little out of sync with the rest of us Oklahomans.* But he was sincere and knowledgeable and I felt his testimony won the jury over.

This wasn't Inman's first rodeo. He had become well-known in California when he helped solve the Freeway Killer and Hillside Strangler serial murder cases. His blood spatter analysis work with the Los Angeles County Sheriff's Office had given him plenty of opportunities to test his skills.

A University of Tulsa professor, Darcy O'Brian, attended the California trials of the Hillside Stranglers and was so impressed with Mr. Inman's work he wrote a book entitled, *Two of a Kind: The Hillside Stranglers.* The book was adapted into a made-for-television film called *The Case of the Hillside Stranglers* starring Richard Crenna. I knew about this book and movie, but it wasn't where I'd gotten the idea to contact Keith Inman. That idea had come from a completely different source.

I had gotten the idea of contacting Keith Inman from Dr. Thomas Noguchi, the famous "Coroner of the Stars." Dr. Noguchi is the controversial California pathologist who is the man the television series, *Quincy*, portrayed. The TV show was based on actual cases Dr. Noguchi had worked on. A little over ten years later from the time of this third trial for Noi, Thomas Noguchi would become even more famous for his work as an independent consultant on the O.J. Simpson murder case in Los Angeles.

A pathologist determines the exact cause of death, I reminded myself, *and I need to know that information.* Dr. Noguchi worked on the Marilyn Monroe case in 1962 and decided that the cause of death was suicide. Almost every famous star's death in the 1960's, '70's, and early '80's was investigated by Dr. Thomas Noguchi. He became controversial when he held press conferences to discuss details of the deaths of certain stars, like John Belushi, for example.

Even though the press and the public appreciated his candor, certain powers in Hollywood did not. After he was fired from his job as County Coroner, he became an independent consultant and instructor to other pathologists for the government. I have considered him to be "The Expert Pathologist," the very best in his field, since the time I was still throwing newspapers in our neighborhood and reading about him while I was sitting on the curb and folding papers next to my bicycle.

I needed someone to determine the actual cause of Bobby's death. *Was it from the gunshot wound, concussions, from the beating to the head, or was it from strangulation?*

Dr. Masood, the pathologist with the Oklahoma Medical Examiner's Office, testified that any one of the three kinds of injuries could have caused Bobby's death, either by itself or in combination with the other two. This was no help at all. I would have to prove Noi's defenses as they related to her actions in the shooting, the baseball bat beatings, and in the injury to Bobby's neck. This is *three times tougher*, as you might imagine, than developing Noi's defense around just one of those ways to die.

Dr. Noguchi was very enthusiastic and supportive when he heard about my case. I needed that desperately. Although he was too swamped to take my case, he gave me lots of good ideas and told me what to look for. He told me one sign of strangulation is petechia, a condition in which broken capillaries in the eyes and cheeks rupture when a person is strangled. The decedent in this case, Bobby Mitchell, III, had no signs of petechia.

He asked me if the Oklahoma Medical Examiners had found evidence of petechia on Bobby's face. I knew that they had not, but the prosecutors had stressed, over and over, the fact that there was evidence of fingernail marks on his neck area and a cracked cartilage in his throat.

In the first trial, I pressured Dr. Masood to admit that a blow by the bat near the chin could have knocked Bobby's head back and fractured the thyroid cartilage (hyoid bone, more commonly known as the Adam's apple). I tried to question Dr. Masood with a copy of a medical treatise to prove that "if there were no petechia hemorrhage, then there was no strangulation". He refused to admit the treatise was authoritative because it was not the very latest edition of the book, even though the relevant passage on petechia had not changed. Judge Dalton and the prosecutors could bet their boots I'd have the latest edition for the third trial, though!

Dr. Noguchi said if I could knock out strangulation as a possible cause of death, then the cause of death would be narrowed down to the beatings and the shooting. These two injuries were so related in time and event, during the struggle, that they probably would be defended together anyway. Dr. Noguchi spent between forty-five minutes and an hour with me on the phone, giving me advice, encouragement, and his sympathy. He knew I had no experience in criminal cases, so he recommended I use Keith Inman, a blood spatter expert, to help with this case.

I silently gave thanks for Dr. Noguchi that night in my prayers. He was such a fascinating person, and I had put him on a pedestal since I was a young boy watching Quincy's adventures on television. I would have very much liked to be able to tell Nancy about this exciting conversation, but, from previous talks with her, I knew she would only be concerned about the big phone bill I had just run up. It seemed like her first question each evening was not about how the case was going, but about how much I had spent on it.

During one argument I complained, "Since I've taken on Noi's case, it's the first time in our marriage that I've not been able to share my experiences with you. This is the first time we are not 'in it' together."

And she said, "Exactly *my* point."

Certainly, I had played a part in this division, this chasm between us, but it was easier to blame it all on her and her lack of understanding. While Nancy was fighting for the welfare of our family, well, I – I was fighting for Justice! Of course, in my own head and in the bottomless pit that is my ego, mine was the bigger, more righteous cause.

Also, due to the fact that she was always so angry with me, I had completely shut Nancy out. It was easier for me to do than fight with her constantly. I'm ashamed to admit that. It was hellishly lonely. Nancy is part of my heart; I missed her. Besides, the guilt I felt over using all our money and all my time to fight this case was overwhelming, but I was just in too deep to stop.

When I called Keith Inman and gave him the facts about Noi's case, he was cautious, at first. He wanted to know my defense strategy. Was it insanity? "If so," he asked "why do you need me? I think you need a psychologist!"

I laughed and said he might very well be right, and on many levels, but that insanity was not one of Noi's defenses. I was placing her hopes for an acquittal on accidental shooting and self-defense.

I sent Inman his airline tickets and he came out the next week in the evening. This was just one day before he was to testify. That evening I picked him up at the Tulsa International Airport and then we drove to dinner at the Pizza Hut across the street from the Mitchell's housing addition in Broken Arrow. We discussed strategy and he shared his experiences as a blood spatter expert with me as we ate dinner. Admittedly, this was not the most appetizing meal-time subject. Still, we got through it.

A blood spatter expert is a forensic expert who determines what caused an impact on a human body and also determines the source of blood by examining blood spatters. With his level of expertise, Inman could determine if a bullet pulled blood out with it while exiting a wound. He could also determine if there was "back spatter" caused by the bullet entering the front of the body causing microscopic droplets of blood to go away from the point of impact. Blood leaving a body due to a bullet leaves a unique pattern and Mr. Inman was a recognized expert on that topic.

That night we had to perform the tests in the Mitchell's home; but there was a full moon and Keith needed it to be dark. This full moon was just like the full moon on the night Bobby died. Since Inman needed it pitch black inside the Mitchell home, we taped up the windows with black, plastic garbage bags to keep moonlight from illuminating the inside of the Mitchell residence.

Inman first used a chemical called Toledine to test for blood throughout the house. He brushed the blood spots with Q-tips soaked in this chemical. He was unaware that Noi had used buckets and buckets of water and household cleaners to try and remove the blood stains. She had soaked the carpet, until the padding beneath it was over-saturated, which made the carpet squish beneath our feet. Noi had taken towels, laid them out and stomped on them, trying to soak up the excess water, even though, it appeared, she had not been very successful at it. She had also used every kind of household cleaner she had on hand to try to get rid of the blood.

After several hours of searching for the blood spatters, Keith Inman figured Noi was either lying about the fight and the blood or she had effectively diluted the blood until it would not activate the chemical. About 2:30 am, he was very puzzled as to why the chemical was not responding as it should, especially where the largest blood spatters should be concentrated. "I assume Noi found the one household cleaner that counteracts the chemical I use," he mused. "Although, that had to have been an accidental discovery on her part."

"Well, what is it?" I asked.

"Nope, I'm not going to divulge the name of the cleaner. What if that information falls into the hands of the wrong people? They might thwart other blood spatter expert investigations." He rummaged around in his gear as he said, "Now I'm going to have to bring out the potent stuff."

"Ooh," I murmured, "It's interesting to watch an expert work."

"There is one problem with the potent stuff. If you breathe it, you could get cancer – that's how toxic it is. And I only brought one mask with me to protect my lungs. You had better leave the room when I spray the carpet."

As I hurriedly left the room he called after me, "And hold your breath."

As it was, the house smelled badly and I had already been inhaling gobs of household dust and mold which made my nose run like a river. Tom Cook, my investigator, couldn't make it here tonight; once I told him about this, he wouldn't feel so bad about missing it.

Inman sprayed the special chemical, which makes blood glow a fluorescent purple color in the dark for about eight seconds. I waited nervously in the living room and just about jumped out of my skin when the bedroom door creaked open and Inman emerged, walking down the hallways with his black mask on, making him look like a monster in some low-budget, Japanese horror flick. The hallway lights were out, of course, and he walked beside spots of blood that were glowing purple. He was following the path of Bobby's last steps, creeping out of the bedroom from the hallway and up to the front porch. It looked like glowing, purple spots coming toward me. It almost made me dizzy to look at them.

As if it weren't already spooky enough, Inman whispered that he felt the presence of Bobby's ghost in the hall and in the bedroom. He believed that ghosts always return to the place where the person died. I stared at him, thinking that this guy from California was really weird.

Inman wanted me to help him cut out some carpet samples by the baby bed, where the greatest puddles of blood were found. By this time, my nose was running and I was sneezing so much I could hardly see in front of me. I spotted some Allerest on the kitchen table and reached for the bottle.

"Wait!" Inman shouted at me. "Don't ever take anything from a death scene!" He reminded me of the Tylenol case in which capsules were laced with cyanide. A relative of the victim visiting the scene of death developed a headache and took some Tylenol there at the crime scene. She died, too, of poisoning. "I make it a cardinal rule," he said, "*never* to take anything found at a crime scene and there are *no* exceptions." I understood and appreciated his caution. I pulled out my totally soaked handkerchief and used that, realizing it was almost as soaked through as Noi's squishy carpet.

Despite being worn to the bone by 3:30 am, I was also exhilarated because Inman and I found even more evidence that Bobby had stalked Noi out of the house. We followed Bobby's foot prints up to the front porch. Rain had washed away the brownish-red stains on the porch, but the police had documented blood on the porch with photographs and testimony in court.

Keith Inman began his testimony the next day by explaining to the jury exactly what a blood spatter expert was and what kinds of tests he conducted.

He said the blood spatters on the baby bed showed that a man's chest was facing the baby bed at close range when the bullet entered. He measured the angle of the bullet from the way the chest faced toward the baby bed and it was directly in line with the baby bed.

He told us the blood found in the house came from the front and back of Bobby's body. From the way the spatters fell, Inman lined up the trajectory of the bullet which shot through Bobby. This was consistent with both Noi's and Lucien Haag's story that the gun had fired accidentally when Bobby had pulled on it. It was amazing that Inman could scientifically show us the position of the bodies struggling over the gun by the way the blood fell.

One bullet whizzed by Bobby's ankle, went straight across the room and into the dresser. The other bullet entered his chest, exited his back, and ended up seven feet, five and a half inches from the floor, at no greater than a twenty degree angle. He said that, in his opinion, it was probable that Noi was on her back when the gun went off. It was good – and critical – to have Noi's story verified by two experts.

In this third trial, Keith Inman also testified on ballistics. In the first trial, Judge Dalton did not think Inman was qualified to do so. But since then, Inman remembered he had given expert testimony prior to even the first trial concerning the characteristics of a bullet as it travels through the air or through human bodies. In truth, Keith Inman was much more effective in the third trial than the first.

This was important to refute the prosecutors' argument that the bullet hit one of Bobby's ribs causing it to shoot upwards and lodge sideways in the wall. Inman testified that bullet turned a little when it went through Bobby's chest and that was why it went into the wall sideways.

It was now Carson' turn to cross-examine Keith Inman.

"Mr. Inman, were you paid by Jim Lloyd for your testimony?"

"No, I get paid for *my time in court*," Inman replied.

"Well, who pays you for your time in court?" Carson asked.

"Jim Lloyd," Inman replied.

"And what are you charging Mr. Lloyd?" Carson asked.

"I have a flat rate of $500 per day and $75 per hour for investigation," Inman answered.

"Mr. Inman, would you be surprised to know when I talked to your supervisor in California, he said that you were quick to jump to conclusions, unreliable and a publicity seeker?" Carson asked.

Inman's jaw dropped. In a very subdued voice, he answered, "Yes, I would be very surprised." It was easy to see this information hurt his feelings, but I'm sure that was part of Carson' attack – to knock Inman off his feet a little bit.

"Where did you find high-impact droplets in the Mitchell home?" Carson asked.

"I found high-impact blood spatters on the east and west walls of the master bedroom near the closet. I found them on both sides of the walls along the hallway. I also found blood back spatters on the baby bed," Inman answered.

"It is my understanding that high-impact blood spots can be caused by beatings or by gunshot wounds. Isn't that right?" Carson then asked.

"Yes, that's true," Inman replied.

"You mean that, from Bobby's trail of blood, he could have been shot anywhere and hit on the head anywhere?" Carson asked.

"Yes, that's right," Inman answered.

"You mean to tell the ladies and gentlemen of the jury," Carson asked, "that it was possible for the blood spatters on both sides of the master bedroom, the baby bed and both sides of the hallway to have been caused by beating with the bat or by being shot repeatedly at all those locations? Imagine, for a moment, that Bobby had not followed Noi out of the house. Imagine, instead, that Noi had chased a mortally-wounded Bobby up the hallway, beating him with a bat all the while. Imagine that…" Carson shouted that out to the jury then his voice trailed off, almost like it was wishful thinking on his part. He walked over to the jury and looked at them intently.

"Yes, certainly, that would cause high-velocity impact spatters such as I saw," Inman agreed.

Carson summed up, "Then, Bobby could have been shot anywhere and hit on the head anywhere within the master bedroom and the hallway?"

"Yeah, that's right," Inman replied.

Carson smiled at the jury and sat down.

I did not like a dark cloud of doubt hanging over the cause of the blood droplets. Carson had painted such a vivid picture of Noi beating Bobby in the hallway that even I, who knew this to be untrue, couldn't shake the image out of my head nor the nausea out of my stomach. I didn't dare think about what the jury must be feeling. I took a deep breath, pretended I was walking into an ice-cold waterfall, and approached the witness stand for my re-direct. I asked only two questions.

"Mr. Inman," I asked, "is it possible that, with the decedent's lung filling up with blood, these droplets in the hallway and master bedroom could have been caused by his coughing and aspirating at the locations about which you testified?"

"Yes, that's possible," he responded indecisively.

"Forty percent of the entire body's blood was found in the decedent's right lung. In your opinion, would the decedent have coughed and sputtered up blood?"

Inman replied, "Yes, I think so."

His testimony ended weakly. This was disappointing to me on so many levels. After we had spent that long, late night at the Mitchell home uncovering blood spatters, I felt that so much of Noi's testimony had been validated – proven to be true with hard evidence and corroborated by an expert in the field. I had been so excited about this! Now, with this expert's flaccid testimony, combined with the doubt I knew Carson had sprayed into the minds of the jurors, I felt so let down, like all of that had been for nothing. Plus, it had cost me a bundle of money, paying for Inman's travel and fees.

But, right now, I had to push that back out of my brain and move forward. Like I said, things can change so quickly in a courtroom fight, not unlike a match-up of two championship teams in a fast-paced basketball game. When you get knocked down or the other side scores, there is nothing else to do but get back up and carry on.

My next witness, Deputy Bob Westover, a former Chief Investigator for the Creek County Sheriff's office, really came through for me in this third trial. The prosecutors had not called him to the stand in the preliminary hearing nor in the first trial, which struck me as odd since he was the first officer on the scene when Bobby's body was discovered. Not only that, but, it seemed to me, they had managed to call everyone else even remotely connected to the case. *Why not Westover? Was it a tactic or was it a mistake?*

So there I was, three days before the third trial began, interviewing Deputy Westover and he explained, "I photographed the decedent's hands before the body was taken to the Oklahoma Medical Examiner's Office." *What?* I thought again, just like I thought the first time he told me this. *I can't wait to see these photos for myself. What are we waiting for?*

Just before the third trial began, when I was actually able to view these photos, I jumped for joy! There it was, gunpowder and soot, just as plain as day on both sides of his hands!

But I was also furious when Deputy Westover told me he had taken the pictures to Assistant D.A. Edward Roosevelt Lewis at the preliminary hearing and Lewis had politely thanked him and assured him that the prosecutors' office would not need him to testify.

I have to repeat this because it is so shocking to me. Assistant D.A. Lewis sent home the first officer on the scene (when Bobby's body was discovered) even though he had important evidentiary pictures! Lewis told Deputy Westover they would not need him for the trial AND then Lewis deliberately failed to inform me of this critical evidence.

Without these photos, it would have been very difficult – if not impossible – for me to prove to the jury that Bobby's hands had been pulling on the gun. They were the second most important piece of physical evidence I had to confirm Noi's story (the first was the bullet in the bedroom wall). *Why had the prosecutors kept the existence of these pictures from me?* This was the big question bouncing around my head. By following a hunch, I had been lucky enough to stumble upon Bob Westover' pictures only three days before the third trial began – just *three* days!

Westover told me that, at the time, he felt the gun powder and soot found on Bobby's hands were so important he took photos and taped clear plastic baggies on the hands so the evidence wouldn't get lost.

Before discovering this major find of Westover' pictures, the jury had to rely on Dr. Masood's testimony that someone had washed Bobby's body before anyone had taken pictures of his hands. Dr. Masood claimed that no plastic bags or any other protective coating had been put on the hands before the body was transported back to Tulsa for testing. He claimed that the hands and body had been washed as a normal routine *before* he had taken pictures.

Dr. Masood claimed he had not tested for traces of gunpowder on Bobby's hands, but that he had made a visual inspection and saw no gunpowder or soot on them. Without proof to the contrary, the jury in the first trial had to accept Dr. Masood's testimony. This type of injustice is a lot like making sausage. No one should have to suffer the indignity of having to watch it being carried out. In our justice system, it's not supposed to happen this way!

I had just begun asking Westover some questions on the stand about the photos he took of the body and the car in Creek County when Judge Dalton called a lunch recess. Westover left the stand holding his photographs.

Lewis asked Westover to come outside to the hallway. Westover and I had a lunch appointment, so I went along with them, too. Lewis said to Westover, "Let's see those pictures, *NOW!*" Then he noticed me hovering around behind him and growled at me, "Take a walk!"

I wanted to hear what he was saying, so I replied, "This is a public area and I am just as entitled to be here as you are."

Lewis snarled at me, "I said take a walk, asshole!"

When I didn't budge, Lewis took Westover into the front room of the Judge's chambers and questioned him about all of my "newly discovered evidence."

During lunch, Westover expressed surprise about the hostilities over State's evidence. He thought it a little strange that the defense attorney – me – wanted to introduce the State's evidence instead of vice versa. *Little did he know just how strange this whole business was!*

After lunch, back in the courtroom, I asked Westover, "Why did you take these pictures of his hands?"

"Because I thought it was significant," Westover replied.

"What did you see that was significant?"

"I saw what looked like gunpowder soot or lead shavings off a bullet on his hands."

"What else did you notice about his right hand?" I asked.

"He had a wound on the fleshy tissue, the web between the thumb and forefinger."

"What was significant about that?"

"I felt like this was possibly caused by a gun hammer striking the tissue."

Boom! Deputy Westover had just given me what I needed.

The District Attorney had contended all along that Bobby never had his hands near the gun since there was no soot or gunpowder residue on them. Thus, the "missing evidence" on Bobby's hands was a critical fact the jury needed to piece together Noi's story.

The prosecutors were visibly shaken by Westover's testimony. Carson' face was a pasty white and Lewis was perspiring heavily.

I'm going to hammer this home, I thought as I stared at a droplet worm it's way down the side of Lewis's face. *I want this jury to understand that the first jury did not get to see these photographs.* So I explained, "I've only recently discovered these pictures." And I didn't hide my fretfulness that these pictures weren't discovered sooner and I let the jury resonate with my relief at finding the pictures just in the nick of time. *Are they as appalled as I am that this could have happened?* I searched the jury's faces for an answer. *Are they beginning to ask themselves if Noi is getting framed for murder?* I took a deep breath before continuing. *I need to drive this home; but I need to be careful, too,* I cautioned myself.

I asked Deputy Westover, "Have you been contacted by the District Attorney's Office for the purpose of testifying in Noi's murder trial?"

"No, sir," Deputy Westover answered, "but the State did subpoena me to the preliminary hearing. I brought these photos with me, but was told my testimony wasn't needed. As I turned around to leave, I handed these pictures to the Assistant D.A. and I asked him, 'What about these?' He told me, 'We don't need them.'"

I paused then asked the sixty-four thousand dollar question, the one on everyone's mind. "Which Assistant D.A. told you that?"

Deputy Westover pointed and said, "Mr. Lewis."

I was finished with my questioning; now, it was Lewis' turn.

Lewis was anxious to discredit Westover. "Deputy Westover," he asked, "what is your current position with Creek County?"

"I am the dispatcher," Westover answered.

"And, what was your former position?" Lewis questioned.

"I was Chief Investigator with the Creek County Sheriff's Office," he replied.

"Were you demoted, then?"

"Yes, about a year ago," Westover said.

"Would you tell the jury why you were demoted?" Lewis asked.

"I had not met the State's continuing law enforcement training requirements," Westover answered. I could tell it embarrassed him a little to say this out loud.

"And, you haven't had training in recognizing gunpowder soot?" Lewis asked.

"No," replied Westover, "but I have seen it many times and I know it when I see it."

"About the pinched web on the victim's right hand – could it have been caused by Noi's fingernails and not by the gun? Isn't that right?" Lewis asked.

"I guess it's possible," Westover replied, "but there was gunpowder soot around the cut and the cut was about the same size as the gun hammer."

"Isn't it possible," Lewis went on, "that Noi's long fingernails could have cut the web in his hand?"

"Anything is possible," Westover replied, as he leaned back and relaxed in his chair. It was obvious to me that he was confident with his knowledge.

As Deputy Westover walked out of the courtroom after his testimony, I thought about how this large-framed man with hazel eyes represented everything that was good and noble in a Peace Officer. *It takes a very courageous man to stand up and be different and, in this case, to tell the whole truth*, I thought. I felt like a better man just witnessing it.

I took just a moment to let that settle and then I concentrated on what was coming. My purpose in bringing my next witness, Dr. Eric Nelson, to the stand was to give the jury a better understanding of Noi's psychological profile. I wanted to prove that Noi acted out of fear, not shrewdness, to cover up a crime. I wanted to show the jury that she had an overwhelming fear of the police based on her experiences in Thailand.

"You can trust the police in America, Noi," I had assured her a year earlier. "This is not Thailand," I had said way back then, although, I must admit I was thinking during this third trial, *with all of the bumbling and, what I consider malfeasance, by the Broken Arrow Police Department in the handling of Noi's case, I am beginning to wonder if what I told her about trusting the police in America is true.*

In Thailand, if a person does not have enough funds to bribe her way out of trouble, a fresh body could be floating down the river that same day. In Thailand, the police are federal officers and are not responsible to the people. They maintain order by force, not necessarily by law, and they carry M-16 rifles. There is little concept of protection of the citizens. A form of martial law exists in which those people suspected of wrongdoing are questioned with the possibility of injury or even death and no consideration given to an individual's rights.

"In the United States," I contrasted, "the police are servants of the people, not the other way around." However, Noi was a confused and frightened girl in a foreign country whose personal experience of how the police investigated crimes in Thailand was ingrained in her. Thus, her fear of the police was real, almost palpable.

Americans would find her fear of police abnormal, even incomprehensible. This fear explained why Noi had hidden Bobby's body, the gun, the bat, the bullets, Bobby's wallet, his keys, and, in short, had acted in a manner that would be considered irrational to Americans. *She seemed so guilty!* However, she was simply terrified.

311

Nothing she did following Bobby's death made her look innocent of a crime. Everything she did – *every single thing* – made her look guilty.

What I needed to make the jury understand, though, was the *WHY* part of this equation. If I could successfully do that, I trusted them to see that she acted out of fear and nothing else, and, if they did that, then they would find her *NOT GUILTY* of murder.

Americans have been raised to trust the police from the time they are small children. American elementary schools invite policemen to their assembly programs where the officers give talks to encourage children to trust them and to believe that the police are their friends. The policeman who came to my school was pot-bellied and probably worked behind a desk all day. He portrayed police officers as kind souls trying to protect the good people from the bad. Before the rash of recent, high-profile excessive force cases were brought against American police, I think most citizens didn't question the integrity of our police officers.

However, Noi was terrified of police in general and she was also terrified that the police would not believe her, and maybe she was right about that. Now, she certainly gave them plenty of reasons not to believe her. Many people considered Noi's covering up of evidence related to Bobby's death and lying to the police as positive evidence of her guilt. They just automatically assumed that innocent people have nothing to hide. I understand that mindset, so I had to explain her bizarre behavior in a new light, not as evidence of her guilt, but as evidence that she was a terrified woman. This was my challenge.

Only three weeks earlier, during the jury selection process, I told the jurors about a personal experience of mine when I was in eighth grade at Whitney Junior High School in Tulsa. I was taking an afternoon typing class from Mr. Smith. Each student had plastic headsets to listen to music at a set tempo. The music would drown out the distraction of seventy-five typewriters all banging away at once.

Before class one day, I went to the front of the room and asked to be excused from typing that day because I had hurt my hand in wrestling practice. My right hand was wrapped in gauze and there was a splint on my finger. Mr. Smith looked down on me and he would not excuse me from typing. He reminded me of a judge because he always dressed in black and his desk was elevated on a platform.

I returned to my desk and knew I was in trouble when I saw my headset snapped in two and lying on the seat. I dragged myself back to Mr. Smith and told him someone had broken my headset. I could feel my solid "D" grade inching downward. Mr. Smith flew into a rage and accused me of breaking my own headset. I was very frightened of his anger, then I thought of a solution and offered to pay for a new headset with money from my paper route. This seemed to make him even more furious and he accused me once more, saying he was sure I was guilty now because only a guilty person would offer to pay for a new headset.

I wanted the jury to remember a time when they had been falsely accused of something by an authority figure. I seemed guilty, even though I had not even touched the headset. Later, Mr. Smith appointed a student proctor to watch and see if anyone was breaking headsets deliberately. There was. The proctor later caught a boy who also confessed to breaking mine. There are not many worse feelings than being unjustly accused, and even though another student was discovered to be the guilty party, I never got an apology from Mr. Smith for his accusation. It still bothers me to this day, which is why I have always made sure I apologize to my own children if I accused them of something it turned out they didn't do. I don't want those feelings to fester in them for a lifetime.

In Noi's case, the only confessions were her own and those of her accomplice. I wanted the jury to understand circumstantial evidence can be very unreliable *and* that things are not always as they appear on the surface. I didn't want the jury to guess Noi right into prison. Evidence of a cover-up should not substitute for evidence of the crime itself.

It was my intention for Dr. Eric Nelson to prove that Noi acted like she was guilty for two reasons. One, because of her extreme fear of police and other authoritarian figures and, two, because of a psychological phenomenon known, at the time, as "traumatic shock syndrome," what has since come to be called Post Traumatic Stress Disorder (PTSD).

The prosecutors were trying to prove that because Noi had acted guilty and had lied, then she must be guilty. Her actions of lying, hiding Bobby's body, and hiding evidence are generally considered to be the actions of a desperate, guilty person.

Dr. Nelson was a noted psychologist who agreed to testify in Noi's case. I had never met him before; had only read about him. His standard retainer was $500 and I knew I could not afford it. I had run out of money. I decided to go ahead and talk with him anyway and see if he would consider waiving his fee.

Dr. Nelson was a wonderful person. After he spoke with Noi and to me, he felt sorry for her and the predicament we were both in. He agreed to testify for free – well, not exactly for *free* since I promised to write his and his wife's wills in exchange for his help in Noi's trial. So, I guess you could say we worked out a trade. I don't mind working out trades, if it's something I really need and the trade feels good for both of us. I just don't want to write someone's will or do other legal work in exchange for a backyard full of chickens and a burro or a leaky boat with one oar and no motor – stuff like that. Still, as I knew all too well, there are times when the bills need to get paid, and it takes money to do that. For the moment, though, this trade was exactly what I needed and Dr. Nelson saved my hide.

Dr. Eric Nelson was sharp, personable, and made a great witness. He was short, about my height, with a young-looking face and a neatly-trimmed full beard. He acted knowledgeable and experienced in a way which projected trustworthiness. He first explained to the jury that Noi was acting out of her extreme fear of police. She had a mindset that was totally terrified of authority. She was sure the police would not believe her. In Thailand, the police did not believe anyone and Noi was well aware of police brutality there. Her fear of police carried over with her when she moved to America. Dr. Nelson said Noi was so fearful of police that she could not be expected to call any authority about what had happened to her husband.

He also educated the jury about "traumatic shock syndrome," which means that people react to extreme psychological shocks much the same way as the body defense mechanism reacts to extreme physical shocks when it experiences traumatic injuries. Nelson gave the jury some graphic examples of a soldier's bizarre behavior in wartime, like when they are facing death or suffer some severe psychological shocks from seeing a good friend killed in battle. He described textbook cases of this effect in Vietnam War veterans and in survivors of natural disasters, such as a hurricane.

Carson had shut me down from discussing the "battered wife syndrome." Judge Dalton would not hear of it and he ordered me not to elicit any opinions from the expert concerning this defense. At that time, this relatively new concept referred to a woman who consistently endures beatings and psychological abuse from a spouse because she lacks self-esteem. The wife often retaliates after the abuse builds up. I did not want to use this defense, anyway, because, at the time, it was classified as a type of temporary insanity.

I did use that as a smokescreen, however. I had hinted in jury selection that I intended to use the "battered wife syndrome" to explain Noi's strange actions. The prosecutors went crazy and researched this area extensively. I wanted to sidetrack them, to throw them off the trail and to keep them from concentrating on Noi's real defense, which was self-defense and accidental shooting. Sure enough, Carson and Lewis convinced Judge Dalton not to allow the jury to hear about the "battered wife syndrome".

I asked Dr. Nelson, "Without discussing the things the Judge told you not to say (concerning the battered wife syndrome), could you please explain the phenomenon which would make Noi do the things she did after her husband's death?"

Dr. Nelson then went on to explain Noi's actions, right down the line. He said her actions were perfectly logical to someone with her psychological make-up. He explained that he had gone to the jail with me to interview Noi and had given her a battery of psychological tests to determine her normal reactions. He said it was quite reasonable for her to lie to the police because of the great fear she had of police, in general, a fear which she had exhibited in the past and, also, because of her cultural background. He said that her fear was a carryover effect from her life in Thailand.

At this point, I did not even have to look at the prosecutors' faces to know that their tactics of proving her guilt by lying and hiding evidence were in trouble. As soon as he could, Lewis fired back in cross-examination.

"Were you paid by Jim Lloyd for your testimony?" Lewis asked Dr. Nelson.

"No," Dr. Nelson replied.

"Did Jim Lloyd promise to pay you money to testify?"

"No," Dr. Nelson answered.

"Have you testified on many other occasions for Mr. Lloyd?" Lewis continued.

"No," Dr. Nelson replied.

"Have you testified on *any* other occasions for Mr. Lloyd?"

"No, I have not," Dr. Nelson persisted.

"Didn't you base your complete diagnosis on one interview with Noi Mitchell?" Lewis asked.

"No," Dr. Nelson replied, "Although I only had one interview with Noi, I gave her a two and a half hour battery of psychological profile tests. She also fits the profile of Asian perceptions of the police."

"Two and a half hours is not very long for complete testing. Did you finish the tests with Noi?" Lewis asked.

"Yes, I gave her the short version," Dr. Nelson replied.

"Didn't you find that Noi was a pathological liar?" Lewis asked.

"No, her fear of police made her lie," Dr. Nelson replied. "She fits the traumatic shock syndrome," he added.

"Dr. Nelson, you have referred to the traumatic shock syndrome several times this afternoon. How many times have you actually seen this syndrome?" Lewis asked.

"I have, personally, never seen it before," Dr. Nelson answered. "It is a very rare occurrence."

"Well, since you have never seen it, how do you know if Noi fits the characteristics of the syndrome?" Lewis asked.

"Noi fits the classical textbook description perfectly," Dr. Nelson responded.

"That will be all, thank you," Lewis concluded.

Next, I introduced Broken Arrow Police Officer, Bob Fuller. Judge Dalton had not allowed him to testify in the first trial. I was able to convince the Judge that Officer Fuller's testimony would be relevant in demonstrating Noi's fear of police.

Over the prosecutors' loud protestations, Fuller's testimony was allowed into the trial. Officer Fuller testified that the year prior to Bobby's death, he, personally, had stopped Noi for speeding. When he turned on his lights and siren to pull her over, she had gunned her car and taken off, never slowing down until she reached her home. Once there, she parked in the driveway and blasted her horn. Bobby came out to see what the matter was and Noi had gotten out of her car and run to her husband, shaking.

Bobby Mack Mitchell, III, was an impressive-looking man who knew all the right things to say to the police, or to anyone else, for that matter. He had a way with words. Bobby handled the officer and paid the fine. Fuller said he was very surprised by Noi's reaction, which was a first for him.

I was pleased with Officer Fuller's testimony and its effect on the jury. The prosecutors had no questions.

Bob Fuller was my last witness. I looked at the jury and said, "Your Honor, I rest our case."

Judge Dalton looked at the prosecutors and asked, "Does the State have any rebuttal?"

The prosecutors called several rebuttal witnesses to testify as to what a nice, non-violent man Bobby had been. The most memorable was Mr. Castro.

I knew I was in for a surprise when, for the first time since the entire trial had begun, Carson walked over to me. He had a gleam in his eye and a sneer on his face when he snarled, "Wait 'til you get the good news on your little girlfriend. You'll see how rotten your little sweetie is."

This was not the first time someone had thought there was something sexual going on between Noi and me. During the trial, I would pat her on the back of the hand or put my arm around her shoulders. Sometimes, I would hug her. For my part, these affectionate gestures were to reassure her, to help give her courage, to let her know we would get through all of this together. Seen through the eyes of others, however, those acts of affection, coupled with my obsession with this case, meant that we were having an affair. Possibly, Prosecutor Carson, a portion of the legal community and several of our friends all thought we were sexually involved, but it was never true. In fact, it was ludicrous. Despite the distance between Nancy and me right now, I was still in love with her. She was my wife, my life partner, and the mother of our children. Besides, it would be pretty difficult to use a jail cell as a setting for a seduction.

Many people do not believe a man and a woman can be friends in a platonic way. Human nature dictates that, if someone sees a man out to lunch with his secretary, it means they are having an affair. People jump to conclusions and then fantasize about whether the dear wife at home knows. It does not matter how innocent both parties might be; people, generally speaking, assume the worst. Noi needed a friend, not a lover.

Carson was enjoying my suspense as we watched Mr. Castro slowly walk up to the witness chair. He was Mexican, or, of Spanish descent, a short man, not much taller than Noi, all muscle and sinew. He looked to be very much the "Latin Lover" type with shiny black hair and caramel-colored skin and he flashed a wicked white smile at the jury as he took the stand.

Castro testified that he was a "good friend" of Noi's from the Monterrey House. He told us that Bobby had walked in on him while he was taking a shower in the bathroom off the master bedroom at Noi and Bobby's house. He said he got out of bed, left his clothes on the floor around the bed and went to take a shower, while Noi was making a snack for them to eat. Supposedly, the children were at the babysitter's.

I almost smiled when he went on to say that Bobby just calmly ordered him out of the shower and told him to get dressed. He said he did so and then left. He said he never saw Noi again. Carson had brought in Mr. Castro in another attempt to show how non-violent Bobby was and how immoral Noi was.

Noi was really angry with Mr. Castro. I only had about thirty seconds to get ready for my cross-examination, so there was not enough time for Noi to explain to me where this guy came from. "He tell all lies," Noi hissed, angrily.

Maybe I was putting Noi on a pedestal, but I just did not believe Mr. Castro. I also knew human nature too well to believe his story. If I caught Mr. Castro with his flashing white teeth in my shower, I would only feel calm after I had knocked a few of them out.

My first question was, "Please describe the shower In Noi's home for us – what color are the tiles?"

"I do not remember," he answered.

"Please give the directions you took from your home or apartment to Noi's home," I requested.

"I think... I am not sure," Mr. Castro said. Then, he proceeded to give us directions that would have gotten him closer to Arkansas than to Noi's home." Someone in the courtroom tittered a muffled giggle to Mr. Castro's response. I waited a second or two.

"Where, exactly, do you live?" I wanted to know.

"I do not know exactly. It is in the Lewiston Apartments," Mr. Castro replied.

"And, what is the address for the apartment?"

"I am not sure."

"How did you get to the courthouse?" I asked.

"Lieutenant Reynolds brought me," Mr. Castro answered.

"Mr. Castro, are you a friend of Lieutenant Charlie Reynolds?" I asked. I wanted to find a reason why Mr. Castro would lie about his relationship with Noi.

"Yes, yes, I am," he said.

"Mr. Castro, are you afraid of Lieutenant Reynolds?" I asked.

He paused for a long time and stared at his clasped hands resting on his lap. Then, he cleared his throat and said, "No... no, he's my friend." He looked like he was very sad, like someone with a broken heart, someone with a tough memory to heal. How often do you suppose these two "friends" got together?

I had pondered, for a moment, about asking Mr. Castro for a description and location of a particular birthmark on Noi's body, one that only a very special friend would know about. I had seen it that night in the jail when Tom Cook and I had to inspect Noi's bruises. Just as I was about to pursue this line of questioning, I realized that, if Mr. Castro made one up, like he was making up this story of his, it would be mortifying to Noi to have to undress for The court in order to prove him wrong. So, I let it go. "That will be all, Mr. Castro. Thank you," I said, as I walked away.

It was 4:30 pm and Dalton asked the prosecutors if they had any more rebuttal witnesses to call.

"No, sir," Carson replied.

"Very well," Judge Dalton concluded. "Ladies and Gentlemen, we will be in recess until 9 am tomorrow." He slammed his gavel down. The sound of it, as many times as I've heard it, still makes me jump and it did this time, too. I hoped no one saw me.

The next day we were to deliver our closing arguments and then it would be up to the jury to decide. That night while Nancy and I were in a deep sleep, the phone rang; the alarm clock showed me it was 11:30 pm. *Who in the hell would be bothering me on the night before my biggest case wraps up?* "Hello?" I said, groggily, into the phone. I heard someone crying on the other end. I couldn't understand what was being said, although it was a female voice I recognized – wait! It was Noi! I could hear her voice between the sobs. "Noi, what's wrong?" I asked. "Calm down and speak slowly."

"I don't have any clothes to wear for court tomorrow and I have no shoes, either," she said, sniffing and snuffling out the words.

"What? What are you talking about? I brought you a week's worth of Nancy's clothes."

"Yeah, but, you see, these girls they like them and so I give them all away… sob, sob… so I have none."

"Wait, wait a minute;" I said, "how are you calling me?"

"On the phone."

"The phone down the hallway?"

"No, the phone inside my cell."

"You have your very own phone inside your jail cell?"

"Yeah."

"When did you get it installed?" I asked her.

"Oh, about a day after the Broken Arrow Police bring me to Tulsa County Sheriff jail."

"OK, I will get up early and bring you another one of Nancy's dress suits and a pair of shoes."

"OK, thank you, Jim."

"Now, go to bed and get your rest," I told her, "we have a very big day tomorrow."

"OK, be here early so I can get dressed."

"See you then, Good night."

What a bombshell! I thought, stunned. *Someone put in that phone. The jailers don't put phones in prisoner's cells for the heck of it. It wasn't Noi. Mr.*

Mitchell, the OSBI, the Tulsa County Sheriff's Office or the District Attorneys' Office could have listened to or had interpreters listen in on every one of her conversations for the past year and I never knew about it until now - the night before the final day of closing arguments!

Then I laughed to myself as I thought back to the phone calls we'd had. *The only calls I remember,* I mused, *are calls about Noi complaining about Nancy's clothes and she probably talked to her kids.*

At least I never talked to her on the phone about her case while she was in her cell - until tonight. If I'd only known... but then, what difference would it make? I guess in the grand scheme of things, it did not hurt my strategies or change anything in the way I would present my evidence. *Was it worth tracking down who ordered the phone for Noi's cell? No, I guess not, but,* I wonder, *is there a limit that... most likely Mr. Mitchell... would go to in order to get her convicted?* I pondered. *Well, time will tell.*

CHAPTER 26 – HOME AGAIN, NO *ALMOST* ABOUT IT

Everything looked different. As I walked into the courtroom, I noticed how very different it all looked from when we had first begun. It reminded me of a stage in a theater with all the props set up. The setting in this case was Noi and Bobby's bedroom with blood-spattered bedroom furniture identified by exhibit stickers. The baby bed, the dresser and the mirror were all placed in the courtroom just as they had been in Noi and Bobby's bedroom. We even taped a white sheet of paper with a hole drawn on it seven feet, five and a half inches above the floor. The stage was set for the final act of Noi's trial.

The actors in this production were weary, but eager for this final act. The battle-worn prosecutors got to court about an hour early. They both appeared to have the confidence that comes from expecting to win. Lewis was wearing a navy, pin-striped suit, with a white shirt and burgundy tie, your basic "Power Look" for men in the 1980's. Carson seemed even taller in his austere, solid black suit. I came in a few minutes later wearing a black suit and pink shirt. I wondered if the jury would hold it against Noi that her attorney was not wearing a traditional white dress shirt. Some law firms are very strict about their dress codes for attorneys. Shirts can only be white, light blue, or ecru. Not my law firm! I usually just wore what was clean and pressed.

No words passed between the two tables of attorneys as we all settled in for the last act.

I looked toward the spectator section as I walked back into the courtroom. I spotted my faithful friend, The Mystery Man, sitting on the "Thai side" of the room. Tom Cook's wife, Mary, was there right next to Tom to hear the closing arguments. A juror from the first trial sat beside her. This woman doesn't want me to reveal her name, and I am honoring that request, but her presence and Tom's and Mary's in the courtroom was a great comfort to me. By this time, I was feeling exhausted and empty; a little let down. Several of my aunts on both sides of the family came to give me moral support throughout Noi's three trials and that says a lot about family. I am so grateful for my family's and friend's reinforcement.

Carson and Lewis divided their closing arguments between the two of them with Lewis going first. I was to be sandwiched in between them. Lewis argued for a manslaughter conviction and Carson would argue for a murder conviction. Lewis' closing arguments had the perfect mixture of facts and sympathy for Bobby. He underscored the things Noi had done and wove them, like a tapestry, into a compelling story. Lewis was good at this, I'll give him that. He asked the jury to consider all of the things she had done and, even if they believed everything that Noi had said, they would still have to come back with a verdict of guilty – at least – of first degree manslaughter.

Lewis emphasized this point again and again. "Who was the aggressor in this fight?" he asked. "An aggressor cannot use self-defense to escape conviction." He broke Noi's story down into four stages of an escalating fight. She argued with Bobby first. She slapped Bobby first. She went into another bedroom, grabbed a bat and hit Bobby with it first. Lewis beseeched the jurors to use their common sense and asked them, specifically, "Who do you suppose would go for the gun? Who would most need an equalizer, like a gun – a man or a woman? Manslaughter is the unlawful killing of a human being." Lewis ended by walking over to the jurors, and slowly pacing from one end of the jury box to the other, asking each one if Noi had the legal right to take another's life. "Did Bobby have to die?" he asked. "What kind of fight was this?

"You know," he continued, "we all have to live with our decisions. I want each one of you to be able to look me in the eyes and tell me you used your common sense when you reached your verdict. I can trust you to come back with a verdict of guilty."

I knew Lewis would do very well with his closing arguments, but I had not expected to be left in a near state of shock. What had caught me off guard, really pulling the rug out from under me, was the prosecutors' change in strategy. They had always gone for – and only gone for – a murder conviction. That was, clearly, their main goal. Secretly, I had always dreaded the possibility of their bringing up an argument for manslaughter and here it was. *What you resist persists, someone had once said to me, and here it was, right in my brain again. Crap.* In my mind, Noi was in much more danger of being convicted of manslaughter than she was for murder. I looked at Nancy who was seated in the second row. Although she winked, it wasn't an *attaboy*, or *good-job!* or, even a *hey, cutie!* kind of wink. It was more of a *just-letting-you-know-I'm-here* kind of wink. I could tell she thought it was over and that I had lost.

I closed my eyes, took a long, deep breath, and exhaled slowly. I tried to picture myself relaxed and smiling. At first, there was only a dark, distant, out-of-focus image. I took another long, deep breath and was able to brighten the image slightly. As I exhaled, my image moved up, closer and closer. What I then saw was a large, gray, close-up of a blurry head. As I took my next breath, I told myself in a clear, firm voice that I would not turn to face Noi until I saw myself relaxed and smiling. With my next breath, the image became bright and warm. The color orange surrounded my image and I came into sharp, clear focus. My image had been facing away and, as it turned around, I saw the features soften into a warm, relaxed smile.

"Mr. Lloyd, you may give the Defendant's closing argument at this time," Judge Dalton said.

I opened my eyes. "Thank you, Your Honor," I replied.

Noi looked at me. I smiled and squeezed her hand to pump some feeling into it. She tried to smile back, but the fear on her face looked almost painful.

327

It was now time for the last discussion I would have with the jury before they would determine Noi's future. I began.

"Ladies and gentlemen, it has been a long four weeks. It has been a long year for Noi Mitchell. You know, I hope you feel good about yourselves. I know I feel good about you. You made a lot of sacrifices to be here. You left your homes, left your families, left your jobs to be with us here today and for the past four weeks. It is people like you who make our country what it is today. It is people who are willing to make sacrifices to make sure our country does have justice – American justice – and make our country this great democratic country that it is."

I walked from the front of the jury box and climbed into the witness chair. There I sat for the next two and a half hours, giving my closing argument from the witness chair! As far as I know, it had never been done before. Basically, this is what I told the ladies and gentlemen of the jury.

"When I was sworn in as a lawyer," I placed my left hand on the Bible and I raised my right hand as to take an oath, "I swore to defend the United States Constitution and the Oklahoma Constitution with my life; and I meant it. I meant it then and I still mean it to this day." I lowered my right hand and then began to take turns holding up each of the 98 exhibits, one by one, while explaining how each related to Noi's being innocent and its importance to her case.

And, after a while, I said, "You folks are going to take a vote to decide, and it's going to take twelve of you to decide, all of you must be convinced beyond a reasonable doubt of her guilt. If one of you is not, then each of you will sign the verdict and there will be a mistrial. It will take all of you to convict. It will take all of you to find her guilty. That's a tremendous responsibility you have, Ladies and Gentlemen, and I'm glad we're in a country that gives us the opportunity, the privilege, to be able, and the freedom, to be able to come up here and say what we feel like and discover the truth together.

"Now, Mr. Lewis has given you a story. He has told you to convict Noi Mitchell based upon linking circumstantial evidence with the facts. Ladies and gentlemen, I submit that it is just another good story ruined by an eyewitness. The eyewitness is Noi Mitchell. She told you what happened.

"I submit that a chain is only as strong as its weakest link, and I've got some forty reasonable doubts, forty weak links, that have broken the chain. They cannot link it up, no matter how hard they try. It won't fit. It won't fit either murder or manslaughter because of these weak links. Let's go over each one.

"If Noi had intended to commit murder, why were both children home when Bobby died? Both children were left with a babysitter the night following Bobby's death when Noi removed his body from the garage, so why wouldn't she hire the babysitter to watch the children if she were planning a murder?

"Evidence shows that there was a fight." I introduced photographs of Noi which showed large bruises and scratches on her thighs, arms, hands and face. "Noi told Detective Anderson when he questioned her that Bobby got the gun first because he was taller and could reach it where it lay on the top shelf in the closet. Noi's fingernail marks were on the back of Bobby's hands which showed that she came up from behind to try and stop him from getting the gun. Dr. Masood testified that there were fingernail marks on the back of the right hand of the decedent's body. Detective Anderson testified Noi told him they were fighting over the gun.

"Blood spatters on the carpet in the bedroom confirm where Bobby and Noi were as they struggled over the gun. Blood spatters on the baby bed show the location of the decedent when the bullet entered his body. A blood spatter expert has testified to the significance of the location of these blood spatters.

"Bobby's hand was on the gun when it went off during the struggle. We have a photograph which clearly shows the decedent's right hand had been pinched, causing a one-fourth inch cut, which supports a struggle over the gun and supports that they both had their hands on the gun when it fired. A Creek County Deputy Sheriff testified that he took a picture of the cut because he thought it was important.

"Evidence shows that there were two bullets fired. The first bullet was found thirteen and a half inches high in the dresser and confirms Noi's position. X-rays taken of the wall prove that the second bullet was embedded in it seven feet, five and a half inches from the floor. The hole in the wall with blood spatters surrounding it was used by ballistic experts to substantiate Noi's position on her backside. The great distance between the two bullets supports that it was an accident. A ballistics expert came into this courtroom and testified that he had run tests which proved the gun had fired twice while Noi was on the floor.

"The path of the bullet, as testified by the experts, had a two inch upward elevation through the decedent's body.

"The gunpowder stippling on the decedent's right shin proved he was on top, in a crouched position.

"Noi told Officers Anderson and Spillman that she hit the decedent after the gun went off. There was evidence of bat marks on the back of his head, suggesting that he went for the gun again.

"Victims of strangulation always have petechia. There was no petechia on the neck, face, or whites of the eyes on the decedent. The autopsy showed no fractures of the voice box or vertebrae.

"A path of blood spots in the hallway, on the front porch, and on the concrete floor of the garage shows that Bobby pursued Noi after he was shot.

"Anderson and the Broken Arrow Police Officers found eight-inch blood stains on the front porch and blood on the door sash.

"And, ask yourselves these questions: 'Why didn't the police photograph Noi's bruises?'

'Why didn't they cut samples from both sides of the mattress? Why did they then bury the mattress?'

'Why didn't the police believe Mia when she told them about the fight which woke her and the baby up?'

'Why did Officer Powell say he thought the bullet hole found at seven feet, five and one-half inches was a scratch?'

'Why would he have a photograph taken of a mere scratch?'

'Why didn't the police cut into the wall and remove the bullet?'

'Why didn't the police test the eight-inch blood stain on the front porch?'

"And, 'Why didn't the police run gunpowder residue tests on the body after Noi told them she and Bobby had been struggling over the gun when it went off?'

"The prosecutors repeated over and over how brutal Noi was when she attacked the decedent with her baseball bat. If she had meant to brutally kill him, why did she pick up the bat by the wrong end and hit him? She was a baseball player; she knew which end of the bat to use for the most power.

"Not only that, Bobby pursued Noi out of the house and around to the side of the garage. He had the gun and dropped it when he fell. Why did she pick up the gun and throw it over the fence into the neighbor's yard instead of pointing it at him and firing again to finish him off?

"For that matter, if she had wanted to kill him, why not use the gun alone from the very beginning, instead of picking up the bat?

"There are many unanswered questions, forty different broken links. Facts don't lie. If one link in a chain of circumstantial evidence breaks, then you've got a reasonable doubt, Ladies and Gentlemen."

Carson objected, "He can't define…"

Judge Dalton quickly sustained his objection and said, "Neither attorney can comment or attempt to define what reasonable doubt is. That is up to the jurors as we've stated in voir dire examination."

"Ladies and Gentlemen," I went on, "you know Noi Mitchell has lost her place of security, lost her husband, lost her home, lost her children. You know she has lost what really makes life worthwhile and there is a stopping point. You can give her those things back. You have the power to say, 'You can go home with your children.'"

Carson hovered over me again with another objection. "Judge, I object to the argument. That is not a comment on the evidence. This argument is intended to appeal to the passion and the prejudice of the jury. It is not a fair comment on the evidence in any form."

Judge Dalton sustained his objection, again. "Ladies and Gentlemen," he said, "you are not to consider 'sympathy' when reaching your verdict."

"Ladies and Gentlemen," I continued, "Noi has all the sympathy she needs from friends and family. We're not asking for sympathy, but I want you to think about… I *don't* want you to think about the children, as Mr. Carson indicated. Don't think about that."

Carson lost control and wildly objected, like he was about to pop a cork. This time, Dalton overruled him.

"Ladies and Gentlemen," I went on, "there is no need for you to think about the one year and two weeks Noi has already spent in jail for a very stupid mistake she made in her life, but I will tell you that the stupid mistake she made does not add up to murder or manslaughter. She made a stupid mistake because she's a backward person. Don't punish her for that, just as you wouldn't punish someone for their personal hygiene and whatever you might think about that. It doesn't have anything to do with the facts of what happened that night. Noi paid dearly for her fear of the police, her distrust of the police, and her thinking that they wouldn't believe her. When it comes right down to it, I don't believe they did."

Carson objected and Dalton sustained his objection concerning my personal beliefs.

"That's right, Ladies and Gentlemen," I said, "you can decide whether the police believed her. You can decide whether they investigated the case based on the facts she told them or if they investigated the case based upon facts as they wanted them to be.

"Do you believe this case should have been handled differently by the Broken Arrow Police Department? Do you think it would have been handled differently if Noi had not had the father-in-law that she did? Do you think it would have been handled differently if she had lived inside Tulsa, as opposed to the suburb of Broken Arrow? You know, Ladies and Gentlemen, I think..."

Carson objected. The Judge allowed me to continue, though, because I had not yet expressed what I thought and he could not rule on the objection. I switched gears.

"I wish I could pass out twelve sheets of paper and pens and ask you to write down what is bothering you about this case. Then, I would know what you want me to talk about.

"Ladies and Gentlemen," I continued, "I think, when you go back in there with this evidence – you are the final judges of this case – and I think with all the law that you have been given, and you have got all the facts, that's all there is, there will be no more, and if I were to give you that piece of paper and have you tell me what you wanted to know, I would hope that I have answered all those questions for you."

At this point, I stepped down from the witness chair after going over the evidence for a full two and one-half hours. I walked directly in front of the jury and made eye contact with each person on my jury.

"Now, Ladies and Gentlemen," I continued, "my time is about up, and I'll not be able to answer Mr. Carson when he gets up here. But, I challenge him to answer each and every one of the reasonable doubts I've given you. Ladies and Gentlemen, I challenge him to answer each and every one of the experts I brought in here to show that Noi's not guilty. I challenge him to prove to you – beyond a reasonable doubt – that she is guilty. I challenge him to that task."

I glanced at Carson. He had a list of things he was going to cover, but, in response to my challenges, he wadded the paper into a ball in disgust and threw it onto the table.

"And," I proceeded, "when the prosecutor gets up here and talks to you next, I'm not going to be able answer and I want you to answer his questions for me because I'm not going to be able to talk to you again. This is my last chance. So, please answer for me.

"You know," I told the jury, "there was once a little boy, a smart-aleck little boy, and a wise old man. You may have heard about it. And the smart-aleck little boy would go to the old man with a brain teaser question and try to stump the old man, but he never could. The wise old man always got the right answer.

"One day, the boy said, 'I've got a way. I know I can beat him.' The smart-aleck boy decided to capture a little bird, put the bird in his hands, take it to the old man and ask the wise man what he had in his hands. If the wise man said, 'Son, it's a bird,' the boy was going to say, 'Correct. Now tell me, wise old man, is the bird dead or alive?' And, if the old man said, 'Son, it's alive,' he was going to crush the life out of the bird and say, 'Wrong. You're finally wrong, old man.' But, if he said the bird was dead, the smart-aleck little boy was going to open his hands, let the bird fly away, and he would say, 'You're wrong, old man.'

"The boy went out, captured a bird, and took it to the wise old man and said to him, 'What have I got in my hands?' The wise old man said, 'My son, you've got a bird.' The boy said, 'Correct, but is it alive or is it dead?' And, the wise old man said slowly and softly,

'My son, the answer lies in your hands.' " (Gerry Spence gave me his "signature" closing argument to use in Noi's case.)

"Ladies and Gentlemen, throughout this last year, Noi Mitchell has been in my hands and, in just a few moments, she's going to be in your hands." My hands were cupped in front of me. "At this time, I want to hand to you Noi Mitchell, my client." I opened my cupped hand, as if to give them a precious and delicate gift. "I hand you Noi Mitchell, my friend, and I hand you Noi Mitchell, the mother of two. I paused for just an extra second. "I give you Noi Mitchell." With this final show of love and trust, I returned to my seat.

Carson bolted from his seat and, in a tone rich with righteous indignation, said, "I, too, want to thank you, Ladies and Gentlemen, and, now that we've got those niceties out of the way, I want to take the forty so-called reasonable doubts and shoot them down." Carson sped over to my posters listing the forty reasonable doubts about this case I had accumulated. He took out a red felt-tip marker, and, very elaborately, marked through each number with a check mark as he began to tear them apart, one by one.

"Noi can commit murder," he said, "and still have her children at home. As I mentioned earlier in the trial, she did not have to decide to kill Bobby the day before the murder, so she could get babysitting arrangements. She could have decided to kill Bobby because he was leaving her. If she formed the intent to kill any time during the fight, it would still be cold-blooded murder.

"Jimmy Lloyd insists that there was a fight – some fight. He says that there is evidence which proves a fight. Would Noi's word be considered evidence? I know, as intelligent people, you would have to consider the hundreds of times she lied to the police. Anybody who killed someone is scared. That does not excuse lying. Noi is a liar.

"Jimmy Lloyd makes a big production of the fact that there were several bruises and scratches on Noi when she was brought into the police station. Remember, Bobby had been beaten, strangled and shot. It doesn't even make sense that someone as small as Noi could beat up Bobby and suffer only a few bumps and bruises because, as she put it, she 'jumped.' That is stretching what happened beyond what is believable, especially when the only person who survived the fight is a proven liar.

"Jimmy Lloyd relies on the fact that Bobby's hands had scratch marks on them to prove Bobby got the gun first. Since when do one or two scratches prove the sequence of events? Noi would have reason to get the gun, not Bobby. Even if Noi were telling the truth, by her own testimony, Bobby had tried to pull away from the fight by pushing her into the hallway and out of the bedroom. Why, then, would Bobby go to his closet and get out a gun? To kill her? That doesn't even make sense. I think it is important to remember, no matter what Jimmy Lloyd argues, as a thinking person, justice requires you to use your common sense to evaluate the evidence. Scratches on Bobby's hands do not prove he got the gun first, and certainly do not prove she had to beat, strangle and shoot him to save her own life.

"Jimmy Lloyd has harped on the blood spatters on the carpet many times throughout the trial. He thinks it proves Bobby and Noi were fighting over the gun. You can remember how Noi washed away as much blood as she could. She washed every towel she had in the house and used a whole roll of paper towels to wash away the evidence of her guilt. Bobby lost a lot of blood in this so-called fight. It dripped everywhere. Jimmy Lloyd's expert has extensive credentials, but I want you to remember he was paid by Jimmy Lloyd. Inman's own supervisor did not have confidence in his findings. He said Inman was quick to jump to conclusions. Remember, too, Inman testified he found high-velocity blood spatters all over the bedroom and in the hall. Bobby could have been beaten by a bat or shot with a gun anywhere in these locations.

"Jimmy Lloyd has also given you a smokescreen concerning the blood-spattered baby bed. We are not even sure the baby bed was in the bedroom. There were seven police officers who swore they did not remember it being there at all. Only one officer thought he remembered it being in the bedroom. Do you think he was mistaken or was the entire police force of Broken Arrow? We are not even sure what the blood spatters would show on the dresser. Noi admitted she washed the blood off the dresser.

"Jimmy Lloyd asked you to use a picture of a bruised hand to determine that Noi accidentally shot Bobby. That is a far-fetched theory, Ladies and Gentlemen. The pictures showed bruises and a small tear. My God, Bobby had been beaten severely, had lacerations, bruises and cuts all over his body. Bob Westover testified that it was possible that Noi's long fingernails could cause the bruises and very slight tear on Bobby's hands. Remember, Bobby had claw marks all over him. Remember, Noi had extremely long fingernails which could easily tear and bruise. Where is Bob Westover today? He has been demoted to a mere messenger because he had not bothered to continue his education. Would you let a killer go with such a single, flimsy piece of evidence?

"And, how is it that Jimmy Lloyd can twist the fact that two bullets were fired to prove it was an accident? My common sense tells me that people do not shoot two times accidentally. The first shot missed Bobby. It almost grazed his skin. She fired again. How could this be an accident? Answer that question for me.

"The fact that there were tattoo marks on Bobby's shin might prove he was on top, crouched over Noi when Noi shot him. But, then, again, it is just a possibility.

"Some of these so-called reasonable doubts are funny. Jimmy Lloyd said because she had beaten Bobby on the back of the head proved that she beat him to keep him away from the gun. It could also prove she came up behind him to bash his head in. We have only Noi's word for what happened, and I do not trust her word.

"Jimmy Lloyd argued that Noi did not strangle Bobby. Even if she did not strangle him, she beat him and shot him. Dr. Masood could not even determine which wound actually caused his death. All we know for sure is that she killed him, with or without strangling him. Dr. Masood did not agree with Jimmy Lloyd's theory that, if there is no petechia, there is no strangulation. Bobby did suffer a cracked

Adam's apple. There were also deep fingernail gouges in his neck which proved she tried to strangle Bobby. Maybe she stopped before she got the job done, so there was no petechia. However, she did work his neck over, as Dr. Masood testified.

"Jimmy Lloyd claims that a path of blood proves Bobby was still trying to kill Noi and stalking her. It could also prove he was trying to get away from Noi. Jimmy Lloyd's own expert agreed that the trail of blood could also mean that she beat him or strangled him or shot him anywhere along that same path. Jimmy Lloyd pointed out the possibility that blood spots could also be caused by Bobby gurgling and spewing out the blood that was filling his lungs. He thought that we would believe that Noi was stalked by Bobby. Imagine, however, this gruesome scene. Imagine poor Bobby trying to get away from Noi. He couldn't have been dangerous to her any more, choking and dying on his own life's blood.

"Jimmy Lloyd thinks that blood stains on the front porch show that Noi was running from Bobby. All that proves is that Bobby was trying to get out of the house. He may have been trying to see if he could get medical help. He did go back into the garage, perhaps to drive his car. Bobby did not have the chance to get his clothes on or even get his keys. He really did not have a chance. Noi selected her time well to start a fight.

"Jimmy Lloyd has attacked the Broken Arrow Police Department. They are not charged with murder. Noi is. Maybe they did think they had enough evidence. They were doing their jobs the best they could. They would have no reason to lie or to hide evidence. Noi would. If we are going to get so critical of the police, why can't we get critical of all the lies and cover-ups Noi used to hide her guilt?

"Jimmy Lloyd thinks that the fact that Noi used the wrong end of the bat makes her guilt go away. Noi was in a hurry, presumably to finish him off. She told Officer Spillman she used the bat so she could make sure Bobby was dead. How does the fact that she used the wrong end of the bat change that? One thing is certain, Noi did finish Bobby off.

338

"And, finally, Jimmy Lloyd's last, so-called reasonable doubt. The fact that she picked up the gun and threw it into the neighbor's yard, instead of shooting him again. What does that prove? Noi may have figured he was not going to last long anyway. He was lying on the ground, face-down, naked and wheezing. She knew he did not have a chance.

"The fact that Noi used more than one weapon to get the job done does not make her guilt disappear. I don't know why she didn't shoot him again. Maybe because she is not a good shot. Maybe she only put two bullets in the cylinder. One thing is certain; she knew how to use a bat.

"You can see for yourselves, there are no more reasonable doubts left. There are no weak links."

Carson ended his closing statement by, literally, shouting at the jury, "I want you to take that chain little Jimmy Lloyd talked about and wrap it around her neck and drag her off to prison for the rest of her life where killers belong!!"

"This case," he continued, in a calmer tone, "is about justice, American justice. When Jimmy Lloyd talked to you about the presumption of innocence, there is something he forgot to mention. That something is respect for law and order. We are a great country, with just laws, and, to respect those laws, there must be juries, like you, who can rise above any sympathies you may feel for the accused, to convict her, if you determine that she murdered Bobby Mitchell. Bobby deserves the same respect you would give someone who is living and sitting over at the table there. I wish Bobby could be here today and give his story. I want you to remember Bobby and the people who will have to live with his death for the rest of their lives. It would be cruel to deny him justice for the sake of his cold-blooded killer, Noi Kanchana Mitchell. In America, we take God's Commandments seriously. 'Thou shall not kill' is basic to human civilization. I believe in God's Commandments and I know you do, too.

"I know it is difficult to send a young woman to prison. In the voir dire, I asked each of you to promise me that you would convict her if we proved that she was guilty. We have proved the case, and I know we can trust you to honor that promise you made when you were sworn in as a juror. That is what makes America a great and unique country.

"Thank you again," Carson concluded.

The trial was over. It was now time for the jurors to make their decision.

Everyone in the courtroom stood up when Judge Dalton excused the jury for the last time on October 21st, 1983. I looked at the clock at the back of the courtroom and it showed 3:15 pm. My hands were resting on Noi's shoulders as the jury filed past us into the jury deliberation room. This room was about ten feet by twenty feet, connected to the front and side of the courtroom. The bailiff locked them in to protect their privacy and to set them apart from the rest of the world. There are two small bathrooms which open up into the jury room.

Dalton asked the bailiff, "Judy, could you help move the exhibits and evidence into the deliberation room?" The prosecutors and I helped pull in the boxes of exhibits which included a baby bed, dresser drawers, twin mirrors and numerous photographs.

Judge Dalton was talking to Carson and Lewis when I came back into his chambers. When I walked in, Carson and Lewis walked out. Dalton looked at me, puffed on his cigarette a few times, squinted his eyes, and asked, "Jim, will you answer just one question for me?" He sounded so serious.

"Yes, sir," I replied, "What is it?"

"Just tell me who helped you with this case."

"Well, Judge, it was Gerry Spence, Bob Rose, Melvin Belli, and a cast of thousands.

340

"That's just what I thought," he said, "I heard you say some things Spence has said."

"Yes, that's true," I agreed, "I don't guess I've ever had an original thought or idea in my life. Everything I've ever said or done, I've gotten the idea from someone else." I don't know if Judge Dalton realized that this wasn't just false modesty on my part; I was telling him the truth. He let out a little chuckle.

Rex helped lug the files back to my office, about four blocks from the courthouse, which was a real chore. It made us both glad he was stronger and of a burlier build than I was. I found myself relying heavily on his bulk and muscle. Altogether, I had assembled almost two hundred pounds of materials and exhibits, and that didn't even include the baby bed, the dresser, the double mirrors, or the carpeting. I lay down on a sofa in my office and Rex brought me a pizza. As we ate, we relived some of the funny moments of the trial. After about twenty minutes, we both drifted off into our own thoughts.

I remembered how I used to be so naïve about trusting the police and the prosecutors. I would have many hours – many years – to reflect on this. My mind raced through the entire trial, thinking about how any of the thousands of decisions I made could change the outcome.

It was over. Carson, Lewis and I had given it our best. In the years to come, I would always think of this third trial as my personal turning point. Up until that time, I had simply been a young attorney trying to do my very best for each client. My parents had instilled in me the notion that I would never be a failure if I tried my very best. Somehow, though, their words rang hollow. I knew I had done my very best for Noi, but I also knew it would not be enough to ease the pain if we lost the case. Some trial masters have said – and I agree – that a lawyer loses part of himself whenever he loses a case.

Somewhere along this path; somewhere during this third trial, although I cannot pinpoint the single event or exact time that it happened, I think I turned into a lawyer. At least, that's what Nancy told me. Imagine, this is the same woman who did yearly audits of my books and threatened to send me back to work for Texaco if my income did not increase by so much per year. Oh, Dear God, not that! *Anything* but that! The slow routine at Texaco dulled my senses; just the thought of it made my shoulders shake like a horse. As it turned out, Nancy was one of my biggest fans by the end of the trial, and nobody was more surprised about it than I was – except for, maybe, Nancy herself.

At about 6 pm, Rex and I became restless and walked back to the courthouse to wait. There were several groups of Thais and Noi's friends milling about. The sound of all the voices mixing together and buzzing in different languages, tones and rhythms sounded like a beehive to my ears. I was surprised to see Lieutenant Reynolds and a half-dozen Broken Arrow police officers waiting in the courtroom.

"Lieutenant Reynolds," I said, "you're not paying these officers double-time to babysit this jury, are you?"

"Yes. Yes, I am," he replied.

"That's a terrible waste of the taxpayer's money, Lieutenant," I teased. He did not like me and I knew that so it was fun to thump his noggin and to gouge him a little bit.

He looked straight ahead and did not reply. After I had given him and his men such a hard time, I'm sure he was looking forward to Noi's conviction – and to my defeat.

At about 7:20 pm, the jury foreman knocked on the door. The bailiff opened it and the foreman handed her a slip of paper. It read, simply, "We have reached a verdict." She called Judge Dalton at his home, where he was waiting. When Judge Dalton got to his chambers, I noticed he had strapped on a .38 caliber pistol. I could not help but notice that it was the same caliber pistol which had killed Bobby Mitchell.

"I've never seen you wear that before, Judge," I said, somewhat surprised.

"Well, it's just in case there's some trouble, you know," he answered.

The Deputy Sheriff was called to bring Noi from the jail. Noi was wearing the same white linen suit she wore that afternoon. Though starved for the sun, her skin was still dark enough to contrast nicely with the stark, white suit. She looked at me and asked, "What does this mean?"

"It means the jury has finished looking at all the evidence and has decided what to do with you," I told her.

"Will I win?" she asked, clasping her hands together so tightly her fingers turned white, as white as the linen suit she wore.

"I hope so," I said, with every fiber of my being.

"Oh, please!" she whispered under her breath, not intending for me to hear. She and I were both slightly trembling all over and my stomach was doing its own jitterbug dance right under my rib cage.

We all stood and held our breath when the jury marched in. The jurors had such blank expressions on their faces it was hard to even speculate as to what their decisions were. Even the most expressive jurors gave no clue as to the verdict. No one looked Noi in the eyes. One juror looked sad, and then I noticed another one did, too.

My heart sank. It began pounding so loudly I was sure everyone could hear it. I could hear it in my own ears, whamming away in my chest like a toddler with a plastic hammer and a bucket... *cathud...* *cathud... cathud...*

"Have you picked a foreman among you?" Judge Dalton asked.

The foreman said, "Yes, sir, we have."

"Have you reached a verdict?"

"Yes, sir, we have."

"Would you please hand it over to the court clerk?" Dalton asked. A man in his fifties with black eyes and gray hair handed the small, white verdict slip to the court clerk. "Would the clerk please read the jury's verdict aloud in open court?" Dalton asked.

She began, "State of Oklahoma, Plaintiff, versus Noi Kanchana Mitchell, Defendant, Case Number CRF 82-3697. We, the jury, being duly impaneled and sworn upon our oath and upon due deliberations do, on this day, find the defendant, Noi Kanchana Mitchell" – *my heart was about to burst* – **NOT GUILTY** of first degree murder…" *I knew we weren't home free yet. They could still convict her of manslaughter.*

I felt like I was dreaming, like I was just a spectator, floating many, many miles away while observing the courtroom drama. It seemed like everyone had suddenly become small and pale, surrounded by a haze. Their expressions were faint, slack and expectant. The courtroom air conditioner clicked on, startling me. I blinked and found myself back in the present, back in the courtroom.

"And, to the instruction of first degree manslaughter," the clerk read, "we find her… *I took a deep breath*… **NOT GUILTY**."

Time seemed suspended and then ground forward into a very slow motion. There was a thunderous uproar as the jam-packed courtroom exploded into applause and cheers.

Judge Dalton rapped his gavel and demanded, "Order in the court! Although I can understand it, we must have order in this court!!"

I had tears in my eyes for several moments. Noi and I hugged each other. As the jurors filed out, Noi put her hands together in the Buddhist symbol for peace and bowed her head respectfully to each one as he or she walked past. All the Thais gathered around Noi and spoke excitedly. Noi just smiled and her eyes were brimming with tears. I said a very heartfelt "Thank You" to each juror as he or she went by. Each one of them looked me in the eye and smiled.

The Deputy Sheriff escorted Noi back to jail for the last time to get her belongings and to process her out.

I remained in the courtroom hugging well-wishers and shaking hands with the excited and joyous crowd, which now swelled around me like two big litters of pups. Everyone was so happy!

Well, almost everyone…

Finally the crowd thinned and Rex and I headed for the elevator. As we stepped out into the hallway, Bobby Mitchell's brother, John, rushed toward me with his hands doubled into fists. His top lip curled up over his teeth as he snarled at me, "GET OUT OF HERE – GET OUT OF HERE RIGHT NOW!!"

I glanced over his shoulder and saw his mother, Bobby's grandmother, sink to her back on the cold marble floor wailing away. Her screams shook my ears, "She murdered my grandson! She murdered my grandson!"

It was hard to bear the cold feelings, the hatred and the pain that washed over me after the warmth and joy I had just felt in the courtroom. Rex jammed his finger at the elevator button and we immediately jumped through the doors as is dinged open. We both wanted to give the Mitchells room for their pain and privacy without us gawking at them.

We rode down to the first floor where we waited for the deputy to escort Noi back to us.

When we finally left the courthouse 45 minutes later, the escort Deputy pulled me aside to warn me there might be trouble. "The Mitchells know some rough men," he said. "I'm just warning you to be careful. Keep a gun somewhere safe in your home, away from the kids, someplace they can't get it, but close enough that *you* can get to it quickly if you need to. Don't go to work the same way two days in a row." He then mentioned the Sheriff's department monitored a phone call made from a courthouse phone to Kansas City. "Someone's called the Mafia and put a contract on you," he said.

I'm thinking, *Lord, can you help me out with this, just one more time? Keep my family safe.*

When Rex and I drove home, Buddy was waiting in his usual spot beside the garage door, jumping up and down. He greeted me with a big hug. "Daddy," he said, "you were the fighter and I was the hoper. I was hoping you would win and you were fighting to win."

I was deeply moved. "Thank you," I told him, "I'm so proud of you, son. You're a special little boy and I love you very much." I thought God created His greatest miracle by making children so forgiving. I just realized Buddy had forgiven me spending the last thirteen months on Noi's case instead of being with him.

I prayed that I could forgive Nancy as quickly and completely for not supporting me as much as I wanted and needed during the most dramatic and traumatic experience of my life. I had realized, though, when I saw her in the courtroom today that while I was off chasing a dream, Nancy was the glue holding our family together. Everything would have shattered had it not been for her. *Everything.* I had shut her out as I focused on Noi's trial. It was all I could think about, not even taking time for those I loved most in the world. I couldn't stop myself. Everything about who I saw myself to be – who I *wanted* to be in life – was at stake.

My embarrassment over being a man of such small stature, my tremendous terror of public speaking, my reluctance to really, truly commit to a life as a good attorney and, most of all, my feelings of impotence at not having been able to save my baby son – all of those things were on the line. But during this process, I began to become David slaying Goliath, and, oddly enough, by stepping into that role, I was molded into the attorney I wanted to be. I would, ultimately, never try another murder case – the cost to my precious family was too dear to pay again. However, by focusing my practice on personal injury lawsuits, I would wind up spending years wrestling and defeating huge companies for millions of dollars and protecting average people from discrimination, bankruptcy, and pain.

I could not see any of this at the time, blinded as I was by all that needed to be done to prove Noi's case and, yes, even by my own selfish dreams of glory. In one of Joseph Campbell's books from the 1980's, he talks about The Hero's Journey, and how, sometimes, we are called to do something so far beyond the realm of what we have ever seen for ourselves that it seems insane. We don't just *choose* to do it, for the choice is not ours. We are *chosen* for this journey. We can shirk from it, but, when we do, some small part of us dies – goes dormant and fallow – maybe it will never rise again. Or, sometimes God just grabs us by the hair and tosses us in the ring anyway. Sometimes, I think that's what happened to me.

Nancy, my wife, had a journey of her own – she needed to hold all of the parts together as a wife, as a mother to our two young children, as the breadwinner and CPA, and as a law student, too. Her torturous grief over the death of Brandon was just as wrenching – maybe, even more so – than my own. The sound of her sobs right after it happened will ring in my mind for all my days. The difficulty of her pregnancy with Jamie was overwhelming and she fought so hard to be able to bring our beautiful daughter into the world. Even if I live to be an old, wrinkled codger of a hundred and twelve, I will never be able to understand how she managed to do all that she did, filling in the void places I'd left behind – and to stay with me! Nancy told me she felt abandoned and dragged along into a fight that wasn't even her own. No wonder she got so mad at me; I wasn't being a very good husband or father, or decent provider for my family.

In the end, what I've come to realize is that while I was busy being David fighting Goliath, Nancy was fighting just as hard for the security of our family. Who's to say which fight was bigger or more important? I think I'd have to vote for my wife on this one. I understood it better after everything was over. I could see *why* she wanted the things that she was desperate for. My family needed the same kind of focus and devotion that I was giving to my quest. She deserved that; they all did.

Right now standing with my devoted son, I felt like a free man once again, one who could be the man my wife and my children needed. Maybe I could be that good man for the first time ever. I missed them.

I missed my wife and all that we had shared. Now, I wanted her back again. Suddenly, there she was, standing right next to our son – my wife, Nancy. She was so lovely. My heart melted at the sight of her again, just like I remembered it could, just like I had longed for it to do again. And, she was waiting for my response. Our eyes met. We all embraced. We were finally home again.

CHAPTER 27 – ANOTHER PAGE, *ALMOST* TURNED

Most people can look back over a long career and see the pinnacle of it all. This one was mine, and it has taken me many, many long years to be able to finally get the story of it into a form that people can read, enjoy and even relate to. I am grateful that time has finally arrived.

Along with my wife, Nancy, there are thousands of people I should probably thank for giving me advice and lending me help along the way, not just through the several months of this particular case, but through my entire career as well. They will probably never know the depths of my gratitude, but it is there, shining like a golden nugget in the clear water of a sparkling river. I hope they all get to see it and that they know it is from me to all of them.

My time as an attorney is in the early stages of winding down for me. Our very successful law practice, Lloyd & Lloyd in Sand Springs, Oklahoma, a Tulsa suburb, is being transferred more and more into the most capable hands of my wife, Nancy, and our son, Buddy, two of the best legal minds I know. I still stay involved with our practice on some level, but find myself looking for ways to enjoy more time with our five grandchildren and in ways to satisfy my own natural curiosity about the world, how it all works and what I can do to help this world work better for all of us.

Quiz, the dragon, still shows up in my dreams sometimes, just to check on me. He had told me once, and, after I understood the wisdom of his words I came to agree with him: "Whenever you go through the most awful pain of your life," he told me, "it will change your life in ways you cannot even imagine."

There had been so much pain for me in losing my baby son, then all of that additional pain I brought to my marriage over this case. Still, in all of the heartache and angst for me and my family during the three murder trials, when I think of it, it's no big surprise that my life changed so much for the better after it was all over. For all I gained from that experience, though, it almost made me think about welcoming even more pain into my life, if that pain was to be balanced out with goodness and light and tremendous change. I know, however, to be careful about what you wish for. It reminds me of a man I knew who suffered through terrible bouts of depression for years and years. When I asked him how he dealt with that, how he could live with something so difficult and debilitating, he got a wistful look in his eye, like he was letting me in on a big, juicy secret.

"Well, the darkness is only the darkness," he said. "When I emerge from those dark spaces, what I've noticed is how much brighter everything is for me. I love deeper, appreciate more, sing louder, and the world feels like mine again. It's a glorious feeling, really, so what I've found myself doing is actually welcoming those dark times because I know how great I'll feel when I get through it."

I can't claim to be as brave or as noble as that guy, but I know that my brain races to discover new ways to be all that I can be in this world, to open my heart and my mind all at once, and, while I'm working on me, to help pave the way for others to discover their own journey of personal growth, too. Within each endeavor, I make sure I ask myself this rhyme: "IS IT GOOD? IS IT TRUE? IS THIS PATHWAY RIGHT FOR YOU?" The dragon's advice has served me well. Quiz is an old guy now, and cranky, so I don't see him much, but that's okay. I don't need him as much. Plus, I'm getting to be an old guy, too, just not as cranky as he is.

In my dream one night, I am walking beside a long stone wall, touching it gently with my fingertips, feeling the grainy, dark red sandstone I know so well as a child of Oklahoma. I hold my face steadily, bravely, as I look toward my future. Rays of light reflect off my own sunset and through the haze of that light, I think I can see

350

him again – the dragon. I blink, not sure, when, suddenly, he's right there! He grabs me by the shoulders, slams me up against the wall, his face right in my own. ***"IS IT GOOD? IS IT TRUE? IS THIS PATHWAY RIGHT FOR YOU??!"*** he shouts it at me. Then, he does something so out of character for him – he seems to mellow. His voice becomes gentle, like it was when I was a boy, when he first showed up.

"Jim," he asks me, "have you done your best? Have you made your time here count for something good? Have you answered all of life's questions? Are you happy with your choices?"

I can feel the heat from his eyes; I can smell the smoke in the back of his throat. I grin at him because it irks him, I know. Quiz always worried that I was just grinning and goofing off through life. I curl my index finger, motioning him closer, because I know that pisses him off, too. I make him bring his big head in close to me so I can whisper my answer in his ear.

I repeat his questions to me, so he'll know I'm paying attention: "Have I done my best? Have I made my time here count for something good? Have I answered all of life's questions? Am I happy with my choices?"

Quiz, of course, will think I'm kidding, but I mean it with all my heart when I tell him the biggest, sweetest secret of my life and I reply, "Almost."

EPILOGUE – NO GOING BACK, *NOT EVER*

Few things in life test our courage and perseverance as this case tested mine. Even though it took place so many years ago, it is still as fresh and recent in mind as if it had all happened last month. Beyond winning the case and keeping an innocent young woman from spending the rest of her life behind bars, it was a turning point for me in terms of my career as an attorney and how I saw myself as a lawyer and, eventually, how I came to see myself as a husband, father, and, even as a person.

My friend, Jody Seay, the woman who's been helping me tell this tale, says she still can't understand why Nancy didn't leave me during that time. I can't understand it myself, sometimes, when I think back on it. "If it had been me," Jody said, "I'd have kicked your skinny ass to the curb."

Knowing, Jody, I'm sure she would have, too.

I would like to be able to say that I went on to become a world-famous criminal defense attorney, like Gerry Spence, Melvin Belli, Bob Rose, or one of those guys I admire so much, those men who helped me more than I can express, but that didn't happen. I was contacted by many defendants after I won Noi's case, but realized I could not represent someone I did not care about. And I couldn't ask my family to go through that again.

My career as an attorney has been spent, mostly, in the field of personal injury law, and I hope I have made a difference in the lives of the clients I've represented over the years. Nancy became an attorney, too, and we worked together at Lloyd & Lloyd for many years. Then we were joined in our business by our son, Buddy, now an attorney. That law firm of ours continues to flourish to this day.

I feel so blessed to have two of the most brilliant legal minds I've ever encountered sitting right next to me at our office in Sand Springs, Oklahoma. Our remodeled building is just a ten minute drive to the Tulsa District Courthouse. We built a courtroom in the building, so if you get a chance to come out this way, be sure to take a tour of our courtroom. You will recognize the motto over the jury box: IN GOD WE TRUST. And, we do.

Noi eventually remarried and moved to Arkansas and had a son. Judge Dalton stayed on as a Judge in Tulsa County and has since passed away. Even though we had our conflicts in the courtroom, I had tremendous respect for him. Prosecutors Carson and Lewis eventually went on to other things. Lewis became a Judge and has since retired and Carson wound up in private practice.

One of the most satisfying things to happen since Noi's trial came from a meeting I had with Mr. Mitchell, Bobby's father, right before Christmas in 1985. We shook hands and had a good visit. Although he looked much older and rather unwell, he had mellowed. He confided in me that the stress of the anger he and his wife carried after their son's death had caused both of them to have heart attacks. He admitted that he had spent thousands and thousands of dollars trying to get Noi convicted of Bobby's murder and he apologized to me for the things he had said and done which had put my own life and career in jeopardy. He had finally come to a place of peace about Bobby's death and, with God's help, he knew he would be just fine. It took a big man to say those things, I know, and I respect him for that. He asked me to be the guardian of his granddaughters' estates, which I did, free of charge, and turned the investments over to them when they reached age eighteen.

Noi's case took a toll on me that civil cases simply do not and I will always consider her case as special and exciting, one of the peak points in my life.

My brother Rex has said for years that helping me with that trial was one of the best times of his life. I am glad for that. He was a tremendous help to me, to Noi, and to the cause of justice.

354

For me, though, the ultimate reward came in the form of knowledge. It sprang forth as a time of my own understanding, finally, of the beautiful and relentless magic adorning the underlying deck of courage which rises up to hold our feet and steady our legs when we dare to be braver than we ever thought we could.

In my friend Jody Seay's first book, an award-winning novel called, *"The Second Coming of Curly Red"*, she writes about courage like this:

> *Transformation can take place in an instant, quicker than a heartbeat, faster than the flicker of a thought. Courage can come out from its hiding place when least expected, when it is needed most. As gently as a whisper through the trees or a shadow across the canyon wall, courage pushes its way through, upward past fear. Then, it settles itself across the shoulders like a comfortable old sweater. Things change, shift, making room for the beating of a brave heart. And, once courage has found its place, there is no going back. Not ever.*

I am grateful for all that I learned about myself and thrilled that my family stayed together in spite of all I put them through. Would I do it all over again? Even though time and blessed spurts of wisdom have given me a different perspective on things, I'd still answer that one as: Probably.

Would I feel guilty about that? I'd have to say: Sure.

But, it changed me, this trial, this fight for justice, and, for that, I am eternally thankful. A different Jim Lloyd emerged from that thirteen month-long battle, a confident, new and improved Jim Lloyd, a guy who I came to respect, admire, and even love. Could I go back to being the insecure person and timid attorney I was before this trial ever happened? That question is the hardest one of all to ask, but also the easiest one to answer: *Not ever.*

J.L., 2017

About the Authors

JIM LLOYD

Jim Lloyd has been named in Who's Who in American Law, and is a member of the Missouri Bar, Oklahoma Bar, and the Oklahoma Association for Justice.

Melvin Belli invited Jim Lloyd to become a Lifetime Trustee of the prestigious Melvin Belli Society. Mr. Belli also requested that Jim write a chapter on the Mitchell case to be included in the *"Melvin Belli's Modern Trials"*, 3rd Edition (sadly, Mr. Belli passed away before Jim could complete the work). Jim is a graduate of Gerry Spence's Trial Lawyers College and its graduate seminars.

The Oklahoma Bar Association honored Jim Lloyd as the Outstanding Young Lawyer for the State of Oklahoma early in his career. In part, he was recognized for his volunteer service to the community.

He was asked to write an advice column, *"Ask a Lawyer"* in the Tulsa World newspaper. Lloyd also ran booths at the Tulsa State Fair as part of a bar association community outreach program to let people know about their legal rights. Jim was also the chairman of the Tulsa County Speakers Bureau explaining to elementary school children through high school students what it is like to be a lawyer.

Mr. Lloyd also performed critical work as an Oklahoma Commissioner tasked with investigating the Tulsa Race Riots of 1921. He uncovered and found 150 lost case files before they were destroyed. This important evidence revealed the scope of loss and devastation of 36 square blocks that had been burned to the ground in the Greenwood District (The Black Wall Street).

Jim, his wife, Nancy, and their son, Buddy, run Lloyd & Lloyd, a "mom-and-pop" law firm in Sand Springs, Oklahoma. Their daughter, Jamie, lives with her family in Kansas and consults with the law firm as a healthcare expert.

Jim and Nancy can be found adoring their five beautiful grandchildren as often as possible.

JODY SEAY

Jody Seay is an Advanced Certified Rolfer and an award-winning author whose first book, a novel called *THE SECOND COMING OF CURLY RED*, won First Prize for Fiction at the Mendocino Coast Writer's Conference, and then went on to become a Finalist in the prestigious Oregon Book Awards.

In addition, Jody has written a memoir called *DEAD IN A DITCH: GROWING UP IN TEXAS & OTHER NEAR-DEATH EXPERIENCES*, a musical called *BUNKIN' WITH YOU IN THE AFTERLIFE*, and numerous essays which have appeared in newspapers and magazines across the country.

Even though Jody swears she loves to write, she also maintains that writing makes her self-absorbed and grumpy for extended periods of time. Sometimes, she also breaks out in a rash, but, usually, that only happens when her computer crashes. Technology is hard for her, which brings her deep shame and makes her mean. She swears she'll get better at it, but, really, she never does. It might be a hopeless cause. Luckily, she has other strengths, and, thank goodness for that! *ALMOST A MURDER* is Jody Seay's third book.

Jody Seay's Other Books

Jody's first novel is titled *THE SECOND COMING OF CURLY RED*. This book is an award-winning and reading it will "expand your mind, your heart and make you see double as if you were hit upside the head". This candid, compelling, and compassionate novel could have been torn out of today's newspaper headings.

> *One minute Texan Jimmy Heron is sitting next to his beloved wife of fifty years eating pie, the next minute she is dead in his arms; killed by a racist, woman-hating, semi-automatic gun-toting maniac. Shattered by Lou's senseless death, Jimmy Heron hits the road – can't sit still; can hardly breathe. He roams the western landscape looking for solace until he lands in the tiny pioneer town of Reliance, Oregon. Here he settles, figuring it is as good a place as any to wait until he dies.*

> *With kindness and perseverance, however, his new neighbors delicately slide into his life. A lesbian couple eagerly awaiting the birth of their first child, a Native American ranch hand, a big-hearted dog, and a small band of generous people gently encourage Jimmy to deal with loss, death and love. Thus, Jimmy Heron begins his healing process.*

This novel will grab you by the heart and not let go. Look for *THE SECOND COMING OF CURLY RED*, second edition – new and improved. Available at Amazon and Barnes and Noble and most bookstores by request. The novel is also available as an eBook (Kindle and Nook).

Also visit Jody's website and blog (http://jodyseay.com) to while away a minute or more of entertainment. She's a riot.

Jody's second book is titled, *DEAD IN A DITCH: GROWING UP IN TEXAS & OTHER NEAR-DEATH EXPERIENCES*. It is a memoir, of sorts; essays to chew on and ponder.

1). Non-Fiction – Short Stories (single author)

2). Autobiography – Memoir – Baby Boomer – Texas Family Life

I come from a large family. My Mother's biggest fear was that one or all of us would die on her watch when we were babies and then children. As we grew up, her fear shifted a little – not just that we would die, but that we would be found Dead In a Ditch.

It was the ditch part that always made it seem so much worse, something drug or alcohol related, to be sure. Mother's children crumpled up and tossed out the window like an old beer can.

"Where have you been?" she would say, "I was worried sick. I thought you were dead in a ditch." This was Mother's mantra.

In Jody's memoir (2011), *DEAD IN A DITCH: GROWING UP IN TEXAS & OTHER NEAR-DEATH EXPERIENCES,* Jody invites the reader to take a look at her 'family story album' – tales that introduce us to a little girl who took every double-dog dare trying to prove her bravery and re-introduces her as an adult who has realized the meaning of a life well-lived. This collection of short stories immerses readers into the wackiness of growing up in a loud and rowdy Texas brood, what it meant to come out as a lesbian in a conservative family, and witnessing the courage it takes to live an authentic life.

Jody always says, "If I can write a story that makes people laugh and cry, then that makes me a happy girl." *DEAD IN a DITCH* is that collection of stories. You will laugh until tears fall and you'll have to sit with your legs crossed. It'll break your heart, too, and make one crazy Texas-born hooligan a happy girl.

This memoir is <u>Available at Amazon</u> and <u>Barnes and Noble</u> and most bookstores by request. The book is also available as an eBook (<u>Kindle</u> and <u>Nook</u>).

Also visit <u>Jody's website and blog</u> (http://jodyseay.com). She looks at the world from a unique perspective.

Jody's Play (A Musical)

BUNKIN' WITH YOU IN THE AFTERLIFE

Each summer, Minnie Rhodes and her Many Roads Ministry – Cowgirls for the Lord, a group of lesbians who ride on horseback through very conservative southern Oregon – spread the good news. Not of having been saved but, indeed, of never actually having been lost. Along the way, we hear their stories of love, joy, sadness, redemption, forgiveness and, in the end, we watch their hearts open with acceptance – for themselves, each other, and for unconditional love from their Creator.

This ecumenical lesbian cowgirl musical begun originally as an idea from one of Jody's books-in-progress: the people to whom we are connected on the earth plane we will be with in the afterlife. *BUNKIN' WITH YOU IN THE AFTERLIFE* has traveled quite a dusty trail to end up where it is today. From a thought to a song it grew into a kernel of an idea, to a full-blown musical comedy that was produced by Melinda Pittman and the geniuses at BroadArts Theatre in Portland, Oregon.

Award-winning author, speaker, and TV host, Jody Seay, wrote this musical about love, loss, redemption, and spiritual awakening to satisfy two issues. One, she wanted to confront, in a humorous and respectful way, any major religion that feels they must be at war with each other all the time in order to prove that theirs is the only path. As Jody sees it, there is just one mountain with many roads. Two, she had grown weary of seeing the spiritual lives of gays and lesbians marginalized. Jody has set out to correct the assumption that the spiritual lives of people who have a different sexual orientation somehow don't matter.

Featuring several original songs and song-parodies, *BUNKIN' WITH YOU IN THE AFTERLIFE* is a rowdy romp.

Jody says, "It is through the writing and telling of stories that we share our common humanity. From that one step, we realize that we are all in this together and more the same than different. This is the essence of enlightenment; it is the learning tool, the implement of empathy and connection, sought throughout human history.

"Our connection to each other is then strengthened with each wonderful story told, and our communities, our nation and our world are all the better for it.

"Indeed, we are more than words, more than language. We are stories – each of us, a collection of tales of triumph and joy, sagas of loss and mourning. We are, individually and collectively, a genetic mish-mash of family history, of well-turned phrases, stories told and then re-told, of crackpot ideas, and even occasional piercing brilliance. The soup pot of stories into which we have all tumbled like chunks of turnips now bubbles and stews with us, softening our centers, turning us golden around the edges, making us vulnerable and oh-so-human, and so very much more the same than different. This is what we learn from the writing and telling of stories."

CPSIA information can be obtained
at www.ICGtesting.com
Printed in the USA
LVHW011751281118
598530LV00012B/238/P

9 781938 282218